THE DIVINE MOTHER

315-1
9

A TRINITARIAN THEOLOGY OF THE HOLY SPIRIT

DONALD L. GELPI, S.J.

BT
121.2
.G44
1984

UNIVERSITY
PRESS OF
AMERICA

LANHAM • NEW YORK • LONDON

Copyright © 1984 by

University Press of America,™ Inc.

4720 Boston Way
Lanham, MD 20706

3 Henrietta Street
London WC2E 8LU England

Library of Congress Cataloging in Publication Data

Gelpi, Donald L., 1934-
  The Divine Mother, a trinitarian theology of the
Holy spirit.

  Bibliography: p.
  1. Holy Spirit. 2. Trinity. 3. Experience (Religion)
I. Title.
BT121.2.G44   1984   231'.3   84-11921
ISBN 0-8191-4034-1 (alk. paper)
ISBN 0-8191-4035-X (pbk. : alk. paper)

All University Press of America books are produced on acid-free
paper which exceeds the minimum standards set by the National
Historical Publications and Records Commission.

For Mother and Daddy
Al and Barbara,
Chris and Adrienne,

who have revealed to me
the faces of the Divine Family

CONTENTS

AUTHOR'S PREFACE

"What are you working on these days?" a colleague recently inquired.

"I am revising a manuscript on the theology of the Holy Spirit," I replied. "I am attempting to understand the Spirit in the context of trinitarian theology."

"Really," came the rejoinder. "That sounds very different from the other things you have been writing."

"That depends," I retorted, "on how you take them. As far as I am concerned, the new book follows directly from the things I have written so far."

Our conversation went no further. But one did not need a crystal ball to guess what my friend was thinking. My publications to date have dealt with problems and issues relevant to an understanding of Christian religious experience. My colleague seemed, like many a student of theology, to suppose that trinitarian theology bore little relevance to identifiable religious experiences. Anyone who has studied the development of trinitarian speculation or plodded through sterile scholastic trinitarian tracts will readily understand such a supposition. But before academic theologians reduced trinitarian faith to a series of abstract and dubiously intelligible propositions, ordinary believers had experienced the Christian God as mysteriously three-in-one. The chapters which follow attempt to probe the experiences that lie at the basis of belief in a triune God.

Like most of the things I write, this manuscript was conceived in a classroom. I hope that it will serve as a useful text in theology. But I have attempted to write it in a way that will appeal to a broader audience. I would expect that any adult Christian interested in understanding more about trinitarian faith would find both challenge and stiumlus in the reflections which follow.

The book you hold in your hands has been conceived in tandem with two other studies: Experiencing God: A Theology of Human Emergence and Charism and Sacrament: A Theology of Christian Conversion. The first attempts to elaborate a theology of the human person; the second, a theology of Christian worship.

Although this volume was conceived in tandem with two other books, all three studies stand on their own. One need not, then, read the other two first in order to understand the reflections which follow. But because the three books are attempting to articulate a synthetic, integrated insight into Christian religious experience, their contents must inevitably throw light on one another.

In writing these three volumes I have attempted to reach a unified insight into the dynamic structure of Christian religious experience. We experience our own persons most immediately. _Experiencing God_, therefore, lays a foundation for the other two volumes by exploring in some detail the psychodynamics of Christian conversion.

Shared worship enjoys a similar immediacy. When Christians gather for spontaneous or for sacramental worship, they experience one another and the reality of God with a directness and vividness similar to personal self-awareness, but more complex because the worship experience is shared. At least Christians do so when their worship expresses converted commitment to God, heartfelt openness to the anointing of the Holy Spirit, and the willingness to share the gifts of the Spirit within worship and in the daily living of life. _Charism and Sacrament_ probes the meaning of such experiences.

The present volume attempts to understand the reality of the God Christians worship.Contemporary Christians experience God in the first instance as Spirit. For no one has ever seen the Father. And ever since His ascension Jesus has not been around to tell us what God is like. But we have contemporary access to both Jesus and the Father in faith through the anointing and enlightenment of Their Holy Spirit. Present experience of the reality of the Christian God begins, then, in a conscious encounter with the Holy Breath of Jesus, the divine Spirit, the sanctifying **Pneuma**, the **Ruah** of God and of His Christ.

Taken together _Experiencing God_, _Charism and Sacrament_, and _The Divine Mother_ cover some of the same theological terrain as Yves Congar's recent three volume work, _I Believe in the Holy Spirit_ (New York: Seabury, 1983). But they differ from Congar's study in that they view the same theological landscape from a different perspective, approach it with a different method, and produce different conclusions. For while Congar's thought advances within a fairly traditional theological paradigm, my own work has attempted to develop systematically a new paradigm for pursuing theology in a North American context. Whether I have succeeded the reader may judge.

I adapt the term "paradigm" from the work of Thomas S. Kuhn. In his studies of the development of scientific thought Kuhn defines a paradigm as a way of posing and answering questions that grounds the pursuit of ordinary science.

Paradigms should not be confused with models. Speculative models mediate between a felt, appreciative grasp of a problem and the formulation of rational hypotheses concerning it. For example, once atomic physicists decided to imagine the atom as a tiny solar system, they could with the aid of that model begin to formulate hypotheses about the bahavior of subatomic particles. Models function within paradigms, but paradigms include more than models. A paradigmatic approach to doing

viii

ordinary science includes assumptions, methods, concepts, symbol systems, models, instrumentation, logical and experimental procedures.

Theologians generally concede that models function within theological thinking. They are, however, only beginning to acknowledge that paradigm shifts also occur in theological speculation analogous to the shift in scientific thought from Newtonian to Einsteinian physics. A paradigm shift in theology occurred, for example, during the second century, when Christian apologists decided to begin to adapt categories from Platonic and Stoic philosophy in order to explain the meaning of the gospel. And until the rediscovery of Aristotle in the west, when Thomism created a whole new way of thinking theologically, Christian Platonism provided the accepted paradigm for doing ordinary speculative theology. A similar paradigm shift occurred in our own century as Christian theologians began to discover continental existentialism. Other paradigm shifts in theological thinking have occurred in the course of the development of Christian doctrine, and still others will occur.

As in scientific speculation, paradigm shifts in theology involve an element of politics. Paradigm shifts effect a revolution in human perceptions. As a consequence, the spontaneous finitude and inertia of the human ego causes practitioners of accepted paradigms to view new paradigms with initial alarm and suspicion. In a successful scientific revolution, Kuhn argues, a small group of individuals spots the advantages of a new paradigm and begins to use it to resolve questions which the old paradigm cannot answer or answer with the same success as the new one. If successful, the new paradigm gains popularity and eventually, usually after about a generation, supplants the old.

Whether the paradigm shift that I have been advocating will ever achieve general acceptance among theologians in this country, heaven only knows. But I have found much encouragement in my work from a group of colleagues who share my enthusiasm for developing a thoroughly inculturated North American theology. We call ourselves the John Courtney Murray Group and gather each summer in a scholarly community of reflection, research, and prayer to share insights and to probe the possibilities of inculturated theological thinking. We ambition constructing a theology in dialogue not only with contemporary religious issues in the United States but also with the American philosophical tradition as a whole.

The new paradigm which I have been attempting to develop in this book and in the two that preceded it tries therefore to draw systematically on the North American philosophical tradition in order to create an inculturated theology that speaks with a Yankee idiom even as it challenges the religious inauthenticities rampant in our culture. Although a few notable Catholic theological thinkers in this country like Orestes Brownson, John Courtney Murray, John A. Ryan, and more recently John Coleman, have also ambitioned such a theology, their work has proved exceptional.

Catholic speculative theology in the United States like American oil has tended to be imported from abroad. If successful, the paradigm which I and my colleagues are developing would change all that.

Although the version of the new paradigm which I myself propose invokes a different epistemology from Bernard Lonergan's, it accepts a number of its methodological presuppositions from Lonergan's ground-breaking work, <u>Method in Theology</u>. With Lonergan I conceive the fundamental task of theology as conceptual mediation between a religion and the culture in which that religion roots itself. I also endorse the main lines of Lonergan's theory of functional theological specialties. I ply especially the specialties called dialectics and foundations. I apply dialectical analysis not only to the development of the Christian tradition, but also to the evolution of religious speculation in the United States as a prelude to formulating a foundational theology of conversion. I also concur with Lonergan's suggestion that revisionist thinking in theology should rest on a sound normative insight both into the dynamics of conversion and into the religious experiences that authenticate the social, affective, speculative, and moral expressions of religious faith.

From a dialectical analysis of the North American philosophical and theological tradition as a whole, I have in the course of this and of the two preceding foundational essays I have written tried to develop a metaphysics of experience that attempts to correct at several significant points the metaphysics of Alfred North Whitehead, even though like Whitehead I attempt to employ the term "experience" as a transcendental category. The construct of experience I am developing, however, incorporates insights from a broad spectrum of North American thinkers, most notably from Jonathan Edwards, Ralph Waldo Emerson, Orestes Brownson, Francis Ellingwood Abbot, C.S. Peirce, William James, George Santayana, Josiah Royce, and contemporary process philosophy. The same construct of experience functions in all three of the foundational studies I have attempted and provides them with an element of conceptual unity.

I have also tried to build on Lonergan's theology of conversion. But my own account of the conversion process contains complexities absent from Lonergan's own thought. Not only do I recognize five interrelated but distinguishable moments within conversion in contrast to the three moments Lonergan originally proposed; but I also invoke the construct of experience I have been developing in order to discuss seven identifiable dynamics within the conversion process. I speak of affective, speculative, moral, socio-political, and religious conversion. I also distinguish more clearly than Lonergan himself between natural and gracious conversion and between initial and ongoing conversion.

Let me state dogmatically some of the basic dynamics of conversion as I conceive them. (1) Religious conversion mediates between affective and moral conversion; at least it does for the converted Christian. (2) Speculative conversion seeks to inform affective, moral, religious, and socio-political conversion. (3) Religious conversion graciously transvalues affective, speculative, moral and socio-political conversion. (4) Natural moral conversion orients natural affective, speculative, and socio-political conversion to realities and values that make absolute and ultimate moral claims. (5) Affective conversion animates speculative, moral, socio-political and religious conversion. (6) Socio-political conversion deprivatizes affective, speculative, moral, and religious conversion. (7) Personal conversion at a religious, affective, moral, and speculative level authenticates political conversion.

I cannot develop the implications of these dynamics in a brief preface like this one; but I mention them because they help ground the reflections which follow. More specifically, I derive both from my construct of experience and from my theory of the dynamics of conversion two operational procedures which structure significantly the argument of this book.

My construct of experience recognizes two ways of grasping reality judgmentally: by logical inference and by felt, intuitive judgments. As a consequence, my construct of experience demands that theologians in approaching divine revelation attend consciously to both kinds of judgment and ensure that their felt intuitive perceptions of any religious or secular reality agree with their inferential perceptions and vice versa. Biblical thought advances primarily at the level of feeling and intuition. It eschews logical system building. That fact imposes specific operational constraints on the Christian pneumatologist. Christian pneumatology must make sure that the judgments of feeling about the reality and activity of the Holy Spirit which it derives from the Bible agree with its systematic, speculative inferences about the third person of the trinity and vice versa. Moreoever, because theology seeks an integrated and integrating perception of God, of oneself, and of one's world, Christian pneumatology must search for means to affirm of the Spirit at an affective, intuitive level what it affirms rationally and inferentially. Failure in the enterprise breeds religious schizophrenia. The search for affective and speculative integration will force us in the final chapter of this work to search systematically for an adequate personal image of the Spirit that connotes and corresponds to speculative belief in the Spirit's personal character.

From my understanding of the dynamics of conversion I derive another operational procedure which structures the following argument in significant ways. I believe that certain forms of conversion--namely, affective, speculative, moral, and socio-political--can occur in complete abstraction from divine revelation. When that happens they occur naturally. Natural conversions and the realities encountered interpretatively within them need to be transvalued by Christian conversion. Christian conversion transvalues natural conversion by providing a novel frame of reference for re-interpreting and judging persons and things perceived and judged only naturally. Christian faith creates that novel frame of reference. In the chapters which follow I will argue that

Christian revelation not only transvalues every other perception of God but that Christian pneumatology imposes on the convert moral obligations that transvalue human conduct. The moral transvaluation in faith of natural and sinful affective perceptions provides an important key for understanding the argument of the final chapter of this work.

From Lonergan's theory of method I derive a third principle which shapes my reasoning in the pages which follow: namely, that a sound theory of conversion needs to take into account not only the insights of philosophy and theology (as traditional theological paradigms do) but also the relevant insights of sciences other than philosophy and theology that study human experience. Because this book deals with trinitarian theology I have no occasion to invoke this principle until the final chapter. The positive sciences have nothing significant to say to trinitarian speculation, since they do not deal with the triune God as such. The final chapter of this work, however, attempts in accord with the operational principle enunciated in the preceding paragraph to coordinate the Christian convert's affective and speculative perceptions of the Holy Spirit. At that point the results of contemporary scientific and clinical investigations of human affectivity assume theological relevance.

I make these observations not to discourage readers but to warn them that they may in the pages which follow find themselves paradoxically from time to time on what may seem alien ground. I say paradoxically because the concepts and insights in this study most apt to seem theologically alien to American Catholics trace their Yankee lineage all the way back to the New England puritans. I would expect such a reaction especially from readers schooled in imported theological paradigms. Chapter II which sketches the construct of experience and of conversion which undergirds my entire argument will probably take readers unfamiliar with the North American philosophical tradition somewhat aback. The final chapter which attempts to set pneumatology in dialogue with contemporary personality theory may evoke a similar reaction. But I would not be suprised were the careful and reflective reader to find an element of the unacanny in all of the chapters which follow. I am, however, willing to run that risk in the hope of exploring a heretofore uncharted area of Christian speculation.

The argument of the present study proceeds down a fairly straightforward path. In Chapter I I invite you to reflect on your own experience of the Spirit of God by recapitulating briefly my own. I doubt that my experience of the Breath of Jesus differs that significantly from the experience of most other Christians. But even if it should differ in some details, the very diversity invites you to understand better the forces in your history that have shaped your Spirit consciousness. The chapter then proceeds to reflect on the forces that cause awareness of the Holy Spirit to flicker. And it suggests that we take a fresh look at the reality of the third person of the Trinity by examining human religious experience. Chapter II attempts to clarify the meaning of the term "experience" by a descriptive exploration of different realms of human experience. It offers both a definition and a construct for understanding experience and focuses attention on aspects of experience important for grasping the argument that follows. Chapter III examines the ways in which the Holy Spirit has come to be experienced historically, and it attempts to elaborate an experiential construct of the divine missions of both the Son and the Spirit. Chapter IV then probes the legitimacy of conceiving the Christian God as an experience. Having concluded positively, we begin to explore the ways in which the divine experience resembles and differs from human experience. In Chapter V we begin to deal with a perplexing problem in contemporary trinitarian theology: namely, can we legitimately speak of Father, Son, and Spirit as divine persons? Our examination of the evidence furnished by the divine missions leads us to conclude that no other conception of the members of the Christian Godhead passes muster. In Chapter VI we face the most fundamental problem of any trinitarian theology: to wit, how can three distinct divine persons subsist as a single divine reality? Having surveyed past solutions to this perplexing problem we offer a response that attempts to draw not only on the Bible and tradition but also on human social experience. In Chapter VII we test the ability of our experiential construct of the Trinity to interpret Jesus' relationship to the Spirit. Then in Chapter VIII we probe the experience of baptism in the Spirit for the information it supplies us about the reality of the triune God and the role of the Spirit within the divine experience. Finally, in Chapter IX we attempt to update our image of the Spirit in the light of the new insights we have reached into Her reality. I have appended a glossary of foreign and technical terms.

I could never thank all the friends and colleagues whose suggestions and criticisms have helped make this a better book than it would have been without their counsel. The following, however, have a special claim upon my gratitude: Roderick A. MacKenzie, S.J., Dennis Hamm, S.J., Elizabeth M. Tetlow, John Boyle, S.J., Thomas Leahy, S.J., John Wright, S.J., Michael Buckley, S.J., Mary Ann Donovan, S.C., Patout Burns, S.J., John Stacer, S.J., Francis Oppenheim, S.J., Barbara Charlesworth Gelpi, William Spohn, S.J., J.J. Mueller, S.J., Robert Heyer, Robert Goeser, Andrew Christiansen, S.J., Joseph Bracken, S.J., and Michael Cook, S.J. I also owe a debt of deep gratitude to Lois McKenna and to Sarah Duhrkopf for their unflagging help in transforming my scribblings into a readable typescript, and to Jill Marshall and Sheila Powers for transcribing the final edited version of the manuscript. With friends such as these I alone must assume responsibility for any defects in the pages which follow.

Donald L. Gelpi, S.J.
Jesuit School of Theology at Berkeley

CHAPTER I:

IN SEARCH OF THE HOLY GHOST

Not long ago, I had occasion to visit the church where I was confirmed. Not much had changed. The same plaster saints presided from their wooden pedestals. They seemed like old familiar friends. St. Michael, smart in his silver mail, athletic biceps swelling, still pinned the throat of the ancient serpent writhing to the earth. And placid St. Lucy still smiled down with strange angelic sweetness as she proferred her latest devotee two large eyeballs on a golden platter. When I was small, I loved her dearly. The sight of Michael giving it to the dragon always satisfied. But those eyeballs were the best. "Won't you just try one?" she seemed to say.

Lucy, Michael, and their companions had presided over my confirmation. I remember it as less than a pentecost. The day before the bishop came, all of us prospective soldiers of Jesus Christ had been told to report to St. Ann's for early mass. That morning as I stumbled from the bathroom still drugged with sleep, I told my mother that I thought that in the course of my dazed ablutions I might have swallowed some water. Quite correctly she told me to stop being silly and get ready for mass. But my conscience resisted her realism. I knew from catechism class that if I went to communion after breaking my eucharistic fast I would commit a mortal sin, and that if struck thereafter by a reckless car or providentially crushed by a falling tree, I would go straight to hell. At the same time my mother's voice brooked no childish nonsense. It was then with reluctance and with a certain stoic fatalism that I took her advice and went to communion anyway.

The next day we filed into the resplendent old church, preternatural in our neatness and white clad like the martyrs of the apocalypse. As we marched proud and scared beneath the fond eyes of our parents and the unblinking gaze of the plaster saints who loomed above and behind them, I was still plagued with scruples about breaking my eucharistic fast. But since the way behind was blocked, I could only move forward. And I filed meekly into the pew.

We performed rather well for the bishop. He liked his catechism questions answered in choral recitation. He wanted to make sure, I believe, that all the children had learned the answers. As a consequence, he resisted the initial attempt of the class smart alecs (among whom I numbered) to blurt out the right response before the duller witted group could remember it. He stumped us only once. I sat there tonguetied knowing I could answer the question the rest had forgotten but reluctant to provoke the bishop further. In the embarrassing silence that ensued, we all looked at our religion teachers. The sisters sat studying their laps, and we knew that we had let them down.

1

The rite filled me with awe: the solemn procession into the sanctuary, the bishop's hands hard pressed on our bent heads. I had never been so close to a bishop and was comforted to have my sponsor with me. My fear of eternal damnation had given me enough to contend with; but as I entered the lighted sanctuary I also nurtured the fear that when the bishop slapped my cheek to remind me that I must be willing to be buffeted for the faith, he might really slug me. He didn't. After it was over, I felt I should probably start thinking about growing up as a Christian. I just hoped I wouldn't roast in hell over a mouthful of water.

We Catholics did not speak a lot about the Holy Spirit in those days. And when we did, we said "the Holy Ghost." Of course, we said the Nicene creed at mass and the apostles' creed at the start of every rosary. And both reminded us to believe in the third person of the blessed Trinity. We were taught too that the Holy Ghost is the soul of the mystical body of Christ and that the Advocate had proceeded from all eternity from both the Father and Son by spiration, not by generation. And we accepted all of that as true. But it certainly didn't seem to make much practical difference other than affording the comfort of being right in knowing it. As we shall see, however, in the pages which follow, these ancient doctrines properly understood make real, practical demands on the Christian conscience.

In my junior year in high school, our home-room teacher was a Jesuit priest named Emmett Bienvenu. He buried our noses in the Acts of the Apostles, called it the gospel of the Holy Spirit, spoke of the Spirit as the forgotten God. It was hard to deny what he said. But somehow the events of Acts seemed as remote as the events of the gospels themselves. We knew that both were true. But times had changed, and as Catholics we realized that the gifts of the Spirit described in Acts had been granted only to the first generation of Christians. And it all made sense when you thought about it. God probably would have to do something special to get the church going; but after the ecclesiastical pump had been pneumatically primed, God only needed the hierarchy to see to it that grace flowed regularly into people's lives through the sacraments. We also knew that to expect widespread charismatic manifestations of the Spirit in our day and age sprang from rank spiritual pride. Worse still, it was Protestant. Little did I realize at the time that a personal encounter with Protestant Pentecostal piety would one day transform the biblical witness to the Spirit into a living word that touched my heart. For the biblical doctrine of the Spirit speaks, as we shall see, directly to human experience. And a religious experience illumined by the biblical witness yields insights into the reality of the Spirit that Christian theologians have for centuries overlooked.

In the course of my theological training as a Jesuit, my classmates and I had plodded through a scholastic treatise entitled De Deo Trino. The text codified Thomistic trinitarian theology and embellished it with proof texts from Scripture, from the fathers of the Church, and from major

2

councils. It all seemed very remote and abstract: one God, two processions, three persons, four relations, five notions, and no proof. Like most Catholics we had no notion that the Christian tradition offers alternative ways of understanding both the Trinity and the Spirit, alternatives we shall examine in the pages which follow.

In 1968 I received the gift of tongues. And as I deepened in the gift, I was drawn into shared charismatic prayer. I began thereafter to experience locutions that seemed to be from God. I had learned from John of the Cross to approach such experiences gingerly. But most of the words survived critical appraisal. They gave direction to my prayer life and to my ministry.

My belief in the Holy Spirit began to be felt, living, and personal, instead of dry, intellectual assent to a dogma. For the first time too, it seemed, my personal piety also began to assume a conscious trinitarian cast. The more I thought of it, the more trinitarian piety seemed to me thoroughly Ignatian. And it felt odd to have discovered the triune God affectively by hobnobbing with Protestants.

The faith in the Holy Spirit which I discovered in charismatic prayer communities lived through practicality. And it became practical through concrete expectation. When charismatic Christians come together to pray they expect the Spirit of Christ to be visibly active in their midst through the presence of the gifts. That expectation, I saw, made all the difference. It brought to life biblical teaching about the Spirit. I began to suspect that the sharing of the gifts creates the vital matrix of authentic trinitarian faith. As we shall see, my suspicion proved true.

But I soon perceived that the Spirit-consciousness of contemporary charismatics suffered from its own human limitations. Charismatic piety is focused on feeling and informed by the rhetoric of faith. The piety of feeling can render one receptive to the movement of grace. And the rhetoric of faith reminds us of the need to follow God's initiative in our lives. But when feeling becomes closed to thought, it ossifies. And then, I saw, the rhetoric of faith can all too quickly be put to sinister uses. The action of grace begins to be confused with unconscious fears and resentments. Receptivity to God degenerates into emotional complacency. And divine sanction and inspiration begin to be claimed for human impulses of rigidity, anger, and apprehension. In charismatic prayer groups, this sad process can bear fruit in fundamentalism, authoritarianism, and sexist discrimination.

In my darker moments I began to wonder if humans can achieve authentic faith in the Spirit in a fragmented church composed of fragmented people. Both personal and pastoral experience have taught me that our human perception of God is filtered through feeling, through image, through language, through spontaneous beliefs and prejudices. And our evaluative filters can either illumine or distort our sense of the divine.

3

Our creedal stance is shaped by ritual but also marred by superstition, neurosis, and human limitation. It is conditioned by history, molded by half-understood abstractions. Our denominational creeds are like the froth that scuds across beach flats in the wake of a storm. The thundering debates that engendered them have subsided into oblivion.

Because it is a form of human awareness, Spirit consciousness flickers. It has flickered in my own life. It flickers in the lives of most Christians. The forces that shape or inhibit Spirit awareness in both individuals and communities interweave in complex patterns. And unless we criticize those forces they will continue to inhibit and distort Christian awareness of the Spirit. One such force is theology.

In the fourth century of the Christian era Gregory of Nazianzus referred to the Holy Spirit rhetorically as the "theos agraptos," the God about Whom nobody writes. Sixteen centuries later the rhetoric still applies. No single reason explains perennial theological neglect of the third person of the Trinity. Even within the New Testament, theological interest in pneumatology waxes and wanes. It burns intensely in many of the letters of Paul, in the gospels of Luke and of John, and in the Acts of the Apostles. Matthew and Mark refer only rarely to the Spirit but do so in suggestive ways. In the other writings of the New Testament references come only occasionally. Often they are peripheral or ambiguous. Sometimes they fail altogether.[1]

In the development of post-Biblical theology Spirit consciousness flickers unpredictably. We find it strong in the writings of Irenaeus, less intense in the works of Justin Martyr, almost absent from the theology of Clement of Alexandria, and confused in the subordinationist pneumatology of Origen.[2] The Arian heresy denied the divinity of both Son and Spirit. But the debate with the Arians focused intially and primarily on Christological questions. As a consequence orthodox concern with the creedal implications of Arian pneumatology developed almost as an afterthought. At Nicea the bishops assembled in council condemned Arius's Christology. His pneumatology was not officially condemned until over a half century later.[3]

Medieval theology manifested a periodic concern to resolve the pneumatological issues raised by the Photian schism.[4] But most medieval theology of the Spirit comments repetitiously on the pneumatology of Augustine's De Trinitate.[5]

During the Reformation both Luther and Calvin sought to revive theological interest in biblical pneumatology.[6] But as Lutheranism and Calvinism solidified into orthodoxies, theological concern with the Spirit languished. It continued to languish until the nineteenth century when Roman Catholic attempts to retrieve and popularize the pneumatology of the medieval scholastics bore fruit in the encyclical Divinum Illud Munus. The letter prescribed novenas to the Holy Spirit. But its scholastic abstractions failed finally to excite extensive popular or theological interest in the third person of the Trinity. <u>Mystici corporis</u> popularized the idea that the Spirit animates the mystical body of Christ. Vatican II further enhanced Roman Catholic awareness of the role of the Spirit in the life of the church. In the course of the conciliar debates the bishops were led to acknowledge that the Spirit abides as the perennial inspiration of the charismatic ministry of both ordained and unordained Christians.[7]

There are speculative motives for the flickering character of Spirit consciousness. In the biblical witness the Spirit performs a clear and indispensable function in the process of salvation. In the Bible the divine Spirit inspires every gracious enlightenment. But as Christian theology came under the influence of the middle Academy and of Neo-Platonism, first rational, then gracious enlightenment was with increasing frequency appropriated to the **Logos,** to the Son, rather than to the Spirit. As a consequence the place and function of the Spirit in the economy of salvation became obscured, confused, and over the centuries all but forgotten. Even to this day interest in Christology overshadows theological concern with the reality and saving action of the Spirit.

Other theological motives have conspired with an encroaching Christology to thwart the development of both theological and popular awareness of the Spirit. Christian pneumatology evolved as a branch of trinitarian theology. But for a variety of reasons trinitarian speculation came over the centuries to be divorced from its foundations within Christian experience. The first Christians discovered saving access to the Father through the Son and in the Spirit. But the Arian controversy in both its causes and consequneces modified significantly the manner in which Christians came to perceive the reality of the God they worshipped. To the rationalizing tendencies of the Arians the Greek fathers opposed a profound reverence for the divine mystery. At first the mystery of God was associated with the Father Whom no mere mortal has ever seen but Who has been revealed to us in the historical missions of both Son and Spirit. But in the acrimony of debate with the rationalizing Arians Christian theologians began to insist on the mysterious and incomprehensible character of the inner, triune life of the entire Godhead. As a consequence, the mystery and incomprehensibility of the Father came to be extended to the Son and Spirit as well and to Their processions from Him within the Godhead. A clear rhetorical advantage attended such a theological gambit. It allowed the anti-Arian forces to accuse their adversaries of rationalistic impiety for refusing to worship the transcendent mystery of a triune God. But the advantage was not secured without its price. The more orthodox theologians insisted on the transcendent mystery of the inner life of God, the more remote the reality of God seemed from the day-to-day living of ordinary Christians. A gap had opened between what would later be called the immanent and economic Trinities, that is to say, between theological understanding of the inner life of God, on the one hand, and of the events of salvation which reveal that life to us, on the other. Despite growing theological insistence on the remoteness and transcendence of the Trinity, eastern orthodox theology would preserve an interest in the saving action of the Spirit. But in the medieval Latin church the gap between the immanent and the economic Trinities widened to a gulf as a systematizing scholasticism transformed the ineffable, transcendent mystery of the Trinity into a metaphysical conundrum. Scholastic trinitarian discussions of subsistent relations, notional predicates, eternal processions, and the tri-personal reality of an infinite divine substance did little or nothing to nourish the lived piety of the ordinary believer. Ordinary folk found the cult of the virgin far more appealing and immediate.

As a Christian theology of the Holy Spirit was absorbed into the movement of trinitarian speculation as a whole, it began to be colored by the latter's remoteness and abstractness. Christians learned to believe that from all eternity the Holy Spirit proceeds from both Father and Son by spiration rather than by generation, but that fact seemed both obscure and irrelevant to ordinary human experience. Living biblical belief in the Holy Spirit as the source of justifying faith, as the inspiration of Christian practice, and as the dispenser of the charisms had been effectively transformed by theologians into the static academic affirmation that the Holy Spirit exists as a facet of a transcendent divine reality. At the same time, the saving action of the Spirit in the lives of Christians had come to be conceptualized theologically in the abstract and impersonal language of grace rather than in the concrete, interpersonal formulas of the New Testament.

But we should not imagine that theology alone causes Spirit consciousness to flicker. A more potent force than academic theology inhibits Spirit awareness: the spontaneous inertia of the human ego. The Spirit of Christ enters experience as a transforming challenge to human egocentrism. Such a challenge most individuals and institutions prefer to avoid. In our own culture secularism, naturalism, and clericalism conspire in different ways with the ego inertia present in popular piety to stifle Spirit consciousness. Secularism forbids people to use the religious terms that will allow them to name grace-filled experiences as Spirit-inspired. In secular circles religious experience is first psychologized, then trivialized. Naturalism so focuses attention on questions of immediate pragmatic interest that religious questions of ultimate concern never arise. Clericalism attempts to direct the action of the Spirit into channels that are socially proper and canonically acceptable to ecclesiastical bureaucrats; but it ends by stifling Spirit consciousness in predictable religious routines. Finally, the ego-inertia present in much popular piety conspires with all three of these forces to domesticate the divine and to keep it within the realm of the familiar, the predictable, and the controllable.

To put the matter baldly Spirit consciousness flickers because the human mind, being finite, can, when left to its own resources, attend only intermittently to the reality of God and of the Spirit. It flickers because the human ego seeks to control its destiny, while the Spirit of Christ challenges us to the naturally distasteful process of abandoning ourselves to God in unconditioned trust and love. And Spirit consciousness flickers because humans being not only finite but sinful oppose, thwart, and suppress the action of the Spirit in themselves and in others.

A contemporary pneumatology faces then a formidable task. In order to counteract those forces which stifle Spirit awareness, it must prophetically challenge individuals and communities to rend their hearts and open them to the illumination of the Spirit. It must speak a word of wisdom that summons Christians to ongoing transformation in the Spirit. It must offer a word of instruction that explains the historical development of Christian pneumatology in the light of a sound normative insight into a Christian experience of the Spirit. It must pronounce a discerning word that discards inadequate or misleading interpretations of God and of the Advocate. It must address not only the minds of Christians but their hearts as well. That is to say, it must offer them an understanding of the God they worship that invites them to heartfelt adoration.

The pneumatology developed in these pages aspires to do all these things. Whether or not it succeeds the reader may judge. It tries to probe the experiences that lie at the foundation of a Christian theology of the Spirit. It begins by examining the dynamic structure of human experience itself. It then reflects on the ways in which the Spirit of God has been experienced by believers over the centuries. It argues that the living reality of the triune God can itself be understood on an analogy with human social experience. It examines the action of the Spirit in Jesus. And it probes the experience of Spirit-baptism for the insight it yields into the reality of the God Christians worship.

The pneumatology developed in the chapters which follow also attempts to engage in normative thinking. Our method is foundational; and foundational theology explores the shape of an authentic Christian conversion. We encounter the reality of the Spirit of Christ within conversion. And conversion imposes specific obligations on the convert. Some of those obligations concern the convert's relationship to God. A foundational pneumatology attempts therefore to answer the question: **How ought an integrally converted Christian to experience that facet of the Christian God we call the Holy Spirit?** Because it engages normative thinking, a foundational theology of the Holy Spirit gives some promise of countering those forces in the Christian tradition that have inhibited the growth of Spirit consciousness.

(1) Christians experienced the Spirit before they formulated pneumatologies. A foundational theology of the Spirit overcomes the abstractness of traditional trinitarian teaching about the Spirit by rediscovering the human experiences that give it meaning. For foundational method not only invites personal reflection on one's own Spirit consciousness, but it also attempts to retrieve in a systematic fashion the

biblical witness to the Spirit's illumination of the apostolic church. Moreover, foundational theology attempts to understand the ways in which the biblical witness to the Spirit both illumines and challenges contemporary Spirit consciousness.

(2) Because it engages in normative thinking, a foundational pneumatology explores the practical consequences of belief both in the Spirit and in the triune God. By making faith in the Trinity practical, a foundational theology of the Spirit highlights its relevance to the day-to-day living of Christians. A foundational pneumatology accomplishes both these ends by taking a stand within the experience of Christian conversion and reaching a judgment about the way in which an integrally converted Christian ought to perceive the reality of the Spirit. That perception transforms human experience and makes of the converted Christian specific moral demands that affect the day-to-day ordering of life.

(3) A foundational pneumatology would fall short of complete adequacy did it not attempt to understand the relationship between the Son and the Spirit. Such an understanding demands that we cooordinate our perception of the reality of the triune God with our perception of the incarnation of the second person of the Trinity. In the process of effecting that coordination we will be forced to examine and revise inadequate theological constructs of the Trinity, to correct the illegitimate attempts of some Christologists to appropriate to the Son experiences that are properly referred to the third person of the Trinity, and to elaborate a construct of the hypostatic union that makes sense of the New Testament's account of the relation of Son and Spirit to one another.

(4) Because it attempts to probe the experiences that lie at the basis of doctrinal affirmations about the Spirit, a foundational pneumatology provides a contemporary context in which to reappropriate the trinitarian soteriology of the New Testament. Although the term "grace" (charis) occurs in the New Testament, it lackes the philosophical and metaphysical connotations it acquired during the patristic and middle ages. New Testament authors explain the meaning of "grace" by speaking of the saving action of the Father creator, the redemptive death and resurrection of His incarnate Son, and the illuminating presence of their Spirit. A foundational pneumatology not only sanctions such usage but provides it with a speculative rationale.

(5) Because it approaches the experience of the Spirit in the context of Christian conversion, a foundational pneumatology offers contemporary Christians both a prophetic challenge and a word of wisdom. It summons them to a converted relationship with the Spirit and to their own ongoing charismatic transformation. It speaks to Christian hope by demanding a re-examination and revision of the images that shape our affective attitudes toward the Spirit. It demands a critical reformulation of inadequate conceptions of Spirit. It examines the moral consequences of belief in the Spirit. And it demands that both individuals and societies be transformed by accepting the lived consequence of such belief.

(6)   Because it reflects on the reality of God, a foundational pneumatology also offers Christians a word of instruction that addresses their minds. It demands that one reach a normative insight into the reality of Spirit that reflects a sound understanding of the development of Christian pneumatology and a grasp of the issues that development raises. We perceive the reality of God, however, with our hearts as well as with our minds. Because it attempts to coordinate an affective appreciation of the Spirit with a speculative understanding of Her reality, a foundational pneumatology also invites a loving adoration of the Spirit as the appropriate complement of a theological understanding of the Spirit's person and activity.

The words we use to speak about the reality of God and of His Spirit stand within experience and color it. Foundational thinking invites the reader to take a fresh look at the realities encounterd in Christian faith and worship. For both these reasons I have in the pages which follow indulged in two linguistic conceits. I have chosen to designate the Holy Spirit by a feminine personal pronoun. And I have elected to speak of Her as God's Breath rather than as God's Spirit. Both choices deserve a preliminary explanation.

The application of the feminine personal pronoun to the third person of the Trinity may strike some as startling. But such usage enjoys the sanction of both Scripture and tradition. As we shall see in greater detail below, divine wisdom is personified as a feminine figure and eventually identified with the Holy Breath of Yahweh that inspires the wisdom born of faith. And in the fourth century, a Roman theologian named Gaius Marius Victorinus suggested that the Son's miraculous conception in the power of the Breath reveals to us that She is His Mother in heaven and on earth. In the pages which follow we will examine his suggestion and probe its theological justification. Moreover, as we explore the experiences which lie at the basis of doctrinal statements about the divine Breath, we shall find in Jungian archetypal theory evidence to support both Victorinus's suggestion and the biblical personification of the divine Breath as a mysterious, feminine wisdom. In the final chapter of this book, we shall argue that the archetype of the feminine, when properly transvalued in faith, has the power to connote the traditional biblical images asociated with the divine Breath as well as basic Christian beliefs about Her person and saving function. I refer to images like water, fire, the descending dove, wind, temple, church. Such images occur outside the Bible, but in sacred scripture they are commonly associated with the divine Breath. As we shall see, Jungian theory suggests that the archetypal imagination associates them spontaneously with the image of the feminine as a transforming, lifegiving principle.

I realize that the legitimacy of applying feminine terms and images to the Holy Breath needs to be argued, just as Her divinity needed to be argued in the fourth century. And I stand under no illusions concerning the complexity of such an argument. First of all, let me say unambiguously that the reality of God transcends human sexual distinctions. But if we humans are to speak of God at all, we must do so in human terms. And the structure of human language reflects the sexual character of those who have invented it. If the Holy Breath is a divine person, we need personal pronouns to refer to Her reality. In English, personal pronouns are either masculine or feminine. The fact that we speak of the first person of the Trinity as "Father" and refer to Him with a masculine pronoun does not mean that He is an old man riding a cloud. By the same token the use of a feminine pronoun and of feminine imagery in speaking of the Holy Breath does not mean that She is literally a woman.

The legitimacy of any linguistic convention for designating the divine persons needs to be argued theologically. The present argument raises a host of interrelated and complex issues. Contemporary theology disputes the advisability of speaking of Father, Son, and Advocate as "divine persons." If then one seeks to justify referring to the Holy Breath with either a feminine personal pronoun or with personal, feminine imagery, one must first justify conceiving Her as a person. One may in principle affirm that the Christian God is triune without holding that the same God is tripersonal. And some theologians have in fact espoused such a position. But if one holds for the tripersonal character of the Christian deity (as one must to speak of the Breath in personal, feminine terms), then one must also offer some account of how three divine persons subsist as one and the same God. In other words, the attempt to justify imagining the Breath as feminine plunges one into the heart of trinitarian theology.

Moreover, a foundational argument for imagining the Holy Breath as feminine must yield a normative insight into the dynamics of Christian conversion. Any image or concept of the divine which the human mind concocts remains constructural. Legitimate theological constructs succeed in interpreting the historical revelation of God which we have in fact received. They must interpret that revelation not only to Christian faith but to Christian hope and love as well. Hope especially thrives on images. A demonstration that feminine imagery correctly interprets Christians' hope in the person and saving illumination of the Holy Breath will remain inconclusive unless it rests on a survey of biblical images of the divine Breath. In other words, the attempt to imagine the Holy Breath as feminine demands that one come to terms with the images and concepts that the Bible uses to interpret Her activity and reality.

Those, then, who expect to find in these pages a narrow or exclusive preoccupation with the "femininity" of God will be sorely disappointed. For the demonstration of the legitimacy of imagining the Breath as feminine can only come as the belated conclusion, not as the premise, of a complex theological argument. That argument must show that one can legitimately think of the Christian God as both tripersonal and triune. And it must propose a construct of the Christian deity that can interpret the biblical witness to the Breath. The subtitle of this volume must then be taken at least as seriously as its title, for it describes a primary concern of its author: namely, the systematic elaboration of a trinitarian pneumatology. The title hints at an important corollary to that central argument.

In the pages which follow, I have not only chosen to refer to the third person of the Trinity as She, but I have also chosen to call Her the Holy Breath rather than the Holy Spirit. This choice too deserves some preliminary explanation. The most common Hebrew term for God's Holy Breath was the feminine noun "**ruah**". Its closest English equivalent is probably "breathing" rather than "breath." For "**ruah**" connotes breath in motion. In its application to God "**ruah**" designates a transcendent, divine life force which nevertheless enters human experience as a source of gracious illumination. The **Ruah** inspires every authentic witness of faith. Through the action of the divine Breath Yahweh becomes present in the midst of His people. A swooping, rushing wind, the **Ruah** comes unannounced and carries with it those whom it engulfs. Far from being remote, abstract, or ethereal the divine **Ruah** enters human experience as an empowering enlightenment, as force doing work.[8]

The Hebrew term "**ruah**" came to be translated by the Greek neuter noun "**pneuma**" and by the Latin masculine noun "**spiritus**." The English equivalent of all three is the neuter noun "spirit." "**Ruah**" both lost and gained something in translation. The Greek and Latin terms had acquired philosophical connotations that eventually replaced for all practical purposes the theological meaning of the biblical term "**ruah**," connotations which continue to accrue to the English word "spirit." Some of those connotations have led to pernicious philosophical and theological misunderstandings which I would just as soon avoid. I have therefore in the pages which follow preferred the term "breath" to the term "spirit" as a designation of the third person of the Trinity. "Breath" approximates better than "spirit" the biblical term "**ruah**." And it lacks the misleading connotations of the term "spirit."

I would name at least three unfortunate connotations accruing to the term "spirit." It suggests the dualistic opposition of spirit to matter. It suggests a fallacious essentialism. And in the writings of transcendental Thomists it designates a non-existent a priori drive of the mind toward Being. In the interests of clarity, let us reflect briefly on each of these misconceptions and banish them forever from the considerations which follow:

(1) **Dualism:** The term "dualism" means different things to different people. Here it refers to any attempt to distinguish two interrelated realities in such a way that their real relationship to one another becomes subsequently inconceivable. In Christian philosophy and theology spirit stands opposed to matter. But Christian thinkers have so heightened the contrast that their relationship to one another eludes coherent explanation. Think, for example, of the attempts of Christian Platonists to explain the unity of the human person as the conjunction of two distinct, essentially different substances, one spiritual, the other material. Or think

11

of the futile attempts of Christian Aristotelians to explain how material sensible faculties can move the purely spiritual faculties of intellect and will. Over the years, I have come to believe that one can describe the dynamics of Christian conversion without employing either the term "spirit" or the term "matter." And in the chapters which follow we shall attempt to describe the reality of the God encountered within conversion without invoking either term. We have, therefore, replaced the term "spirit" by the term "breath."

(2) **Essentialism:** The dualistic fallacy stands related speculatively to another one. The latter has different names. It has been called both the essence fallacy and the fallacy of misplaced concreteness. It naively reifies abstract essences instead of recognizing that they are only modes of perception, not things, not principles of being. Classical philosophical use of the terms "spirit" and "matter" illustrates this common fallacy. "Spirit" is defined classically as that which is essentially immaterial. Whatever "matter" consists of, that by its essence "spirit" cannot be. When these conceptual distinctions are reified into distinct realms or principles of being, a dualistic vision of the world results. Since we wish to avoid both the essentialistic and the dualistic connotations of the term "spirit," we have replaced it with the philosophically innocuous term "breath".

(3) **Transcendental Thomism:** In the world of transcendental philosophy and theology, "spirit" connotes the "essential, a priori dynamism of the mind toward Being." Since Being in this philosophical tradition is supposed to be infinite, the a priori drive of the mind toward it is usually characterized as virtually infinite, or as an unrestricted desire to know. How blessed we would be if this inflated conception of the human mind had any relationship to reality! Think of what a pleausre teaching would become: classrooms filled with students with an insatiable longing for knowledge. Unfortunately, however, the existence of such an intellectual drive is belied by human behavior. The human desire to know remains hopelessly finite and historically conditioned. The dynamisms which shape it result, not from some essential, a priori orientation, but from the specific habits the mind has acquired in the course of its total historical development. As a consequence, the relationship of any given mind to being, to the real, remains partial, haphazard, and variable and not isomorphic and universal as transcendental philosophy suggests. Because we wish to avoid the fallacious psychological connotations of the term "spirit", we have in the pages which follow elaborated a construct of human experience in which it does not function. And in referring to the third person of the Trinity, we have replaced the term "spirit" with the term "breath".

We have, then, embarked on an ambitious venture. We are attempting to probe the experiences that give warranty to Christian faith in a triune, tripersonal God in order to reach a normative insight into the person and reality of God's Holy Breath. We should not underestimate either the difficulty or the complexity of the problems which face us. But

12

God is faithful. And we may be sure that if we draw near to the throne of grace with loving reverence and humility, then the Breath of Truth Who loves the lowly will enfold us in Her merciful light.

1. In the pages which follow we will have occasion to survey all the important texts from sacred scripture which describe the activity and reality of the Advocate. Because we seek an integrated perception of the divine, we will examine different strains in biblical pneumatology chapter by chapter for the light each strain sheds on the problems we will be considering.

2. We shall return to these matters in greater detail in Chapter III.

3. We shall examine the pneumatological implications of the Arian crisis in Chapter V.

4. One of the saddest incidents in the development of Christian pneumatology was the division of eastern and western Christianity. The division had both political and theological motives. It has endured for centuries fed by mutual anitpathy and suspicion, despite repeated attempts at reconciliation. But ecumenical dialogue has renewed the hope that this ancient conflict may finally reach resolution.

In the year 858 a.d. Emperor Michael deposed the reigning patriarch of Constantinople and appointed Photius (c. 820-c. 891) in his stead. Michael's successor confirmed the appointment. Photius assumed office in the wake of the iconoclast controversy. The political struggle and intrigue which had accompanied the overthrow of the image smashers had left the new patriarch in a politically weakened position. At the time the power of the papacy was on the wax. The pope had succeeded in imposing his rule decisively on the occidental bishops. And papal diplomats sensed that the time might be ripe to extend papal influence in the east. The relations between the two sees degenerated. And in 867 Photius convened a synod at Constantinople that anathematized Pope Nicholas I as a heretic. Two years later a second council of Constantinople presided over by papal legates excommunicated Photius as "an intruder" and annulled all his official acts and synods.

The controversy possessed a theological dimension as well. Athanasius of Alexandria and the Cappadocian fathers had been somewhat vague concerning the origin of the divine Pneuma within the Godhead. Did the Advocate proceed from the Father alone or from both Father and Son? [Edmund J. Fortman, The Triune God (Philadelphia: Westminster, 1972) pp. 87-90; Francis Dvornik, The Photian Schism: History and Legend, New York: Cambridge, 1948; see also Hans Küng and Jürgen Moltmann, eds., Conflicts About the Holy Spirit (New York: Seabury, 1979) pp. 3-30.]

Latin theologians had been more explicit. Augustine, Ambrose, and Jerome had all taught that the divine **Spiritus** proceeds from Father and Son. Before them Tertullian had taught that the Advocate proceeds from the Father through the Son. And Hilary of Poitiers, though vaguer, seems to have held a similar position. The term **Filioque** was accordingly inserted into the Latin creed. (cf. Fortman, op. cit., p. 332.)

Photius denounced the insertion as a western aberration and transformed it into a doctrinal bone of contention with the papacy. He defended the position that the divine **Pneuma** proceeds from the Father alone but is called the **Pneuma** of the Son because sent by Him and consubstantial with Him. He attempted to marshal biblical, patristic, and conciliar support for his position. He established without difficulty that the **Pneuma** proceeds from the Father. That the Advocate proceeds from the Father alone eluded clear exegetical proof. Accordingly, in order to support his arguments from authority, Photius constructed a barrage of dialectical arguments as well (Ibid., pp. 93-94; Myst. Sp. S., 3-4, 7, 8-12, 15, 19, 31, 36). In constructing his theological case, however, Photius assumed that Latin theologians taught that the Son produces the Advocate independently of the Father. In fact the Latins taught that the divine **Spiritus** proceeds from Father and Son as from a single principle. Moreover, Photius's arguments also presupposed that the historical mission of a divine person reveals to us nothing about that person's origin in the Godhead. In Chapter III we shall argue that the missions reveal the processions.

The most important medieval treatise dealing exclusively with pneumatology was Anselm of Canterbury's De Processione Spiritus Sancti (On the Procession of the Holy Spirit) . In it Anselm undertook a polemic defense of the **Filioque.** Anselm pointed out that if the Son in generation receives the fullness of divinity from the Father, then He can communicate that same divinity to the Advocate. He also argued that if the Son sends the divine **Spiritus** as God He must be related to the Advocate as God. Among the divine persons, however, relationship is established through procession. If, then, the third person of the Trinity is sent by the Son, the Spirit must proceed from Him as well (De Processione Spiritus Sancti, II-IV, XIV). Anselm also noted that several of the Greek fathers had held that the divine **Pneuma** proceeds from the Father through the Son. He argued that "through the Son" means "from the Son" (Ibid. IX). Anselm also realized that Latin theologians had never regarded the Son as an independent source of the Advocate. Instead they had held that the third person proceeds from Them as from a single co-principle (Ibid., X, XIV).

Anselm's little treatise reads like a dress rehearsal for the Council of Florence. Florence, convened in the year 1439, was a council of reunion. Its all too brief success was prepared by two other important councils: Lateran IV (1215) and Lyons II (1274). Although thte Latin Church had added the **Filioque** to its creed, until Lateran IV no council had explicitly endorsed the doctrine its addition implied. But in 1215 Lateran IV taught that the third person proceeds from both Father and Son (**ab utroque**) (DS 805). Lyons II published two important pneumatological

14

statements. A constitution on the Trinity declared that the third person "proceeds eternally from Father and Son, not as though by two spirations, but by a unique spiration" (DS 840). The council also received the profession of faith of the Greek Emperor Michael Paleologus. The document affirmed that the three divine persons are co-essential, co-substantial, co-eternal, and co-omnipotent (DS 851). It endorsed the **Filioque** and insisted that the Trinity is "not three Gods but one God, omnipotent, eternal, indivisible, and unchangeable" (DS 853).

In the fifteenth century political pressure once again drove pope and patriarch to seek church union. The inaugural sessions of the council were held at Ferrara (1439-1445). The progress of the debates was fitful, punctuated by moments of breakthrough. First it was agreed that the Latins did not hold, as Photius had charged they did, that the divine **Spiritus** proceeds from the Son as from an independent principle within the Godhead. Father and Son function as a single co-principle of spiration. A comparison of Greek and Latin codices revealed as Anselm had insisted that Greek fathers had spoken of the procession of the **Pneuma** from the Father through the Son. On the dubious principle that saints cannot contradict one another, agreement was reached that the difference between "from" and "and" was nugatory. The council removed to the city of Florence where in 1445 the documents of reunion were signed. But on their return to their respective sees, the more conservative of the eastern patriarchs denounced the accords and charged that illegitimate pressure had been brought to bear on the Greek delegation. Once again union evaporated in the acrimony of charge and countercharge Cf. James Gill, The Council of Florence (Cambridge: Cambridge University Press, 1959); Dietrich Ritschl, "The History of the **Filioque** Controversy," Michael Fahey, "Son and Spirit: Divergent Theologies between Constantionple and the West," Theodore Stylianopoulos, "The Orthodox Postion," in Conflicts About the Holy Spirit, pp. 3-30 .

5.   We will attempt to reflect on some of the major issues raised by medieval pneumatology in Chapters V and VI.

6.   In his trinitarian theology Martin Luther (1483-1546) was doctrinally conservative. Sacred scripture, he believed, supports the doctrine of the Trinity in the form articulated in the traditional Christian creeds. Accordingly he confessed that the Advocate is both personal and divine, a reality distinct from Father and Son but co-equal with them R. Prenter, Spiritus Creator, translated by John M. Jensen (Philadelphia: Muhlenberg, 1953) pp. 174-184 .

But his pneumatology was innovative in its attempt to link pneumatic inspiration to specific kinds of religious experience. His understanding of religious experiences was, however, colored by his own anguished search for God. His early struggle with scrupulosity had convinced him that faith is bought at the price of conflict. One must not only face before God one's radical sinfulness but ratify the divine judgment of condemnation with a self-hatred (**odium sui**) that is really self-love. For

15

entic self-love is hatred of everything within oneself that is an acle to grace (Ibid., pp. 3-15).

Having confessed one's guilt before a just and terrible God, one must then claim in faith the "alien righteousness" of Christ. The power to cling to the crucified savior in faith is worked in us by the divine **Spiritus**, Who is the living presence of Christ in our hearts. Through the Advocate's illuminating presence, the gospel message of repentance and of hope is appropriated, internalized. It becomes an experienced reality (Ibid., 56-67).

Not only is our justification through faith the work of pneumatic enlightenment, but the third person of the Trinity abides within us as a source of sanctification. And in the struggle against sin, the Advocate teaches us to cling to Christ as our only hope of salvation (Ibid., pp. 70-88; Works, II, 516-517, 527, 560-561, 587-588, 592-595; XL^2, 167-168).

John Calvin (1509-1564) distinguished three spheres of pneumatic activity: in creation, in those who are not predestined to salvation, and in those who are Werner Krusche, Das Werken des Heiligen Geistes nach Calvin (Göttingen: Vandenhoeck and Ruprecht, 1957) pp. 9-63, 67-101 . He taught that all three divine persons created the universe and sustain it in being. He also regarded the third person of the Trinity as the agent that leads the course of history to the ends that God has predestined. In the predestined, pneumatic enlightenment restores the divine image lost through sin. But the Advocate also works in those who are lost, through a common grace that undoes in some measure the effects of sin, even though it falls short of justifying faith (Institutes, III, i, 4; ii, 7-8, 11).

The Advocate is especially active in Jesus and in the elect. Through the action of the Advocate Jesus becomes present to the Church in His threefold ministry of prophet, priest, and king (Krusche, op. cit., pp. 150-159). The divine **Spiritus** inspired the scriptures. In the elect the Advocate effects justification through repentance, conversion, and faith in the God of scripture, also rebirth, sanctification, and resurrection. Through the faith, hope, and love the third person of the Trinity inspires, the saints are transformed into the living body of Christ. The Advocate unifies that body creating it through charisms of service that bind the saints to one another in community. Pneumatic enlightenment also endows the sacraments with their efficacy (Krusche, op. cit., pp. 160-329; Institutes, III, i, 3-4, ii, 7-8; IV, xiv, 17).

7.   Apostolicam actuositatem, 3, 30; Lumen gentium, 4, 7; Ad gentes, 28.

8.   For a more detailed discussion of these matters, see Chapter IX.

CHAPTER II:

ON BEING AN EXPERIENCE

We seek to elaborate a foundational theology of God's Holy Breath. The foundational theologian takes a stand within a personal experience of conversion and tries to understand its conditions, its consequences, and the realities that give it shape. Realities encountered within conversion are interpreted; and the interpretation of any reality shapes the way we perceive it. A foundational pneumatology ambitions therefore an adequate and integrated perception of God's Holy Breath.

No one, of course, can completely comprehend the reality of the triune God. The divine mystery eludes the strategems of the human mind to encompass it in finite categories and images. But a foundational pneumatology can and should aspire to an applicable and adequate account of the historical self-revelation of the divine Breath which we have in fact received. An applicable interpretation of Her reality should have something to say about that revelation. An adequate pneumatology will not fail to account for every facet of the same revelation.

There have been theologians in the history of the Church who would look upon such an undertaking as an irreverent exercise in futility. When confronted with the living reality of God they have, like the repentant Job, preferred to place their fingers on their lips and sit in humble, contemplative silence before a mystery that cannot finally be expressed. They follow the path of negative theology. Praise God, they counsel, for the creatures He has made and acknowledge Him as their source. But when asked to describe the reality of God Himself, confess your humanness and be content to say only that He is not like anything He has made.

The history of theology has, however, known other bolder spirits whose reverence for God is more richly incarnational. These bolder minds have not only looked into the human face of Jesus and found there the face of God revealed, but in the joy of that encounter they have also realized that a deity who is capable of revealing Himself to us in human form cannot be utterly unlike the humanity that discloses Him. They have seen that the living reality of God can express itself in human flesh because humans, who are made in the image of God, are also called by grace to mirror His likeness. A robust incarnational faith and the theology it inspires live therefore not by negation alone but by every analogical resemblance between creature and creator. Such a faith affirms that the living reality of God both resembles and differs from the things He has made.

An analogical approach to the reality of God advances through three moments: a moment of affirmation, a moment of negation, and a moment of transcendence. In the moment of affirmation, one asserts some likeness between God and His creatures. For example, I may assert with Jesus that

God is my Father. By that I mean that something about a human child's relation to its father interprets my relationship with God. In the moment of negation one denies of God those traits present in the creature which are irreconcilable with God's way of existing. For example, if I assert that God is my Father, I must simultaneously deny that He is my biological father, even though there are other ways in which my relationship to my father resembles my relationship to God. In the moment of transcendence one asserts that despite the acknowledged differences between creature and creator, nevertheless there are some traits in creatures that find their supreme exemplification in God. For example, while I recognize that God is not my biological father, as a Christian I believe that the divine Father typifies all created fatherhood (Ep. 3:14-15). Indeed, He is its supreme exemplification. If human fathers at their best are loving, nurturing, lifegiving, and faithful, the divine Father exemplifies these traits in the most perfectly conceivable way.

There may be those who concede that philosophers may legitimately approach God through the way of analogy but who may wonder whether analogical access to the supreme mystery of the Christian faith is either possible or desirable. Jesus' **Abba** experience certainly presupposes the legitimacy of discovering in human parental relationships an analogical revelation of God's saving intentions toward us. But the doctrine of the Trinity in its traditional systematic formulation seems at first glance a mystery pretty far removed from ordinary human experience. Human persons we know, but a tripersonal reality that is simultaneously triune simply has no created counterpart. For it is one thing to aspire to an analogical understanding of the reality of God but quite another thing to discover the analogies.

The Thomistic attempt to understand the divine essence through the analogy of being is familiar. But most people find such a metaphysical approach to God through technical philosophical notions like act and potency, essence and existence pretty abstract and remote. Worse still, as a way of understanding the triune God the analogy of being falters at important points. For example, in Thomistic metaphysics the divine essence is pure Being, pure act, and therefore by its very nature simple. What is simple lacks all internal complexity. A tripersonal God is, however, internally complex. Moreoever, the God of classical metaphysics cannot in principle be related to His creatures. But the triune God has entered into covenant with us; and covenant relationships are reciprocal. For both these reasons, one may then legitimately question whether Christians actually worship the God metaphysically described as pure Being.

Contemporary process theology has also been concerned to discover an analogical resemblance between creature and creator. Like Thomism, process speculation is no stranger to abstraction. But the analogy it discovers between the divine and the human is more attractive in its immediacy than is the metaphysical analogy of being. In process theory creature and creator resemble one another because both are experiences. Certainly nothing is more immediate to humans than their own personal experience. Were it then possible to conceive the triune God on an analogy with human experience, the attempt might conceivably rescue trinitarian belief from the abstract remoteness to which ancient and medieval theology has consigned it. The possibility is fascinating enough to merit exploration.

But one should not be too sanguine about interpreting the reality of the Christian God in experiential categories borrowed from process speculation. The Christian God is triune and therefore triadic. But experience in process theory is dipolar. Its first pole is concrete and efficacious; its second, abstract and conceptual. As the supreme exemplification of experience, the God of process theology is dipolar, not triadic.

There are other difficulties attending the understanding of experience defended by process theologians. For in addition to being dipolar, experience in process theory is also atomic in its structure. Each atomic unit of experience emerges only to perish within a fraction of a second. Any observable individual is conceived as a society of atomic occasions of experience. The society is unified by a common subjective aim that is carried on from one occasion to the next.

The social atomicity of experience leaves the strict Whiteheadian somewhat hard pressed to come up with a unified conception of a human person. If, for example, I attempt as a Whiteheadian to think a historical person like George Washington, I must decide whether I mean the pure possibility of George Washington, the society of actual occasions that was George Washington, or one particular occasion within the society. There may be those who find here an adequate account of the unity and continuity of human personal experience. But I must confess that I do not number myself among them.[1]

More directly to the point, the atomic structure of experience also poses a serious dilemma to a process theology. The orthodox Whiteheadian must hold either that the divine experience is atomic in its structure or that it is a single actual occasion of experience. If God is a single occasion of experience, then God's relation to the world becomes inexplicable. For as long as a single actual occasion of experience is in process, it is impervious to outside influence. As a single actual occasion God would, then, be eternally indifferent to whatever transpires in the world. If, on the other hand, the divine experience is atomic in its structure, then the cosmos dissolves into atomic fragments bereft of any ultimate divine principle of unity.[2]

I do not intend to harrass the reader with detailed reflections on the strengths and weaknesses of process theory. Rather, I am only attempting to dramatize the fact that in the pages which follow neither the category "experience" nor the category "God" means the same thing as it does to the orthodox Whiteheadian. I say so despite the fact that my own speculative approach to the Christian God is analogous to that taken by process thinkers. For I have come to believe that the God Christians worship can indeed be conceived on an analogy with human **social** experience. I have also come to believe that a theology of the Holy Breath provides us with the means for approaching the triune God experientially and for understanding the divine society as an experience.

Only Christians experience God as triune. The Hebrews believed in one God and experienced the Holy **Ruah** as the saving presence of Yahweh. But it took the incarnation for the one God to be perceived as tripersonal. The experiential basis of that faith was Jesus' experience of His unique filial relationship to the Father, His communication of that experience to His disciples, His subsequent revelation to them in the resurrection as Lord, and the Christian community's experience of the divine Breath as the presence of both Father and Son. Once the implications of that complex historical event were clearly understood, place had to be made within the Godhead for Father, Son, and Breath; and the relationship of all the members of the divine triad had to be conceived on an analogy with the Son's relation to the Father.

But while all orthodox Christians perceive God as triune, they do not all perceive the triune God as an experience. Both the speculative legitimacy and the creedal orthodoxy of such an affirmation need to be argued. But then so did the affirmation that God is three in one.

In process theory the perception of God as an experience follows from Whitehead's equation of experience and reality. He made the equation in enunciating his reformed subjectivist principle. An examination of some of the important implications of his principle promises us initial clarity. The principle states that "apart from the experiencing of subjects there is nothing, nothing, nothing, bare nothingness."[3]

First of all, we should recall that Whiteheadian subjects differ from Aristotelian subjects in significant ways. Aristotelian subjects underlie change and endow it with essential continuity. In an Aristotelian understanding of human growth, for example, the human substance with its perduring substantial essence is the subject that underlies its every accidental modification. Among those accidental modifications are the human subject's personal experiences. But Whiteheadian subjects emerge within the process of change. They are a developing complex of physical, conceptual, and propositional feelings. They do not have experiences. They incarnate a way of experiencing the world. And they are the very experiences they incarnate.

Every systematic philosophy must at some point offer a descriptive account of reality. The classical Thomist defines being, or reality, as that which exists and divides it into act and potency. Act is an intrinsic principle of specification; potency, an intrinsic capacity for being specified. The Whiteheadian defines reality as experience and divides it into what is experienced and the way in which what is experienced is experienced.

The Whiteheadian equation of experience and reality raises a number of important philosophical questions, questions that are relevant to the reflections which follow. Whitehead uses the term "experience" quite idiosyncratically. Let us then probe some of its peculiarities.

In the language of common sense "experience" means practical, cumulative wisdom acquired through more or less prolonged acquaintance with some reality or with some way of doing things. This usage of the term occurs in a phrase like: "Only experienced personnel need apply." But the term "experience" has also acquired a number of technical philosophical definitions.

One may, for example, take "experience" to mean the knowledge gained through sensory cognition. In this sense, what is experienced not only supplies the data for human understanding, judgment, and decision but is superceded by them as insight is transformed first into validated knowledge and then into concrete activity.

An analogous use of "experience" distinguishes the data of sense from the data of consciousness. The data of sense supplies the information needed to understand and judge the world around us; the data of consciousness supplies the information needed to understand one's own thought processes. Both the data of sense and the data of consciousness are, however, taken to be the object of "experience." "Experience" in this third sense is no longer correlated exclusively with the operations of the "lower" powers of the mind. Instead, it is restricted to the first stage in the mind's advance to insight and judgment. But in this third sense of "experience," understanding, judgment, and decision continue to sublate and supercede experience itself.

A fourth and broader understanding of "experience" contrasts experience with whatever is known in any way. What is known is the object of experience; experience itself, the way things are known.

A fifth understanding of the term "experience" would restrict it to conscious acts of the mind. Some philosophical epistemologies rule out in principle the possibility of unconscious cognition. And some contemporary positivists seem quite content to discard the idea of an unconscious experience as speculatively useless.

A sixth and final restrictive use of the term experience limits its applicability to living, sensing, or thinking beings. These may legitimately be said to experience themselves and their world. But inanimate realities are themselves without experience, though they are objects of experience.

21

But Whitehead's reformed subjectivist principle points the way to a use of "experience" that encompasses all of the previous senses of the term and goes beyond them. For in equating reality and experience the reformed subjectivist principle transforms "experience" into a transcendental category, i.e., into a term universally applicable in intent. In such an understanding of "experience" the cumulative wisdom of which common sense speaks would be an instance of experience but not the only instance. The data of sense and of consciousness would be objects of experience; but understanding, judgment, and decision would no longer be looked upon as sublating and superceding experience. Rather they would be transformed into modalities of experience itself. Instead of being opposed to the things it knows, "experience" used transcendentally would include them. For in a world of experiences reality divides into what is experienced and the way what is experienced is experienced. Both however are aspects of experience itself. When used transcendentally "experience" would encompass both conscious and unconscious acts. And it would apply in intent to both living and non-living things.

That the term "experience" can be extended even to inanimate processes can, of course, be debated, although Whitehead's position can also be argued. But his attempt to transform "experience" into a transcendental category remains theologically suggestive. It suggests a new way of perceiving the reality of God, one which attenuates somewhat the distance that separates us from the divine mystery. For if both God and I are experiences, we share something immediate and intimate in common. For nothing is more immediate and intimate than one's own experience.

But anyone who ambitions constructing an adequate trinitarian theology by parroting the insights of Whitehead will end in sore speculative disappointment. The problems are both linguistic and speculative. Whitehead's language for describing the dynamics of experiential development is couched in terms so technically abstract that it sounds to most people like unintelligible jargon. Even could we conceive the Trinity in technical Whiteheadian categories, the resulting doctrine would be as speculatively remote from the experience of most believers as the airiest abstractions of medieval trinitarian thelogians. Moreover, as we have already seen, we have reason to believe that a dipolar construct of experience can never interpret the reality of a triadic God.

No. If we are to understand the Christian God as an experience we must make a fresh speculative start. We must attempt a descriptive analysis of experience that avoids as much as possible technical philosophical jargon. And we must see whether or not one can derive from such a description an interpretation of the term "experience" that applies not only to humans but to the God Christians worship.

In a sense nothing is more obvious or immediate than our own experience: our felt sense of ourselves and of the persons and things we see; our visceral and kinetic sensations; whatever we hear, taste, touch, and smell; our joy and our sorrow, rage and frustration, dreams and fantasies; our beliefs, calculations, predictions; our disappointments and triumphs; the myriad things we do and suffer each day.

Yet despite its immediacy few realities resist easy generalization as effectively as experience. We all experience something, but we do not always experience the same things. And even when we do, we all too often experience them in different ways. Two friends may go to a movie: one will find it a triumph; the other, a flop. What one person experiences with heightened consciousness, another will overlook with bland indifference. A geologist and a six-year-old may both view the Grand Canyon, but they will not see it with the same eyes. A symphony conductor and a rock-and-roll teenager may listen to a Brandenburg concerto; but one will hear much more than the other. Even our senses play tricks on us: they decay with age, are warped by disease, are duped by habit and expectation. And what different kinds of things we experience! The space age scientist and the Australian aborigine would probably find one another's worlds equally baffling.

The very profusion and diversity of human experience have caused some to despair of making any generalizations about it at all. But things are not so serious as all that. For up to a point we can describe its shape with a measure of security. Certainly, every human experiences something. We experience ourselves. And we experience other selves with whom we interact. Among those other selves we correctly distinguish those who are persons and those that are less than persons. We call the latter "things."

In point of fact, if we attend carefully to the dynamic shape of human experience, we can discover there three shifting and interrelated realms. We respond evaluatively to ourselves and to our world. Our evaluative responses range from concrete sensations to abstract conceptions. In the pages which follow we shall call the realm of human evaluation the experiential realm of **quality.** Besides responding evaluatively to reality, we also interact decisively with persons and things we encounter. We bump into them, and they bump back. Let us call the realm of decisive action and reaction the experiential realm of **fact.** Through our evaluations and decisions we engage the selves that populate our world. They play the alter to my ego. For I myself am a self like them. The selves that react and respond evaluatively and decisively cannot be reduced to the evaluations and decisions they generate. For reasons that will become apparent, we will call the selves that people experience the experiential realm of **law,** for they can be described as habitual tendencies to react or respond in specific ways. And habitual tendencies are laws. Let us begin to explore these three realms of experience. For as we shall see, their character is transformed by the gracious illumination of God's Holy Breath.

23

We experience the selves around us initially through sight, sound, touch, taste, and smell. We experience our own bodies through visceral and kinetic sensations, through pleasure and pain. These sensory experiences seem vivid, especially when we contrast them with mere memories or fantasies. But when they are compared to a nuanced and warranted explanation of their meaning, they appear somehow blurred by comparison. Millions of Americans have, for example, watched TV coverage of a liftoff at Cape Canaveral. And space scientists have watched the same event from mission control in Houston. The flash and roar of the engines, the slow rise of the massive rocket, its arching curve as it hurtles heavenward. But the space scientist's perception of what is happening at that moment and the perceptions of the average American are light years apart. Both see and hear roughly the same sensory image; but one perceives its meaning in detail and the other does not. What appears to each is, then, finally quite different.

The key word is "perception." For we must distinguish within experience between sensation and perception. Our sensations are forced upon us. We cannot wish away the glowing hues, the bustling sounds, the varied smells, tastes and touches, the titillating delights and startling pangs that crowd in on us at any given moment. We may ignore many of them. Within limits we can choose among a spectrum of possible sensations. But in the moment of sensory encounter itself, things force themselves upon us without so much as a by your leave. And that force is a fact.

But we exercise more direct control over our perceptions. For in our perceptions we interpret the significance of the things we sense. And in the act of interpretation we endow that significance with meaning. For meaning is the evaluative grasp of significance. As we shall see, when human experience yields to the gracious illumination of God's Holy Breath, it acquires a sacramental significance. And that significance, too, can be perceived.

Some perceptions resemble sensations. They occur spontaneously and resist manipulation. When I sit in a moving vehicle, things seem to slip past the window willy nilly, no matter how often I tell myself that I, not they, am moving. Such perceptions seem to be sensed; but they betray their interpretative character by deceiving us. They are, then, perceptions in the strict sense, primitive and deceptive perhaps but perceptions nonetheless. As our perceptual interpretations of the things we sense become more differentiated, however, they acquire suppleness and begin to yield to conscious control.

Within the spectrum of human perceptual responses, we can distinguish two realms: affectivity and inference. Human affections are linked to motor reactions. A sudden noise will make me jump. Unexpected contact with a slimy object will cause me to recoil. But affections are also modes of perception. They interpret the significance of sensory stimuli. Moreover, because they interpret reality, they trigger motor activity. Both the sympathetic and the negative affections illustrate these two facets of human affectivity. Pain, for example, tends to give rise to the negative feelings of fear or anger. I react fearfully to a painful stimulus when I perceive it as both threatening and beyond my power to control. Fear breeds the impulse to flee. I react angrily to a painful stimulus when I perceive it as conquerable. And anger breeds assault. Similarly, I perceive with fond affection those who comfort and befriend me. And affection breeds the deeds of love.

We have described the affective perceptions of sensed realities as interpretative. And so they are. But we should not be too quick to sunder sensation from perception with abstract artificiality. Studies of human sensation suggest that they are themselves emotionally tinged. For human sensory experience, despite its extraverted character does not consist in the experience of bare objects unrelated to any sensing knower. Sensations involve complex transactions between sensible realities and sensate organisms. In sensation one experiences not only the sensed thing but the complex transaction by which it comes to be sensibly present to the one who knows it. Hence, when light radiating from a surface strikes the retina of my eye and when that event is communicated to my brain, I experience not only a colored surface but also in a vague way the kind of reality it is for me. The latter feeling is a germinal perception. Our subsequent affective perceptions of the things we sense prolong the inchoate affective component already present within sensation itself. In the process they allow us to begin however gropingly to grasp the significance of sensory events.

Our affective perceptions of reality do not obey the laws of logic. But they judge reality. When I perceive some sensed reality as painful and threatening or as pleasant and desirable, I pass primitive judgment upon it, a judgment that resembles analogously logical affirmations or negations. A judgment of feeling resembles logical judgments only analogously for its motives are affective and irrational. Still, a sympathetic affective judgment affirms; and a negative affective judgment denies. Judgmental acts based on irrational feeling often cannot be defended on strict rational principles; but they occur nevertheless. Though vaguer than logical judgments, they stand closer to the biological rhythms that shape experience. In the balanced psyche affective and logical affirmations and negations reenforce one another. In the sick, disturbed soul they stand at loggerheads. As we shall see, judgments of feeling are graciously transformed by the charism of discernment.

Affective perceptions focus experience on some reality of importance to the perceiver. They render the perceived reality attractive, fearful, or hateful, but always somewhat interesting. That is to say, affective perceptions render the perceiver attentive. Through attention experience acquires an enhanced sense of purpose.

But our attentive perceptions are not mediated by vague feelings only. They are also mediated by images. Some images are remembered. In our more primitive memories we recall some past event. Primitive memories resemble after images that linger in the wake of a vivid sensation. They occur spontaneously, occasioned by some occurrence that reminds us of them. On seeing the photograph of a loved one, I may, for example, be suddenly flooded with the vision of some shared intimacy. On climbing a mountain top, I may recall other similar peaks and vistas I have seen. Habit and recent occurrence condition the survival of remembered images. So do physical resemblance, juxtaposition in space and time, and conceptual, linguistic, or symbolic associations.

But not every memory involves a simple act of recall. Other memories are more contrived. Instead of being spontaneous, they are reconstructed. I may, for example, try to remember where I left the car keys, or whether I locked the front door, or exactly what someone said or did on a given occasion. Reconstructed memories can err. They engage interest. Sometimes they engage self-interest. And self-interest easily transforms itself into self-deception.

Memories perceive past events. All events are transactions. As long as the transaction continues, the events themselves are actual. Events become present to me, however, through sensation and perception. Once the transaction ends, an event ceases to be actual. But as long as I myself survive, it can become present to me through memory. For memory serves as the incremental repository of the way events were sensed and perceived.

There is a more general truth worth noting here: namely, that our evaluative responses ground our experience of the present moment, for through them we become present to ourselves and our world, and they to us.

Reconstructive memory resembles fantasy. Memory reconstructs something that actually occurred. Fantasy constructs something that never was but conceivably might be. The threads of the tapestry fantasy weaves are spun by memory. In moments of fantasy we dream of what may be or might have been. But what we hope for always bears a family resemblance to what we have known. Even our most creative fantasies build upon the past, mating in thought images that never met in actuality.

Besides remembered and created images we experience archetypal ones. They too give shape to our affective perception of the real. Archetypal images occur spontaneously. They do not recall specific events. Nor do they seem to be the children of creative fantasy. Archetypal images happen to us. When they surge into consciousness like a breaching whale, they vibrate with affective energy. As a consequence, they grip the imagination with an authority and a power not to be ignored. Our attempt to imagine the Holy Breath as feminine builds on archetypal theory. Let us then try to understand how they function within human experience.

Every archetype possesses at least four facets: each displays an affective, a symbolic, an apparent, and a structural component. The **affective** component of an archetypal image consists in the vaguer, more primitive feelings it endows with new conceptual clarity. Since an archetype can illumine either sympathetic or negative feelings, it can be charged with either creative or destructive energy.

The **symbolic** element in an archetype consists of the image which gives it meaning: images of heroes and or heroines, of benign or conniving mothers and fathers; of clown suits and weaponry; of dark, menacing figures, of gods and of devils; of mandalas and hermaphrodites; of dragon fights and marriages.

The **apparent** component of an archetype consists of the conscious meaning we attach to it. But conscious insight into archetypal symbolism does not exhaust its meaning. For the archetype has deep intertwining roots in the unconscious psyche. Being affectively charged, every archetype has the power to gather to itself a host of conscious and unconscious images and feelings.

The **structure** of an archetype consists of the network of images and affections, both conscious and unconscious, which the archetypal image attracts to itself in meaningful clusters. In virtue of its structure, every archetype has a heuristic function, namely, a capacity to organize an affective perception of meaning. Perhaps the experience of synchronicity best illustrates the heuristic function of an archetype. We experience synchronicity most commonly as a meaningful coincidence: as the chance juxtaposition of things, persons, images, events which assume unexpected symbolic meaning. The meaningful coincidence has no logical explanation. For it obeys, not the laws of logic, but those of human affectivity. Synchronistic perceptions of meaning are often organized by an archetype.

An example may help concretize these abstractions. Eight years ago I helped plan a river trip which resulted in the accidental death of a friend. I was shattered by the experience. The day before the funeral I went into the chapel to pray. As I wrestled there with God and with my own feelings of grief and of guilt, I felt moved to open the New Testament and read. I found my finger resting on the account of Jesus' burial in Mark. Crucifixion functions as a standard archetype for ego disintegration; the risen Christ functions as a standard archetype of the self. The passage spoke to me with a power I continue to feel every time I read it. What gave it power was the complex archetypal image of a crucified, yet victorious Christ. It spoke to me of my friend and of myself, of God and of human brokenness, of sorrow and of hope, of realism and of faith, of forgiveness and of compassion, of dying and of rising. It was not a rational experience. But it was a profoundly meaningful one.

27

We often describe images as concrete. Images are certainly more concrete than abstract universals. Remembered images are utterly concrete. I may, for example, recall the house where I grew up or dancing at my senior prom. Anticipatory images are also concrete. I may anticipate that the water on the stove will boil if left long enough over the fire. And eventually it does. But in the case of both remembered and anticipatory images the concreteness of the image is a function of the reality it attempts to interpret. Images, however, function in a variety of interpretative contexts. And sometimes our images intend meanings that are universal rather than concrete. Such, for example, are the images which structure the parables of Jesus or myths of the origin and end of all things. We know the good Samaritan as a character in a parable; but he confronts us not as a concrete, historical individual but as an image of what every human is called to be. In the story of Adam and Eve, Adam symbolizes every man, Eve symbolizes every woman.

As we shall see, the gracious transformation of intuitive, imaginative perceptions of reality is effected by the gift of prophecy. And in the final chapter of this book, we shall try to understand how the archetype of the feminine organizes Christian hope in the divine Breath.

The concrete universals that structure imaginative thinking form a cognitive link between irrational thinking and inferential forms of perception. For logical inference presupposes the ability to grasp abstract universals as such.

Abstract universal concepts result from definition. We intend defined terms to apply to all the members of a given class of things. Our abstract classifications of things express human purposes. They seek to expedite our dealings with the realities around us by allowing us to anticipate the way in which they may be expected to behave. Our best and clearest definitions are as a consequence operational.

Inferential thinking grasps relationships rationally, through logical implication. Implication is a conceptual relationship expressed by the correlatives "if...then." Significant events acquire logical implications when they come to be interpreted by a predefined set of interrelated, abstract symbols. A crime, for example, acquires legal implications only when it has been shown to stand in violation of a predefined code of law in which specific misdemeanors and felonies are carefully defined and their punitive consequences indicated.

Inference seeks to establish the truth or falsity of specific propositions. A proposition expresses an inference in linguistic shorthand. A true proposition applies to events in the sense in which it was defined. A false one fails to apply to events as defined. A probable proposition applies as defined only to a portion of those events it attempts to interpret.

The establishment of the truth or falsity of propositions engages three different kinds of inference: abductive, deductive, and inductive. Abductive inference formulates the proposition whose truth or falsity needs to be established. Deductive inference explicitates the implications of a formulated hypothesis. Inductive inference tests the predicted implications of a deductively clarified hypothesis against events. And interrelated sets for propositions form a logical frame of reference. As we shall see, the charisms of teaching wisdom and understanding graciously transform human inferential responses.

Perhaps we should at this point pause and take stock of our progress. We are attempting a foundational pneumatology. Our approach is experiential. That is to say, we are attempting to understand how the converted Christian ought to experience the reality of God's Holy Breath. We need therefore to clarify the meaning of the term "experience." We are trying to do so by exploring descriptively the different realms of human experience.

We have discovered within human experience an evaluative continuum stretching from sensation to abstract inference. The continuum consists of a spectrum of evaluations that blend imperceptibly into one another like the colors in the visual spectrum. We have found that sensations which disclose the impact of impinging actualities are emotionally tinged and blend into affective forms of perception. Memories of sensed events are transformed by the creative imagination into fantasy. And imagistic thinking endows affective perceptions with an enhanced degree of clarity and differentiation. Images of universal import form an interpretative bridge between images that are concrete and abstract, inferential modes of thinking. Appreciative insights are linked by spontaneous connotations; inferential insights by logical implication. The continuum of evaluation is reflected in the structure of human language. The terms we use to describe the things we sense have both affective connotations and logical implications. In other words, they engage both affective and logical frames of reference.

Moreover, within the spectrum of human evaluation we have discovered both conscious and unconscious evaluative responses. But once again we are confronted by a continuum of evaluative responses. Attention focuses consciousness through interest. But we are conscious of more realities than those to which we attend. As we approach the periphery of conscious perception, clear distinctions evaporate and consciousness fades into memory and the subconscious. Subconscious evaluative responses blend into obscure psychosomatic and biological rhythms that shape us as organisms.

We may on the basis of the preceding descriptive analysis hazard a number of generalizations about human experience. First of all, it possesses an evaluative component. Second, that evaluative component endows experience with a sense of quality, for it tells me what things are, their character for me or for any other human mind. Third, qualities are of necessity particular, for this felt characteristic is never that. Red is not blue, green, orange, or brown. Orangutan is not giraffe is not kangaroo is not platypus. Being particular, qualities endow experience with a feeling of suchness. Qualities become universal through use, through intentional application to all, not to just some, of their referents. Fourth, the evaluative component within experience also mediates our experience of the present moment. For through our evaluative responses to persons and things they become present to us and we to them.

But if we attend to the structure of human experience, we will quickly realize that in addition to responding evaluatively, we also react decisively. Our decisions are all transactions. They retaliate to the brusk intrusions of the world.

Transactions happen. They are events. They contribute concreteness to experience. Some decisions may resemble one another because they terminate similar evaluative processes. I may, for example, on a series of muggy afternoons decide to take a cool shower. But in the last analysis each decision taken in its full concrete reality can never be repeated. At the very least, it would occur at a different time. Taken all in all, it remains forever itself and nothing else, a unique, irreversible, incremental addition to the repository of history and experience, a datable, locatable happening that is this occurrence and no other.

Not every decision deals with alternatives. Knee jerk reactions lack evaluative discrimination. But to the extent that we do opt among discriminated alternatives, our decisions are free. For freedom consists in the ability to act or not to act, to do one kind of thing or another.

The fact that we act with more or less freedom on different occasions tells us some important things about the relationship between evaluation and decision. First of all, it points to the fact that the character of our decisions is a function of the kinds of evaluative responses they terminate. When, for example, I choose to take a stroll rather than to study, I choose between two courses of activity that confront me as realistic possibilities. Before I choose one over the other, both possibilities are only evaluative perceptions of my immediate future. In choosing one and rejecting the other, I render one of those possible futures actual and concrete, the other eternally impossible for that particular segment of space and time. As we shall see, charisms like leadership and administration together with the other action gifts graciously transform human decisions and endow them with a sacramental character.

Second, because the character of a decision is a function of the evaluative response it terminates, the relative freedom of any human decision is grounded not in the decision itself but in the evaluative process it ends. The more differentiated my evaluative perception of the alternatives confronting me, the freer will be my choice. For I cannot choose this over that until I recognize that the one is not the other. Consciousness too grows through evaluative discrimination and synthesis. Hence, freedom and consciousness wax and wane together.

We may conclude that those things will enhance freedom which foster the evaluative discrimination of realistic alternatives for action. By the same token, what inhibits such evaluative dscrimination will diminish freedom of response. A New Yorker may, for example, choose among a broad range of classical concerts almost any night of the year. The same options do not exist in Opelousas, Louisiana. But the New Yorker who ignores the concert schedule will be no freer to attend than the Louisiana Cajun. And New Yorkers who know the schedule but who have never learned to listen to classical music or who have been trained to despise it will be free in principle to attend one of the concerts. But they will be prevented in practice by the lack of differentiation in their habitual perception of the available musical opportunities. Their present tendency to misprize classical music results, moreover, from previous decisions to ignore or despise it.

We may, then, identify five factors that enhance or inhibit the degree of freedom present in any given human decision. Those factors are environmental, conceptual, perspectival, habitual, and decisive. They condition one another. But each of them fosters or stifles freedom by **either increasing or diminishing the degree of evaluative discrimination antecedent to any given choice.**

A sound insight into the sources of human freedom will enter in significant ways into our understanding of what it means to be a human person. It will therefore also condition our understanding of the Holy Spirit as a divine person. For the category "divine person" must be extrapolated from reflection on human personal experience. Moreover, understanding the sources of human freedom will assume enhanced speculative importance when we consider Jesus' relation to the Holy Breath and His freedom under grace. Let us then attend in some detail to this important facet of human experience.

Our environment defines the range of realistic possibilities for choice. Every choice responds to something. The smaller my world the fewer the things to which I may respond. A teenager in Topeka may dream of becoming a movie star; but the dream will remain a pipe dream without a change of address. A marine in boot camp enjoys limited recreational opportunities. The slumdweller and the heiress have in the concrete access to very different educational opportunities.

But even an environment rich with potential options can emprison one without the evaluative equipment to deal with it. For realistic possibilities for choice must be discriminated before they are selected. One may, for example, turn a six-year-old loose in the Library of Congress, but that bored child will find few books to excite its interest.

31

Acts of discrimination occur within frames of reference. Frames of reference consist of interrelated propositions. They express either affective or logical perceptions depending on whether they follow the laws of emotion and intuition, on the one hand, or of logic and reason, on the other. Frames of reference are neither true nor false; but they can be more or less adequate to interpret different realms of experience. An inadequate frame of reference will inhibit my capacity to discriminate realistic possibilities. An adequate frame of reference will facilitate discrimination. For example, as long as humans thought of the earth as flat, the possibility of sailing around it remained unthinkable. It became a real possibility with a more adequate conception of the shape of the planet.

Most of the evaluative discriminations we make are habitual. Evaluative habits can become rigid and inflexible through routine, neurosis, and inhibition. When that happens, the ability to differentiate possible courses of action may diminish; and freedom may languish. But healthy habits are useful skills that create realistic possibilities for action and flexible powers of discrimination. The skilled harpsichordist has a rich repertoire of pieces to play which baffle and frustrate the novice musician. Similarly, the accomplished political scientist can without effort point out the possible strategems that might save a troubled situation.

Finally, the freedom of any given decision is conditioned by antecedent choices. The antecedent decisions may be my own or another's. Those decisions will stifle freedom which create constricting environments, which prevent the acquisition of useful skills or foster inadequate habits of evaluative discrimination, and which leave one trapped in an inadequate frame of reference. Those decisions, on the other hand, will enhance the growth of freedom which create interesting and stimulating environments, which encourage the learning of useful skills and of discriminating evaluative responses, and which expand the horizons within which evaluation occurs.

We are attempting to understand the relationship between evaluation and decision within human experience. We have found that both the character and the freedom of any decision is determined by the kind of evaluative processes it terminates. There is, however, another facet of the relationship between evaluation and decision to which we must attend. For it will shape our understanding of human personhood and of our relationship to the Holy Breath.

Although all decisions derive their character from the evaluative processes they terminate, some decisions are not concerned directly with persons or things as such but with our attitudes and beliefs about them. We also decide about our evaluative stance itself. We fix attitudes, beliefs, and frames of reference. These preliminary decisions about one's personal evaluative stance toward reality prepare one's final reactive impact upon one's world. The decision to fear or to befriend another, will, for example, ultimately determine the way I deal with the individual in question. I will relate in one way to God if I believe that He is vindictive and in another way if I believe that He is compassionate and loving. An analyst who is a convinced Freudian and one who is a convinced Jungian will each relate very differently to patients.

Of special importance among those preliminary decisions that shape one's evaluative stance to reality is conversion. For not only does conversion affect the character of one's decision; but it also has a special impact on the freedom with which they are made.

Conversion in its most generic sense is the decision to assume personal responsibility for the quality of one's subsequent development in some area of human experience. Initial conversion occurs when one first takes such a decision. Through ongoing conversion we attempt to live out the consequences of initial conversion.

Through conversion human decisions become personally responsible. Responsible behavior reflects critically upon itself and submits to ideals that it acknowledges as personally binding. In responsible behavior I measure the quality of the things I choose to do against the ideal self that I know I ought to become. Responsible behavior, therefore, concerns itself especially with the causes and consequences of one's personal choices. For when the consequences of my choices fall culpably short of my self ideal they become irresponsible. When they advance toward that same ideal in the measure humanly possible, they are responsible. And a sound insight into the causes of human behavior clarifies the realistic limits of choice.

We should distinguish four kinds of personal conversion. They correspond to four distinct realms of human experience in which responsible behavior is possible. Let us name those realms: affective, moral, speculative, and religious. Affective conversion submits to sound ideals of emotional development. Speculative, or intellectual, conversion submits to sound logical and methodological norms. Moral conversion submits to sound ethical ideals and principles. And religious conversion, to ideals revealed by God. Through socio-political conversion I assume responsibility for the decisions other than my own over which I exercise influence. Socio-political conversion culminates in devotion to a cause.

In the pages which follow, we shall argue that the capacity for responsible behavior distinguishes persons from selves less than personal. We shall also argue that religious conversion transforms and transvalues the other forms of conversion and endows them with ultimate meaning and purpose. Moreover, since the Holy Breath inspires religious conversion, we shall argue that She enters human experience as its ultimate personalizing principle.

The human experience of conversion remains incredibly complex. We cannot therefore examine all of its dynamics. We are presently concerned only with the relationship between evaluation and decision

33

within human experience. Conversion affects the quality of one's evaluative responses. For the integrally converted individual is concerned not only with the truth and falsity of human belief and hope but also with the uprightness of moral decision, the quality and intensity of religious love, the adequacy of the frames of reference within which attitudes, beliefs, moral choices, and religious acts occur.

Every conversion, whether initial or ongoing involves conscious acts of self-appropriation. I cannot take personal charge of my affective, intellectual, moral, socio-political, and religious growth without engaging in strictly normative thinking. For strictly normative thinking shifts the focus of consciousness initially from one's world to oneself. In the process it opens the door to a differentiated understanding of unacknowledged possibilities for personal growth.

By creating the possibility for strictly normative thinking, conversion significantly enhances the development of human freedom. Through ongoing conversion I understand and master the obstacles to healthy affective, intellectual, moral and religious growth. I learn to distinguish critically between life-giving and destructive choices; and I learn to recognize the frames of reference that lead to either life or death. Inevitably, then, the convert advances toward the future with a clearer perception of different kinds of human options. Such perception cannot but enhance freedom.

We have dwelt at some length on the human experience of freedom. **Of crucial importance is the realization that the freedom of any human decision is grounded not in the decision itself but in the degree of differentiation present in the evaluative processes which the decision terminates.** To put the matter in grammatical terms, freedom when viewed experientially should be understood not as a noun or as an adjective but as an adverb. I am free or enjoy freedom only because I choose free**ly**. For freedom is in the last analysis an aspect of the evaluative shape of an experience.

There is another facet of the relationship between evaluation and decision that we need to consider, for it will help explain the sacramental character of graced experience. I refer to the fact that that decision punctuates evaluation by both initiating and terminating evaluative response. Sometimes the termination of evaluative response advances in stages. In the preliminary stages I opt for this or that frame of reference and fix my attitudes and beliefs. In the terminal phase of decision one acts out of fixed beliefs and attitudes. Decisions or facts are either initial or final with respect to the evaluative processes they punctuate.

Initial facts may be self-caused. I may jump into a lake only to discover to my dismay that the water is far colder than I had anticipated. I must then decide whether to endure its rigors or return to the sunny bank. But initial facts are never exclusively self-motivated. For my choices create new situations in which realities other than myself intrude themselves upon me. Their impact starts me sensing, feeling, thinking anew.

Final facts terminate evaluative responses. One always initiates them oneself, even though they may be motivated by events beyond one's personal control. I may, for example, lapse into a reverie while trying to decide whether or not to take a job with a particular firm only to be startled by a gunshot. It is not the gunshot itself, however, that terminates my reverie but the split-second decision I make to attend to it rather than to the details of my financial future. If I am deeply absorbed in my reverie, I may, of course, scarcely hear the gunshot.

Facts, decisions, always initiate or terminate specific evaluative responses. As a consequence, a final act which terminates a sequence of evaluations when once posited may become initial with respect to a novel evaluative sequence. Every preliminary choice either establishes a revisable attitude or belief or accepts a frame of reference that can be critically set aside. Similarly, every terminal decision is sensed; and every sensation initiates a new process of perception. Morever, as we shall see, every final fact which terminates an evaluative response illumined by the Holy Breath is graciously transformed into a sacramental symbol of Her indwelling.

We have been exploring the relationship between evaluation and decision within experience. Our evaluations constitute an identifiable realm of experience. We have called it the realm of quality. Qualities are values, and endow experience with particular suchness. Decisions, however, constitute a different realm of experience. Let us call it the realm of fact.

The realm of fact is the realm of action and reaction. Facts make experience concrete. They effect this rather than that. They are irrevocable and unrepeatable: having been done they can never be undone. Nor can the same concrete act be performed twice. At the very least it must be done at a different moment. Facts shape one's environment: they establish social links between interacting selves. Facts are hard: they set realistic limits to future growth and development. The consequences of the decisions I and others take today we must live with tomorrow.

Facts, however, are not "pure objects," things divorced from any other reality. They are relational realities, even though by defining the actual shape of experience they endow it with what has often been called "objectivity." But their "objectivity" does not consist in their unrelatedness to anything beyond themselves. Rather what has been improperly called objectivity consists both in the concreteness of facts and in their ability to define the realistic conditions for future decision and evaluation.

Quality and fact define two important realms of experience. But there is a third realm. The **selves** that act decisively and respond evaluatively people it. How then are these selves to be characterized? How are they experienced?

Every self is a law unto itself. It is a developing, autonomous tendency to react decisively or to respond evaluatively. It is a general tendency; for no self can be reduced to its concrete acts or particular evaluations, even though these influence the kind of self one becomes. Each self endows its own evaluations and decisions with significance by linking them to one another in intelligible habits. When we understand actions and evaluations, we perceive the self that performs them. For each self abstracted from its actions and evaluations is a general, habitual impulse to react decisively or to respond evaluatively in a specific way. How often have we all felt the desire, when a friend acts or speaks in a specific way, to remark: "That was typical." The friend is much more than the single gesture or word, more than a series of them. They typify my friend because the habit of responding thus is so deeply ingrained.

A self subsists when it functions autonomously. Autonomy is the abiding ability to initiate either evaluative or decisive responses. Each self consists then of two interrelated sets of developing habits. Evaluative habits interpret; decisive habits react.

Habits can diminish consciousness. When I am first learning to type, I must attend carefully to each movement of my fingers over the keyboard. Once I have acquired habitual typing skill, my fingers fly over the keys without my having to mark how they move. The habit does not prevent me from attending to my finger movements, if I choose. It only makes the attention optional. As a consequence, healthy habits allow us to function effectively while attending to matters of greater importance than our own functioning.

Habits blend. Children are born with a sucking instinct and with the capacity to thrash about with their arms and legs. As they transform thrashing into coordinated movement, they acquire motor habits. And when the child masters the complex acts of inserting its thumb into its mouth, it blends an innate, habitual instinct with an acquired motor skill in a way that yields hours of subsequent bliss. Thumbsucking is a basic act of coordination. But even the sophisticated grace of the ballerina results from the patient blending of interpretative and motor skills, even as the subtle wisdom of the sage blends complex linguistic skills with nuanced human perceptions.

Habits also result from evaluation and decision. Every decisive and evaluative response, whether conscious or unconscious, either reinforces an old habit or creates a new one. In either case the self is modified. Old habits are perfected and strengthened through repetition: practice makes perfect. New habits are established through innovative decisions. The

36

fixation of beliefs and of attitudes illustrates the formation of new habits. Having been wounded by another, I may remain undecided as to whether or not to forgive the offense. As long as I linger in the limbo of indecision, my reactions to the offending party will be random and confused. Once I decide to forgive, I create in myself a tendency to respond to my former enemy with compassion. Similarly, as long as I puzzle over conflicting accounts of the same reality, I will lack an habitual way of dealing with it. Only when I decide what the true account of it is, do I fix my belief about it and in the process create within myself a tendency to deal with it in a specific, predictable way. Motor skills too are the fruit of decision. They are acquired in the doing.

Each developing self subsists, then, as the habitual, incremental repository of decision. Each decision is specified through its antecedent evaluations. Each self initiates its own evaluations and decisions. Each self is, therefore, a self-defining process. Moreover, as we shall see, when human evaluations and decisions express a graced enlightenment, the graced self defines itself into a revelation of the divine. The selves encountered in experience are either persons or things. We shall have occasion later to reflect in some detail on the diagnostic traits that distinguish the two. For the moment, it suffices to note that human persons can choose between responsible and irresponsible behavior while animals and other subhuman species cannot. Animals react unreflectively, instinctively, and habitually. But they give no behavioral evidence of being critically self-aware. Since human behavior becomes fully responsible through conversion, we may describe human persons in a preliminary fashion as autonomous selves capable of conversion.

Persons and things share autonomy in common. Autonomy is the bare capacity to initiate reaction or response. Autonomy creates the self. When a self loses its autonomy it ceases to be a self. It is incorporated instead into a larger and more complex reality that so rules and controls it that it forfeits its very identity. This fact will assume enormous importance in our reflections on the hypostatic union.

Digestion illustrates the loss of autonomy. It used to be said that the human body was made up of about ninety-six cents worth of chemicals. In an inflationary economy we are no doubt worth more on the chemical market. But the old aphorism points to an important facet of the way human selves develop physically. In the course of biological growth we absorb life-sustaining food from our environment, break it down into its nutritive and non-nutritive components, integrate the former into our biological structure, and eliminate non-nutritive waste. The chemicals that are present in the human body can within limits be traced; they are identifiable as such. But once they have been completely ingested they lose their capacity to function autonomously and cease as a consequence to be selves in their own right. Instead I am the ruling self of which they are now integral parts. The human body may then be described as that portion of the impinging environment which has been successfully organized to support and advance personal life and growth. Non-human bodies support life, growth and activity that is less than personal.

But human biology follows specific laws. The chemicals that I ingest and incorporate into myself continue to behave in predictable ways even though they now compose my body and function differently from the way they did prior to digestion. They follow now the laws of organic chemistry. We must then distinguish two kinds of tendencies present within experience. Some are autonomous selves; others are not. But both function as habits, as general inclinations to react or respond in specific ways. A generalized tendency is a law.

We have then identified a third realm of experience distinct from the realms of quality and of fact, yet dynamically related to both: namely, **the realm of law.** Freedom being rooted in the degree of evaluative differentiation present in a given response knows either more or less: it flickers as consciousness flickers. For ordinary consciousness grows through evaluative discrimination and through the interrelation of discriminated realities and values. Autonomy, however, being rooted in law does not flicker: autonomy knows only either or, never more or less. Either a given feeling, thought, word, or deed is mine, or it is somebody else's. It all depends on who invoked the individual autonomy to feel, think, speak, or act. The distinction between freedom and autonomy functions in important ways in the argument that follows. We shall return to it in reflecting on Jesus' relationship to the Holy Breath within the hypostatic union.

Laws are directly perceived; for through perception we grasp first affectively, then inferentially, the general tendencies, the vectors, the habitual inclinations that shape experience and endow sensed facts with significance. Because we perceive every reality both affectively and inferentially, we can reach an integrated insight into it only by coordinating those two perceptions. Since we seek an integrated insight into the divine self called the Holy Breath, this fact will assume special methodological importance in the final chapter of this treatise.

Facts signify. The laws in which they are grounded and which they express make them significant. For significance is the relational structure of an event viewed in its capacity to be evaluatively grasped by some experience. The evaluative disclosure of significant relationships reveals their meaning. Through perception, therefore, we experience the meaning of a significant law.

Every law is a general tendency; but it is not an abstract principle. Laws enjoy a real generality that sets them apart from both qualities and facts. Every quality, every concept, every evaluation is what it is and nothing else. Pink is not kangaroo is not fear. The realm of quality is particular, however, not general. But if laws are not abstractions, neither are they facts. Facts are not general but concrete. This movement, this word, this gesture, this caress, this blow is unique and unrepeatable.

38

Because of their generality laws endow experience with continuity, both individual and personal. They constitute the selves that interact evaluatively and decisively. A tendency to act precedes activity, grounds it while it occurs, and survives it after it has ceased.

General tendencies also bind the past to the future, for they orient each self beyond any concrete act or particular feeling or thought to other reactions and responses yet to be achieved. Facts are transactions that link selves socially. As the causal ground of facts, laws are then spatial; as vectors groping toward the future they are temporal.

Laws develop. Habits grow strong through exercise or atrophy through neglect. They are acquired only to blend with other habits in order to create complex arabesques of activity.

Laws are specific, the incremental fruit of evaluation and decision. Decisions shape them directly by either creating or reinforcing specific habitual responses. And the character of each decision is determined by the kind of evaluative response it terminates. A decision perishes as soon as it is effected, but not the self it creates and transforms. For the habits decision creates endure.

There are then three distinct but interrelated variables that shape the progress of human experience: qualities, facts, and laws. They function simultaneously within experience but are analytically distinguishable. They cannot be reduced to one another. Facts are concrete; qualities, abstract. Laws are dynamic and general; qualities, inefficacious and particular.

The three variables that shape human experience stand dynamically interrelated. Laws cause efficacious and evaluative responses. Facts are presented by particular sense qualities. Laws are perceived by affect, image, inference. Qualities specify decisions; and decisions either create or reinforce laws, or habits. In consequence of their dynamic interrelation, the three experiential variables stand inseparable. There are no floating qualities or facts unanchored in a law, no laws which do not result from evaluation and decision.

We are also in a position to hazard a definition of experience in general. An experience is a process comprised of structured relational elements. Let us call those elements feelings. Human experience boasts of three different kinds of feelings: qualities, facts, and laws. In Chapter IV we will reflect on the legitimacy of applying this conception of experience to the reality of the triune God.

Human experiences are spatio-temporal. As such they have a certain number of describable traits. They are finite, relational, symbolic, and transactional. Their developing structure is constituted by real rather than by clock time. And they are mutually inexistent. Let us reflect on each of these traits, for each casts light on the dynamics of experience. Moreover, an insight into the dynamics of spatio-temporal experience will condition our judgment concerning the legitimacy of describing the triune God as an experience.

Spatio-temporal experiences are finite. That is to say, they are bounded by other experiences with which they must interact in order to become the kinds of experiences they prove to be.

Spatio-temporal experiences are relational. Human spatio-temporal experiences are constituted by three kinds of relationships. Factual relationships are efficacious and concrete. Legal, or habitual, relationships are dynamic and general. Conceptual relationships are either emotive, imaginative, and connotative, on the one hand, or inferential, rational, and logical, on the other. All experienced relations are feelings.

Spatio-temporal experiences are symbolic in their structure. Evaluative responses are interpretative symbols, for they endow events with meaning. Meaning is the evaluative disclosure of relationship. But events signify in their own right; for every decisive act expresses and reveals the law or self that initiates and grounds it. Because events signify, they too are symbolic in their structure; but they are expressive rather than interpretative symbols. For the significance they express needs interpretation in order to become meaningful. Linguistic and artistic events mediate between the realms of expressive and interpretative symbolism. From the standpoint of the speaker a linguistic event is an interpretative symbol, for it incarnates the evaluative grasp of the meaning of an event. So too is the meaningful gesture, or the creation of an art object, or the enactment of an artisitic performance. From the standpoint of the interpreter or spectator, however, linguistic and artistic events are expressive symbols; for they are physical acts that incarnate a relational structure capable of further interpretation. A symbol which both expresses intent and interprets reality communicates. All cultural events are communications.

Spatio-temporal experiences are transactional, for action and reaction link finite selves. When they bond persons together, spatio-temporal experiences cease to be merely transactional and become social.

The developing structure of spatio-temporal experience is constituted by real rather than by clock time. We measure clock time with artificially constructed scales: seconds, minutes, hours, light years. Real time is the developing process that is measured.

Within human experience the structure of real time results from the dynamic interplay of the three realms of experience. Experiences less complex than ours manifest a temporal structure that is correspondingly vaguer.

Initial facts stimulate human sensory awareness. But a fraction of a second elapses between the time the light strikes my retina and the point when I see it as a colored object. Only when I sense it, do I finally experience it as present to me. For evaluative response, from sensation to inference, endows experience with presentational immediacy. It grounds one's experience of the present moment by mediating a sense of individual presence to oneself and one's world. Because they precede the experience of presentational immediacy, initial facts endow experience with **a felt sense of one's immediate past as actual.** The immediate, actual past defines the realistic limits of future development

As the evaluative continuum grows in differentiation, our felt sense of the present acquires differentiation. Through sensation I experience **my immediate past as present to me.** That present contrasts with similar remembered events that have long since ceased to be actual. In recalling the ways in which I once reacted or responded to events no longer extant I render my remote past more or less vaguely present.

Through vague affective perceptions of the laws that shape experience, my feeling for the present moment begins to expand toward a future. For through affective perceptions I begin to **anticipate the further impact** upon me of the selves that inhabit my world. Fantasy endows my perception of the future with new vividness, as I begin to dream of possibilities that might yet be.

Inference **clarifies time perception and enhances control of the future.** Hypothetical explanations sharpen perceptions of the forces with which one must deal; in the process one becomes present to them with new vividness. Deductive predictions focus feeling for the future on specific anticipated events. Inductive verification transforms that same deductively anticipated future into an experienced present.

Final facts terminate different strains of personal evaluative response. Being unique and unrepeatable, historical decisions **transform dreaming, calculating feelings of the present** moving toward a future into an irrevocable past. But when final facts are sensed they become initial with respect to a new strain of evaluations and **then yield a sense of one's immediate past as actual.**

Finally, each self is a generalized tendency to react and to respond in specific ways. Being autonomous each self functions as a law unto itself; and being a law, a dynamic, habitual tendency, each self **orients experience toward the future as future.** Indeed, each self may be accurately described as the relationship of an individual past to its future.

Each self is the sum total of its history. Each self's history is the sum total of its experience. As a consequences, each self is its experience. It does not **have** experiences. When I say, "I have experiences," I distance myself linguistically from the experiences I say I

41

have, as though I enjoy some kind of reality apart from them. In point of fact, I sum up all that I experience. I am the cumulative product of my experience. Whatever I am is the totality of my experience. The persons and things that have changed me have become part of me, flesh of my flesh, bone of my bone, just as I in changing them have become part of them.

Because I am an experience, **not only do I exist in my world but my world as felt, as experienced, exists in me.** To say my world exists in me simply means that it makes me to be the kind of self I am. When it impinges on me and I respond to it, we exist in one another because we experience one another.

The term "inexistent" does not in this context mean "non-existent," but "existing in some other reality." It is a technical term derived from the Christological and trinitarian theology of John of Damascus (c. 675-c.749). It renders in English the Greek term **"perichoresis."** The term implies the mutual interpenetration of two realities which remain nevertheless distinct. When, for example, wine and water mingle in a chalice, the two interpenetrate one another without being transformed into a third reality. In the incarnation, the Damascene believed, the divinity and humanity of the divine Word interpenetrate one another in an analogous fashion. And John invoked the same concept to explain how the divine persons subsist as one God. Their mutual inexistence **(perichoresis)** functions in his theology as the equivalent of their unity.[4]

In the present context, "mutual inexistence" means the unity in distinction of two interrelated realities in consequence of their mutual interpenetration. I and my world interpenetrate one another every time we have a transaction. In the course of that transaction, I do not lose my identity to the selves with whom I interact, nor do they to me. For throughout we each retain the autonomy that makes us individual selves. Yet we are one. Through the immanence of my world to me I become the kind of experience I am, even as my decisive immanence to my world reshapes it into a different kind of place to be. We are wedded, my world and I. We find union in our mutual embrace. These reflections will assume enhanced importance when we come to consider the divine unity.

Let us pause once again to take stock of our progress. We are attempting to elaborate a foundational pneumatology. We are seeking an answer to the question: how ought an integrally converted Christian to experience the reality of God's Holy Breath? Our approach to this question claims to be experiential in a double sense. It probes the normative structure of Christian religious experience while simultaneously testing the legitimacy of conceiving the realtiy of the Christian God as an experience. In the construction of an experiential pneumatology, our first speculative challenge has been to understand the dynamics of human experience, for those dynamics when properly understood give the term "experience" its meaning. After exploring the realms of experience we have concluded that the term may be defined as "a process that effects the ongoing integration of relational elements called feelings." In human experience we have discovered three kinds of feelings: qualities, facts, and laws. But can we truthfully describe the God Christians worship as an experience? In order to answer that question we must begin to examine the way in which the Christian God comes to be experienced in faith. To this problem we now turn.

1. For an examination of these and other related issues, see: Donald L. Gelpi, S.J., Experiencing God: A Theology of Human Emergence (New York:Paulist, 1978), pp. 52-121. Moreover, the construct of human experience elaborated in this chapter is discussed in the same work in much more descriptive and empirical detail.

2. For a lucid handling of the problems attending a Whiteheadian conception of God, see: Robert C. Neville, Creativity and God: A Challenge to Process Philosophy (New York: Seabury, 1980).

3. Alfred North Whitehead, Process and Reality, edited by David Ray Griffin and Donald W. Sherburne (New York: Free Press, 1978), p. 167.

4. Leonard Prestige, "Perichoreo and Perichoresis in the Fathers," The Journal of Theological Studies (April, 1928), pp. 248-249; John of Damascus, Fid. Orth., III, 8, 17; De Imag., 1, 21; Jacob., 81.

CHAPTER III:

ON EXPERIENCING A HOLY BREATH

We experience both the Lordship of Jesus and the Fatherhood of God in the enlightenment of Their Holy Breath. As a consequence, in any experiential approach to the God Christians worship, pneumatology holds the key. How, then, ought we to perceive the reality of God's enlightening Breath? In the present chapter we shall attempt to show that because the historical mission of the divine Breath is experienced as a gracious enlightenment, She ought to be perceived as the mind of God.

The Church claims the Bible as its Book, as a norm of Christian faith. Those, therefore, who seek a normative insight into the reality of the Christian God will discover in the biblical witness their most basic theological evidence. For every Christian doctrine seeks in some sense to interpret both the meaning of the biblical witness and the significance of the events to which it testifies. If, then, we want to know how Christians ought to experience the reality of God, we must first seek to grasp how that reality was perceived by the authors of sacred scripture.

But here we face a perplexing challenge indeed. For the writings of the Bible span centuries of religious history, preaching, and reflection. Its authors do not always share identical angles of vision. Their perspectives on God and the world expand and contract. Their flickering awareness of the Holy Breath waxes and wanes. Can we then expect to find in the pages of the scriptures a unified account of the divine Breath?

If we expect to discover there a systematic pneumatology, we will meet sore disappointment. For the biblical writers did not think systematically in the ordinary sense of that term. They saw reality with coherence often enough. But they were poets, prophets, preachers, religious historians, apocalyptic visionaries, community leaders, not speculative theologians with the systematizing passion of philosophers.

But if the Bible contains no systematic pneumatology, the witness of the biblical authors to Her reality and saving presence displays a remarkable convergence of themes and consistency of perception. In the present chapter, we shall attempt to trace one of those themes through both Testaments in some detail. We shall examine the tendency of biblical writers to describe the Holy Breath as a divine principle of saving enlightenment. As a source of gracious illumination the divine Breath functions within salvation history advancing it toward the saving ends God has decreed. But eventually some of the biblical authors realized that the Breath's activity within salvation history reveals to us something about Her transcendent divine reality. The Hebrew sages portrayed Her as the transcendent wisdom of God. And in the New Testament the fact that the Breath reveals to Jesus the saving intentions of the Father leads Paul the apostle to declare that She is the mind of God and of Christ. Let us then examine this strain in the biblical witness, for it will provide us with a norm for evaluating post-biblical interpretations of the activity and reality of the Advocate.

Much Old Testament pneumatology is couched in images. Very early in the development of Hebrew theology, the image of breath came to be associated with both life and religious enlightenment.

"In the day that the Lord God made the earth and the heaven....the Lord God formed man of dust from the ground and breathed into his nostrils the breath of life (**nishmat hayyim**)" (Gn 2:4b, 7).[1] The story of the creation of Adam antedates the priestly account of cosmic origins which opens the book of Genesis. In the course of the story, the reality of life is interpreted by the image of breath. The living breathe; the dead breathe no more (Ps 104:27-30; Ws 15:11, 16).[2]

Adam enjoys a special interpersonal relationship with God. Because Adam receives his breath as a free gift from the very lips of God, there is a sense in which it continues to belong to the Lord of life. Adam therefore rises from the earth constrained to cling in obedience to the God from whom he draws his life or suffer the deadly consequences (Gn 2:16-17).[3]

The creator God retains, moreover, the power to cancel or curtail his free gift of life at any time. After the sin of the first couple Yahweh justly forbids them access to the tree of life; and the arrogant pride of their offspring leads Him to impose yet another punishment: no individual shall enjoy the breath of life more than one hundred and twenty years (Gn 6:32; cf. Ws 15:11).[4]

Both punishments entail poignant consequences. The life breath given by Yahweh may return to Him in death (Ps 31:6). But once it goes, no human power can command its return. Humanity stands impotent before the mystery of its own death-bound, sinful state; but the Creator does not. For human self-alienation from the living God is countered by the intervention of the divine **Ruah**, by the living Breath of Yahweh (Ws 2:2-5, 11:26-12:1, 16:14).[5]

The earliest traditions of the Jewish people link the action of the **Ruah** with the dawning of religious consciousness. Before the conquest of the Promised Land, for example, the **Ruah** of God inspires the prophet Balaam to utter his oracles concerning the destiny of Israel. The action of the Divine Breath does not abolish the prophet's intelligent processes. But his submission to Her clears the eye of his mind to perceive the truth about God's saving intentions (Nm 24:2).[6]

The enlightenment of the **Ruah** takes many forms. She inspires both the practical wisdom of Joseph and the prophetic words of Balaam (Gn 41:38; Dt 34:9).[7] Later on She will infuse religious artists with creative insight (Ex 31:33ff). She will evoke prayer that is pleasing to God (Ze

12:10). And at critical moments in the history of God's people the **Ruah** will raise up inspired leaders to mobilize Israel to concerted action: Moses, Joshua, and the judges (Nm 11:17-30; Jg 3:10, 11:29, 13:25, 14:6-19; Dt 34:9).[8]

The images used to describe the action of the Breath suggest, moreover, that receptivity is indeed the proper human stance in the face of Her activity. The Breath of God resembles a rushing wind that sweeps along the one whom it enlightens (1 Sm 11:5, 16:13-21).[9]

The biblical writers recognized that not every form of allegedly religious enlightenment need come from God. The Deuteronomic tradition, for example, distinguishes between the activity of a good and of an evil **ruah.** When the divine Breath abandoned Saul in consequence of his disobedience to the prophetic word of Samuel (1 Sm 15:1-31), an evil **ruah** settled upon the doomed king. He became subject to violent moods (1 Sm 16:14-23).[10]

The breath of evil is dark, violent, hypocritical, lying. It blinds one to the saving action of God in the events of history (Is 29:10). The Holy **Ruah** by contrast inspires faith, covenant fidelity, sensitivity to God's saving deeds--all of them forms of religious enlightenment.

If the Breath of God inspires the visions of the prophets, one would expect the great Hebrew writing prophets to provide us with a rather detailed portrait of Her illuminatig action in their own lives. But paradoxically several of the pre-exilic prophets fail to link their ministry directly to Her inspiration. Amos, Isaiah, and Jeremiah make no mention of the divine Breath as the source of their teaching.

But two of the pre-exilic prophets, Hosea and Micah, do acknowledge Her as the inspiration of their preaching. Hosea is content to be known even derisively as a man of the Breath--**ish ha-ruah** (Ho 9:7b).[11] And Micah derives from Her illumination his prophetic authority to confront God's people with their sins (Mi 3:8).[12] Moreover, in exilic and post-exilic prophecy, the divine Breath is more freely credited as the source of prophetic inspiration. Ezechiel illustrates the tendency. A powerful mystic with a penchant for complex and even bizarre imagery, he testified freely to the power of the **Ruah** of God over his psychic functions (Ez 2:2, 3:2ff, 3:12, 14, 11:1, 5, 37:1, 43:5).[13]

We have seen how Hebrew theology very early linked the action of the divine **Ruah** with the dawning of religious consciousness. But in Ezechiel we find a hint that Yahweh's own presence to the world is mediated by His Breath. In the inaugural vision which opens the book of Ezechiel, Yahweh comes to the prophet in human form riding in something like a chariot whose wheels are moved by four cherubim. But the wheels and the cherubim are moved by the divine Breath (Ez 1:1-21).[14] In other words, somehow through the action of His Breath Yahweh Himself becomes present to His creatures. How that presence is effected remains obscure.

47

A similar insight can be extracted from a complex passage in Deutero-Isaiah, but with greater difficulty.[15] In a reflection on the exodus, the prophet observes:

> It was not a messenger or an angel but He Himself who saved them. Because of His love and pity he redeemed them all the days of old. But they rebelled and grieved His Holy Breath; so He turned on them like an enemy and fought against them. (NAB, Is 63:9-14)[16]

One "grieves the Breath" by disobeying Her inspirations. Such disobedience transforms the presence of Yahweh into a threat, for our rebellious choices make Him an enemy. But by the same token, the illumination of the **Ruah** makes Yahweh present to His people either in salvation or in judgment: in salvation when they respond to His prophetic word, in judgment when they contemn it.

Eventually, Hebrew wisdom would transform the Breath into the transcendent wisdom that enlightens God. This important development in biblical pneumatology was prepared by the Breath's association with divine creativity. The priestly account of creation which opens the book of Genesis was written during the exile. It vindicates a place for the divine **Ruah** within the creative act. Unlike the Babylonian creator who must struggle against the forces of chaos and conquer them, Yahweh creates by the naked power of His word (Gn 1:3). But the Breath of God is already active before the divine word is spoken. It hovers over the restless waters of chaos, apparently disposing them to listen in obedience to the voice of God.[17]

The creative activity of the Breath is also celebrated in the psalms. Psalm 104 describes Her as effecting the ongoing creation of life in nature. When Yahweh breathes, life is created in the animal kingdom. When He inhales, the animals perish. More to the present point, through the ongoing creative activity of His **Ruah,** Yahweh is present to every living being (Ps 104:27-30).[18] Psalm 109 goes even further. Through the action of the **Ruah,** God knows everything that exists. "Where shall I flee from your Breath?" the psalmist asks, "or where shall I flee from your presence?" (Ps 139:7) Here the term **"Ruah"** envisages more than God's saving enlightenment of those who believe in Him. It designates the living reality of God Himself viewed as a principle of scrutinizing omniscience.[19]

One passes easily from the vision of Psalm 139 to the pneumatology of the Hebrew sages. The wise men of Israel were fond of speaking of the life breath in humans as a source of enlightenment, often a fallible source to be sure, but a source nonetheless (Pr 16:1-9, 20:27; Jb 32:8). And they insisted that the wisdom of God offers the chief antidote to human fallibility.

48

The transcendent character of divine wisdom demands that the sage seek it as a gift from God. In Proverbs wisdom effects our illumination from on high (Pr 1:23). The book of Job likens wisdom to a "Breath (**Ruah**) of the Almighty" moving the human heart to an understanding born of more than human experience (Jb. 32:8). Ben Sira discovers in "fear of the Lord" wisdom's foundation (Si 1:14).[20]

The Wisdom of Solomon attempts to characterize the kind of wisdom which is the fruit of divine enlightenment. Wisdom is described, of course, as a light to the mind. It dispels ambiguity and brings certitude. One can trust it. It frees the mind to penetrate to the heart of things. Divine wisdom can also be recognized by the attitudes it engenders. It heals anxiety and brings peace to the heart. It instills kindliness toward others, especially towards those less advantaged than oneself. It produces sensitivity to value in all its forms. It overlooks nothing and inspires readiness for any good work. The wisdom from on high also yields a distinctive kind of understanding. Its subtlety too creates sensitivity in one who seeks it. It opens onto the complexity and mystery of life. It never leads to what is harmful. Above all it is a knowledge which sanctifies. Finally, true wisdom is transcendent in its origin and operation. Begotten only of God, it reflects the divine glory, guarantees divine benevolence, and imparts a share in the divine wisdom which "reaches from end to end mightily and governs all things well." It can permeate different kinds of people and motivates every authentic expression of piety and prophecy. Gracefully flexible, it pervades a world of movement. It is, however, transcendently mobile, mobile beyond all motion (Ws 7:22b-8:1).[21]

It should be clear that for the Wisdom of Solomon divine wisdom not only effects human enlightenment but is itself the very omniscience of God. That same wisdom is also the **Ruah** of God. In the Greek text the word **"pneuma"** replaces the Hebrew word **"ruah"**. The sage observes:

> For the holy **pneuma** of discipline flees deceit and withdraws from senseless counsels; and when injustice occurs it is rebuked. For wisdom is a kindly **pneuma,** yet she acquits not the blasphemer of his guilty lips; because God is the witness of his inmost self, the sure observer of his heart and listener to his tongue. For the **pneuma** of the Lord fills the world, is all embracing and knows what man says. (NAB, Pr 1:23)[22]

Here the use of the term **pneuma** is cumulative. Not only is the "holy Breath of discipline" cultivated by the sage both approved and sanctioned by the "kindly Breath" of divine wisdom, but that Breath encompasses all and knows all.

Clearly, then, for the devout Hebrew, the Holy **Ruah** functions as a divine principle of lifegiving illumination. She inspires every religiously wise and righteous act. This She can accomplish because She is within God the source of divine wisdom. A scrutinizing principle of omniscience, she presides over God's providential dealings with His creation. These basic Hebrew beliefs provide the proper context for understanding the New Testament witness to the divine **Pneuma.** But New Testament pneumatology transposes these insights into a Christological context. The Holy Breath that inspires Christian faith and worship frees the heart and mind to recognize Jesus as incarnate Son of God and as the final and full revelation of God's saving intentions.

In Pauline theology, for example, the Holy **Pneuma** illumines the apostle and presides over his witness to the risen Christ. Paul conducted his mission of proclamation in the name of the God who had sent him, namely, the Lord Jesus Christ and the Father who had raised Him from the dead. But the force animating and sanctioning his words was, by his own testimony, their Holy Breath. (Rm 1:1-7, Ga 1:11-24, Eph 3:1-6).[23]

That the divine Breath animated his apostolate was manifest in the heartfelt conversion of those who heeded his message and in the signs of healing that accompanied his preaching. Paul also testified that the Breath dwelt with him as an abiding source of personal support (1Th 1:4-6; 1Co 2:4-16; Phil. 1:19).[24] As an apostle, he enjoyed a personal charismatic authority directly derived from his encounter with the risen Lord (1Co. 12:28).[25]

The Holy Breath that enlightens and sustains the apostle also illumined the Christian community as a whole (1Th 1:4-6, 4:1-8; 2Th 2:13; 1 Co 3:1-3, 12-13, 16-17).[26] But while the apostle's initial pneumatic anointing probably resulted directly from his encounter with the risen Christ, the community enjoys access to the Breath of Jesus through faith in the Lord proclaimed in apostolic preaching (Ga 3:1-5, 14).[27] Moreover, the same divine Breath Who inspires the apostle's witness inspires freedom to consent in faith to the Lordship of Jesus (1 Co 12:1-3).[28] And, as Paul argues at length in Romans and Galatians, this consenting faith justifies the believer in the sight of God, rather than fidelity to the law of Moses or to one's natural conscience (Rm 1:8-5:21; Ga 3:1-6:16; 1 Co 6:9-11).[29]

Paul's theology of justification was elaborated primarily to vindicate his pastoral practice of admitting gentiles into the community without demanding that they be circumcised.[30] But it also rejected outright rabbinic teaching that the **Ruah** of God might on occasion be granted to exceptional individuals as the reward of a lifetime of fidelity to the Torah. The law, Paul insisted, was never intended to justify us, only to tutor the conscience concerning right conduct before God and to convict the disobedient of sin. The disobedient Jew, who is bound by the Law, stands under its curse. The divine **Pneuma,** on the other hand, is given freely to us even in our sinfulness. And justification by faith in response to

Her illumination is available to all: male and female, gentile and Jew, slave and free (Rm 3:1-31).[31]

Justification for Paul consists, then, in the righteousness of God actively transforming the sinner through faith. The Holy Breath works justification in us. Justification begins personal moral transformation in faith.[32] Both result from the Breath's gracious enlightenment.

For the Christian the faith which justifies culminates in ritual baptism. "You were washed, you were sanctified in the name of the Lord Jesus and in the Breath of our God." (1 Co 6:9-11; cf. 1 Co 12:12-26; 2 Co 13:13)[33] Not only does baptism seal the faith of the convert, but it gives the Christian neophyte ecclesial access to the divine Breath who is charismatically active in the Christian community (1 Co 12:1 ff; 1 Th 4:7-8; 2 Th 2:13).[34]

The sanctifying impulse of the Breath can be recognized in its fruits: faith, hope, love, joy, peace, patience, kindness, goodness, faithfulness, gentleness, self-control (1 Co 13:1-13; Ga 6:22-23). It frees us, for it inspires a spontaneous desire to do what is pleasing to God. As a result, the freedom born of the Breath leaves our liberty intact. Our relation to Her remains one of cooperative docility (Rm 8:14-15).[35]

Indeed, the Holy Breath of Christ is Herself the law (**nomos**) which ensures Christian covenant fidelity. The indwelling **Pneuma** governs the believer, not as an external principle of constraint, as did the Mosaic code. Instead She rejuvenates believers through an enlightenment that fixes the mind and heart in freedom upon the things of God (Ga 5:5-6, 13-26; Rm 5:1-5, 8:1-13; 2 Co 3:4-18).[36]

An important facet of the enlightenment imparted by the Holy Breath is Her charismatic inspiration of the services which bind the Christian community together in conscious, practical faith. In Pauline theology the term "**charisma**" is linked etymologically to another term: "**charis**" (grace). "**Charis**" denotes God's saving action not only in the past but especially here and now in the eschatological present as it moves toward the future prepared by Him. "**Charisma**" is a particular instance of **charis**. The **charismata** are given by the Breath for the building up of the body of Christ which is His church (1 Co 12:4-7).[37]

Charisma becomes diversified as different members of the community manifest their openness to the Holy Breath in different ways. Some are outstanding examples of faith. Others pray or speak in tongues. Others still interpret tongues. Prophets summon the community to respond to the present saving action of God in their midst. Some teachers proclaim the divine wisdom revealed in Christ, while others instruct the community in other ways. Some are the instruments of divine healing and of miracles. Discerners authenticate genuine **charismata** and unmask inauthentic religious impulses. Some are called to a celibate ministry, others to marriage. Apostles, administrators, community leaders, and appointed officials bear the burdens of pastoral organization and leadership. They are assisted by helpers, ministers, those who supervise the distribution of alms, and those who serve the needy (1 Co 12-14; Rom 6-8).[38]

In comparison with the Pauline corpus, synoptic references to the Holy Breath occur rarely. They make it quite clear, however, that Jesus Himself experienced Her as a source of divine enlightenment. In all three synoptics She descends on Him at His baptism in order to begin His public manifestation as messiah, Son of God, suffering servant, and Breath baptiser (Mk 1:9-13; Mt 3:13-4:11; Lk 3:21-4:13, 10:21-22).[39] Because She comes to Him as a principle of illumination that reveals to Him the scope of His mission by the Father, She endows His teaching with divine authority (Mk 1:22; Mt 7:28-29; Lk 4:14-15). Her presence is manifest too in His power over evil spirits (Mt 12:27-28). Moreover, because She functions in Jesus' ministry as the source of His self-awareness as Son (Lk 10:21-22), the Holy Breath is historically revealed to us as the interpretative link between the Son and the Father. As we shall see, Paul the apostle grasped more clearly than any other New Testament author the trinitarian implications of this important fact.

Moreover, in all four gospels, the Holy Breath is promised to believers as a source of personal illumination. In Mark's gospel, as Jesus in His Jerusalem ministry moves inexorably to betrayal and death, He utters a brief eschatological discourse. In it He warns:

> But take heed to yourselves; for they will deliver you up to councils; and you will be beaten in synagogues; and you will stand before governors and kings for my sake, to bear testimony before them. And the gospel must first be preached to all nations. And when they bring you to trial and deliver you up, do not be anxious beforehand what you are to say; but say whatever is given you in that hour, for it is not you who speak but the Holy Breath. (Mk 13:9-11)[40]

Jesus' disciples can expect to share his own violent fate. But the Breath that dwells in Him will sustain them in the midst of persecution and suffering. She will strengthen them to bear testimony despite the futile violence of their enemies. The same theme is taken up by Matthew. In Mt 10:20 Jesus promises His disciples that in times of persecution "the Breath of your Father" will speak in them the words that will confound their adversaries.

In Luke/Acts the Pentecostal Breath descends upon the Christian community to inspire their persevering witness to the risen Christ. Her inspiration is manifest too in the diffusion of charismatic gifts throughout the community: tongues and prophecy, cures and exorcisms, preaching and works of mercy (Ac 2:1ff, 3:12, 4:32-37, 5:12, 21:10). The apostolic witness is especially confirmed by signs and wonders (Ac 5:12). Luke also portrays the Holy Breath as the source and inspiration of Paul's gentile mission (Ac 13:2, 9, 19:1-7, 21).[41]

That the divine Breath is conceived by the synoptic evangelists as a source of gracious illumination is also implicit in Jesus' warning, repeated in all three gospels, not to "blaspheme" Her. In Mark's gospel the warning occurs in the course of Jesus' reply to the charge that He casts out devils by the power of Beelzebul. For Mark the blasphemy against the Breath that Jesus rebukes consists of the sin of attributing to the Evil One exorcisms done in the power and inspiration of the divine **Pneuma**. No one inspired by Her would confound the deliverance She brings with the activity of demons. Matthew situates Jesus' warning in the same context, but he prefaces the false accusation of Jesus' adversaries with a reminder of the large number of people whom the Savior cured. He does so in order to underline the unbelief of Jesus' enemies (Mk 3:28-29, Mt 12:24-32).

Luke's handling of this same saying of Jesus contrasts somewhat with Matthew's and Mark's. Jesus, having warned His disciples against the hypocrisy of the pharisees, begins to instruct them concerning their proper relation to each member of the divine triad during times of persecution. For the Father they must preserve a reverential fear and a trust strong enough to carry them through martyrdom. They must confess the Son of Man fearlessly. And under persecution they must avoid the unforgiveable sin of blasphemy against the divine Breath. Luke, therefore, in contrast to Matthew and to Mark, here associates the "unforgiveable sin" with the apostasy of the Breath-baptised Christian (Lk 12:1-11).[42] But in all three synoptics blaspheming the Holy Breath can occur because She is experienced as a divine source of illumination which reveals to us the truth about God's saving action in Jesus.

In Johannine theology the divine **Pneuma** inspires authentic worship. She is also the illuminating principle which guides the disciples' faithful witness to the risen Christ.

John's Jesus insists twice on the pneumatic character of true worship. To the Samaritan woman He promises:

> Yet an hour is coming and is already here when true worshippers will worship the Father in **Pneuma** and truth. Indeed, it is just such worshippers the Father seeks. God is **Pneuma**, and those who worship Him must worship in **Pneuma** and truth (Jn 4:23-24).[43]

The phrase "God is **Pneuma**" resembles Jesus' reply to Nicodemus: "Whatever is born of the **Pneuma** is **Pneuma**" (Jn 3:6). In both texts the term **"Pneuma"** without the article is descriptive and generic. In both passages **"Pneuma"** designates a reality in which all three members of the divine triad participate. But the present passage makes it clearer that **Pneuma** is the very life by which God lives. Authentic worship must then incarnate enlightened participation in the very life of the Godhead.

Pneumatic worship transpires "in truth." In Johannine theology truth consecrates and sanctifies (Jn 17:17-19). Truth is the Wisdom of God incarnate in Christ; for He is "the way, the truth, and the life" (Jn 14:6-7), the very reality of the Father made visible. Pneumatic worship, therefore, seeks the face of the Father revealed in Jesus with a wisdom begotten from above by the indwelling **Pneuma**. Such worship will render temple worship passe, whether in Jerusalem or on Gerazim.[44]

Moreover, John's Jesus insists that the freedom to eat His flesh and drink His blood in faith is also effected by the divine Breath. At the close of the Bread of Life discourse, when many former disciples abandon Jesus, He rebukes them for their lack of faith. He says: "It is the Breath that gives life; the flesh is useless. The words I have spoken to you are both Breath and life" (Jn 6:60-71).[45]

Once again we meet an interweaving of the two senses of the word **"Pneuma"**. "The **Pneuma**" (**Pneuma** with an article) is described as a principle of life (**zoopoioun**). Her lifegiving potency contrasts with the impotence of the flesh, when the latter is confronted with the truth that comes from above. That this explains the division between Jesus and His unfaithful followers becomes clear in the question which prefaces His rebuke to them: "Does this offend you? What then if you were to see the Son of Man ascending where He was before?" (Jn 6:61-62) Their inability to believe that Jesus can give them His own flesh and blood as food and drink betrays the fact that they have yet to recognize His true origin. Were they born from above they would have known the truth that descends from above. Their mocking, sceptical unbelief, words born of flesh in its impotence, contrast then with Jesus' own words which are **"Pneuma** and life."** Jesus' words are **Pneuma** because they are inspired by the **Pneuma** who abides within Him and Whom He will send when He is lifted up in glory. They are the very words, the very testimony of God. For they incarnate **Pneuma**, the life of the divine triad. And they give access to pneumatic life to those who hear them in faith.

Jesus' reply to His faithless disciples suggests then that the testimony of the **Pneuma** and of the blood (Jn 19:28-37) also encompasses faith in His eucharistic presence. Those who refuse to believe in His power to give them His body to eat and His blood to drink are moved not by God's **Pneuma,** but by a **pneuma** of this world.[46] By implication, in eucharistic faith **Pneuma** triumphs over **sarx.** For it links the believer to the risen Savior and frees the true disciple to confess the saving power of what Jesus said and did while still in the flesh.

In the course of His last discourse, John's Jesus promises more than once that after He is gone He will send the Paraclete. Nowhere else in John's gospel is the Paraclete mentioned. Moreover, the term is peculiar to the pneumatology of the fourth evangelist.

The term "Paraclete" (**ho parakletos**) has a rich variety of connotations. The first two are forensic and legal. A **parakletos** is an advocate, an attorney at law. And indeed, the Paraclete whom Jesus promises comes to convict the world of its guilt before God. In this respect the Paraclete has functions analogous to a prosecuting attorney. But in the mind of the fourth evangelist, the activity of the Paraclete resembles finally that of a legal witness. By testifying to Jesus the Paraclete will give the lie to His enemies and confirm the faith of His disciples.

A Paraclete is also an intercessor, a spokesperson. But the Paraclete never intercedes for Jesus or for His disciples. Rather, as spokesperson for Jesus, the Paraclete will testify in the faith witness of those who confess Him to be the Christ.

The **Parakletos** may also be said to be a comforter, a consoler. But in Jesus' final discourse, the personal consolation which the Paraclete will bring is not stressed.

Finally, a Paraclete teaches or exhorts. The Paraclete will teach and guide the disciples of Jesus, instructing them concerning the things they must teach others in His name.[47] As Paraclete, She brings the enlightenment from above.

In His last discourse, Jesus promises that He will send His disciples "another Paraclete" (**allon parakleton**) (Jn 6:61-62). The phrase suggests that Jesus Himself was the first Paraclete. The second Paraclete will, then, come to prolong the witness of Jesus, to instruct the disciples as Jesus Himself had done, and to inspire their confession of Jesus in a way that conforms it to His own confession of the Father.

It is therefore significant that the fourth evangelist refrains from introducing the forensic title "the Advocate" until Jesus' "hour" has arrived, His hour of testing and of glory, when He will be put on trial, put to death. Both events foreshadow what awaits those who follow Him into glory. When their own "hour" arrives, His disciples will need to rely on the Advocate He will send. Their trial will prolong the judgment of this world begun in Jesus' own.

The Paraclete is named the breath of truth (**to Pneuma tes aletheias**). The Paraclete is also the Holy Breath (**to Pneuma hagion**) (Jn 14:16-17).[48] Both phrases describe the Holy **Pneuma** Who abides in Jesus in inexhaustible plentitude (Jn 3:31-34). But they highlight specific facets of Her action in the disciples. As Paraclete She will come as witness, spokesperson, exhorter. She will dwell with the disciples, She will be in them. As the **Pneuma** of truth She will teach the saving wisdom from on high, the divine wisdom incarnate in Jesus. And like the "spirit of truth" described in the documents of Qumran, She will do battle in the cause of truth, inspiring the disciples' faith witness to Jesus and confounding the powers of darkness.

In her function as Paraclete the Breath will abide with the disciples as She abode with Jesus. Indeed, She will abide with them forever (Jn 14:16). As She dwelt with Jesus, She will now dwell with them. Through Her indwelling, the disciples will know Her with a new kind of intimacy and immediacy. For Her indwelling will reveal Her living, life-giving presence (Jn 4:14, 14:17). Moreover, where She is present the risen Christ will be present as well (Jn 14:18).[49]

The Paraclete will come to the disciples to teach them. She will "teach all things" (**didaxei panta**) and "remind" (**hypomnesei**) them of Jesus' own instruction. This recall of Jesus' teaching will be more than just factual. Through the illumination of the Paraclete the disciples will reappropriate Jesus' doctrine with new insight into its meaning.

The historical Jesus could not teach His disciples "all truth" because they could not bear to hear all He could have told them. They need the presence of the Paraclete to bear the weight of wisdom from on high and the burden of suffering that it brings. But the coming of the Paraclete can occur only after Jesus Himself has departed. Only then can She come to teach the disciples all things and guide them to all truth. Nevertheless, even these new insights taught by the Paraclete will be Jesus' own teaching. She will teach only what She receives from Him. The Paraclete's submission in teaching only what She hears from the glorified Jesus imitates Jesus' own fidelity in saying and doing only what He has heard from the Father (Jn 4:34, 5:30, 6:38, 18:13-19, 37-40).[50]

The teaching of the Paraclete will have a double focus: the revelation of divine truth and prophecy. For She will not only teach divine wisdom, She will "announce to you the things to come."[51] The revelation of divine truth will unfold gradually. Moreover, the future which the Paraclete will disclose is eschatological. It encompasses not only historical events still to come, but life eternal with the victorious Christ.[52]

We have been attempting to show that in the biblical witness to the divine Breath She is uniformly portrayed as the source of gracious, life-giving enlightenment. A survey of the pneumatological texts in the Bible will disclose no exceptions to this biblical pattern. We have also seen that for the Hebrew wise men, the divine **Ruah** was experienced not only as the immanent source of the wisdom from on high, but also as a divine principle of scrutinizing omniscience. In the gospels, the Holy Breath guides Jesus in His proclamation of God's reign. She links Him cognitively to the Father. After the resurrection She is the enlightening presence of God and of the risen Christ. It was, however, given to Paul the apostle to articulate the implications of these insights.

56

There are a number of passages in Paul in which he explicitly names Father, Son, and Breath. But on occasion he also affirms a close identity between the divine **Pneuma** and the risen Lord. One such text occurs in Second Corinthians. There Paul affirms quite boldly: "The Lord is the Breath" (**ho de kyrios to pneuma estin**) (2 Co 3:17). One might be inclined to dismiss the phrase as a slip of the pen, were it not immediately reiterated, albeit ambiguously. But the same idea surfaces less ambiguously in a parallel passage in First Corinthians. In the latter text the apostle insists that by His resurrection Jesus, the new Adam, has become "a life-giving Breath" (**pneuma zoopoioun**) (1 Co 15:45).

The phrase "the Lord is the Breath" has been subject to at least six exegetical readings. Most scholars believe that "the Lord" refers to the risen Christ. But it has also been suggested that He is God the Father, or the Lord of the exodus. Moreover, those who agree that "the Lord" of whom Paul speaks is the risen Christ cannot seem to reach a consensus on the meaning of the term "**pneuma**".[53]

Paul's affirmation occurs in the course of an extended allegory. The apostle is contrasting the glory of the new covenant revealed in the risen Jesus with the fading glory of the Sinai covenant. Unlike the divine glory reflected on Moses' countenance at Sinai, the glory of the new covenant revealed in Christ does not fade; it abides forever. Moreover, the divine glory that shone on the face of Moses did not effect the justification of those who saw it. Those who know the glory on the face of the risen Lord are justified; for they share by faith in the same divine **Pneuma** that animated Him.

Paul's meaning in asserting an identity between the Lord and the Breath would, then, seem to be the following. The new covenant is sealed through faith in the risen Christ. That faith is the work of the divine **Pneuma**. Jesus' resurrection was, however, the apex of His transformation in the power of the Breath, a transformation so total that it overflows to all who confess His Lordship in faith. "All of us," Paul concludes, "gazing on the Lord's glory with unveiled faces, are being transformed from glory to glory into His very image by the Lord who is the Breath" (2 Co 3:18).

To say, then, that the Lord is the Breath means that the Lord who sends the **Pneuma** is Himself present and active wherever the Divine Breath is present and active. They are distinct, yet mysteriously one. The action of the divine **Pneuma** is the action of the risen Lord who is Her mediator. Her action in us resembles Her action in Him. It is, indeed, our present participation in the divine glory of the risen Savior, the beginning of our resurrection in His image.[54] But while Jesus' total transformation was immediate and personal, ours is collective and must wait until He returns upon the clouds of heaven (1 Co 15:51-58).

The identity which Paul discovers between the Lord and the divine **Pneuma** is more than just functional. Rather their functional identity within the salvific process is a present revelation to the believer of their **vital identity.** By His resurrection Jesus has been forever filled to overflowing with a divine pneumatic life that is imperishable (1 Co 15:45).[55]

Clearly, for Paul the apostle the illuminations of the divine Breath disclose to us Her living reality. Her touch is God's own. She is the living presence of both Jesus and the Father. Transformation in the Breath is transformation in the living reality of the Godhead (1 Co 14:45-50, Rm 8:9-17).[56]

Moreover, in First Corinthians Paul explains the character of the vital identity that unites the Lord and the Breath. The apostle writes:

> But we impart a secret and hidden wisdom of God, which God decreed before the ages for our glorification. None of the rulers of this age understood this; for if they had, they would not have crucified the Lord of glory. But, as it is written, "what no eye has seen, nor ear heard, nor the heart of man conceived, that God has prepared for those who love Him," God has revealed to us through the **Pneuma.** For the **Pneuma** searches everything, even the depths of God. For what person knows a man's thoughts except the **pneuma** of the man which is in him? So also no one comprehends the thoughts of God except the **Pneuma** of God. Now we have received not the **pneuma** of this world, but the **Pneuma** which is from God, that we might understand the gifts bestowed on us by God. And we impart this in words not taught by human wisdom but taught by the **Pneuma,** interpreting truths to those who possess the **Pneuma.** The man who is not pneumatic does not receive the gifts of the **Pneuma** of God, for they are folly to him, and he is not able to understand them because they are pneumatically discerned. The pneumatic man judges all things, but is himself judged by no one. "For who has known the mind of the Lord **(noun Kyriou)** so as to instruct Him?" But we have the mind of Christ **(noun Christou).** (1 Co 2:4-16)

The **pneuma** in each human person searches the depths of the psyche. It is the human mind attuned to its own deepest dynamisms. The divine **Pneuma,** therefore, stands within the reality of God as the human **pneuma** stands within the reality of personal experience. Both are noetic in character. Both encompass the deepest movements of conscious personal life. The divine **Pneuma** is then the mind (**nous**) of the Christian Godhead. She is the mind common to both Father and Son. Through Their union with the Breath They share an identity of conscious divine life. The action of the Breath of God in Jesus ensures, therefore, that the wisdom He incarnated is God's own. In His life, teaching, death and glorification, the divine plan of salvation, God's wisdom, stands finally and fully revealed.

Jesus incarnates Divine Wisdom not only because He reveals to us the Father's abiding and irrevocable love (Rm 8:38-39), but also because He incarnates for us the plentitude of pneumatic enlightenment. The mind of Christ is conformed to the mind of God, for it is ruled by the fullness of the divine **Pneuma** who searches the depths of God's saving intentions.

Clearly, Paul's proclamation of Jesus as the wisdom of God closely parallels his insistence later in the same letter that by His resurrection Jesus became a lifegiving **Pneuma**. The two affirmations illumine one another. Jesus incarnates for us the divine wisdom because His conscious transformation in the **Pneuma** Who is the mind and wisdom of God was total, so total indeed that He and He alone had been divinely appointed to mediate Her to others in eschatological fullness. By baptising us in the divine Breath, the risen Christ imparts to us the wisdom that is His. Through justifying faith, personal sanctification, and the sharing of Her charismatic inspirations, we who believe in Christ are assimilated consciously and collectively to the mind (**noun**) and wisdom of God incarnate in Him. This is the goal of our baptismal participation in the communion (**koinonia**) of the saints and of our sharing the **charismata**. Of course, the Divine Mind surpasses the community in enlightenment. We see now only in a glass darkly. But we who know Christ through openness to His Breath have already begun to probe the mysterious depths of the divine intelligence. When fully transformed in the **Pneuma** of God, we will know God even as we are known by Him (1 Co 13:8-13).[58]

Let us once again pause and take stock of our progress. We have been examining the biblical witness to the Holy Breath in order to discover how She is perceived in living faith. We have discovered a remarkable convergence and consensus. Biblical pneumatologists perceive the Holy Breath as an immanent source of gracious enlightenment. That enlightenment takes a variety of forms: the wisdom that descends from on high, the faith that inspires authentic worship, the gracious impulse to serve others as an expression of faith in God. Pneumatic enlightenment yields the ability to perceive the saving action of God present in Jesus and in the obedient witness of His disciples. The Holy Breath sheds light on every corner of human experience. She graces the heart with discernment. As She breathes upon the human imagination it glows with prophetic words and inspired visions. She guides the study of the sage and endows the words of religious teachers with divine authority and healing power. From Her flow the courage of leadership and the exalation of devout prayer.

Moreover, in biblical pneumatology one cannot experience the enlightenment of the Holy Breath without perceiving something of Her reality. Through Her enlightenment we know Her inferentially as **divine wisdom itself,** as **a transcendent principle of scrutinizing omniscience.** Moreover, Her enlightenment of Jesus reveals Her to be **the mind of God and of His Christ,** the cognitive link between the Father and the Son. By inspiring the faith, the hope, the love, and the charismatic service of Christians, the Holy Breath stands historically self-disclosed as **a matrix of divine life** that encompasses and transcends the community of believers. An abiding source of authentic religious insight, the Breath functions as **a principle of continuity within salvation history.** Individual religious leaders come and go; but the same divine Breath inspires them all. Because She effects our sanctification, She is Herself **the law** to which authentic religious behavior must conform. She stands revealed as both a **life-force** and a **life-source,** as an empowering enlightenment.

We have dwelt at some length on this particular strain in biblical pneumatology. And we have done so out of set purpose. For sadly enough, contemporary theological conceptions of the divine Breath often remain untouched by these fundamental biblical insights into Her reality. Instead, they reflect trinitarian doctrines popularized during the middle ages. And by the middle ages, for a variety of historical reasons, many of the biblical truths we have just examined had been largely forgotten. A perception of God derived from the eclectic fusion of Christian faith and platonic metaphysics had largely replaced biblical teaching about the Holy Breath. Let us examine briefly how this fusion occurred and what it signified.

The writings of the apostolic fathers failed to advance Christian pneumatology beyond the insights of the biblical witness which we have just examined. They acknowledged divine inspiration, especially of the Bible, as the work of God's Holy Breath. She guarantees religious truth and effects union in faith and love. She inspires true rather than false prophecy and sanctions the authority of the ordained leader. She is the presence of the risen Christ. Biblical texts dealing with Her activity are cited as normative for faith. And She is conceived as a matrix of divine life. (I Clement, 13:1, 16:2, 42:3, 45:2, 46:6, 47:3; Ignatius of Antioch, Letter to the Philadelphians, 7, Letter to the Ephesians, 18; Hermas, The Shepherd, Mandates 10 and 11, Parable 5; Didache, 7:1, 3; The Martyrdom of Polycarp, 14:3; Epistle of Barnabas, 6:14, 12:2, 19:17).[59]

But when we turn from the apostolic fathers to the church apologists of the second and third centuries, we find writers of a very different metal. Urbane, educated, argumentative, they strove to interpret the gospel to the intellectuals of their day and to defend the Christian community from slanderous charges of political subversion and immorality. They also exhibited on occasion a flair for theological innovation.

One eloquent Christian apologist was Justin Martyr (c. 100-c. 165). A man of his time, Justin thought more eclectically than systematically. But he was especially fond of the later dialogues of Plato. And he did not hesitate to speak of the God Christians worship in terms borrowed largely from Platonic speculation. The Middle Platonism which inspired Justin adapted the insights of other philosophical systems to its own speculative needs and interests. And with hints from the Stoics, the philosophers of the Middle Academy had eventually located the ideal world of Plato in a transcendent intelligence. They thus transformed Plato's archetypal forms into the thoughts of a divine mind.

Philo of Alexandria (30 b.c.-45 a.d.), a Jewish theologian whose works Justin seems to have known, had drawn on these insights to understand the word (**logos**) and wisdom of the Hebrew God. He had equated both with the divine intelligence described by the philosophers of the Middle Academy. Justin turned these same insights to theological advantage by using them to explain to a pagan world the **Logos** Christology of John the evangelist.

Justin spoke of the Son of God, the Word (**Logos**) made flesh, as a reasoning power begotten by the Father before creation but with a view both to creating the world and revealing God to humankind. Moreover, in the world of Middle Platonism, humans become rational (**logikos**), capable of reason and of speech, through conscious participation in the divine **Logos**. Accordingly, for Justin, the **Logos** of the fourth gospel is the transcendent ground of all human rational endeavor, including the best expressions of Greek and Roman philosophy. By the same token, human reason is like a seed of the divine Word. It is a seminal **logos**, a **logos spermatikos** (First Apology, 5, 32, 63; Second Apology, 10, 13; Dialogue with the Jew Trypho, 63).[60]

But the **Logos** is not the only source of divine enlightenment. The divine **Pneuma**, Who for Justin occupies the "third place" in God after the Father and the Son, inspires all prophetic illumination. The Breath of prophecy speaks in Her own name, but She can and does inspire words from either the Father or the Son. She has inspired the sacred scriptures as well as the apostolic witness. She imparts the light of faith and keeps the prophetic gift alive in the Christian community after it died in the Jewish. Moreover, without Her gracious illumination no one can assent to divine revelation (First Apology, 13, 13-33, 39; Dialogue with the Jew Trypho, 7, 19, 34, 36, 38, 43.)

In portraying the divine Breath as the source of gracious enlightenment Justin remained faithful to biblical pneumatology. But he diverged from it in one important respect. For Paul the apostle, the Holy Breath is, as we have seen, the mind of God and of Christ. For Justin the divine intelligence is the Son.

61

In the writings of Clement of Alexandria (c. 159-c. 215) some of the theological motifs which Justin had introduced into the Christian tradition were extended and embellished. And their implications for Christian pneumatology were clarified. Like Justin, Clement interpreted the Johnanine **Logos** Platonically and believed that Greek philosophers could be enlightened by the Christian deity. He reserved his warmest praise for the Pythagoreans and especially for Plato.[61]

Justin had spoken of two principles of enlightenment within the Christian Godhead: the **Logos** and the Holy Breath. Clement, however, speaks of only one. As the seat of the divine ideas, the **Logos** grounds all cosmic and moral order and intelligibility. As such He mediates between the material universe and the absolute and unutterable mystery of God. For Clement divine enlightenment is effected by the Son alone. He has no developed pneumatology.[62]

The absence of concern with the divine Breath which one discovers in the writings of Clement is theologically significant. For it gives clear evidence that the **Logos** Christology which Justin had introduced and Clement had developed was in fact changing theological perceptions of the Christian God. Moreover, those changed perceptions were subtly alienating Christian thought from important aspects of the biblical witness. Once theologians began to attribute to the Son divine functions which the Bible attributes to the Holy Breath, they found themselves hard pushed to explain how the latter functions within the economy of salvation. At the same time their perception of Her place within the Godhead became confused. These unfortunate tendencies emerge clearly in the trinitarian writings of Clement's most brilliant disciple, Origen of Alexandria (c. 185-c. 254).

In the economy of salvation, Origen's **Logos** holds the primacy in divine enlightenment. The saving function of the divine **Pneuma** is therefore correspondingly obscured. Even within the Godhead She is shapeless until informed by the order and intelligibility of the **Logos**. She saves us by disposing the soul to receive the gracious illumination of the Word. But He, rather than the Breath, effects gracious enlightenment.[62]

In the West, Augustine of Hippo bears chief responsibility for popularizing the **Logos** Christology introduced by Justin and developed by Alexandrian theologians and other Greek fathers. But Augustine was more successful than Origen had been in explaining how the divine Breath functions in the Christian economy of salvation. Augustine's trinitarian theology was shaped both by his longing for God and by his passion for philosophy.[63] His espousal of Neo-Platonism combined with his own conversion experience to convince him that divine Wisdom is discovered by turning inward. Adapting Ciceronian language to the needs of trinitarian speculation, he had also come to imagine the wisdom of God as the supreme measure (**modus**) of everything that exists. The Father is the seat of Wisdom. The Son is His **Logos**, His perfect image, eternal truth, the light of unchanging intelligibility. The Breath is a ray from that eternal light that penetrates our hearts. She summons us to a love of interiority. She is the lure of wisdom from on high. (Commentary on John, II, 6)[64]

Ambrose of Milan (340-397) in his treatise De Spiritu Sancto had identified the Holy Breath as the one who inspires Christian love (On the Holy Spirit, I, 8, 9). Amborse was echoing an important theme in Pauline pneumatology. But Augustine found his suggestion both psychologically and theologically suggestive. Might not the divine Breath be understood as a cosmic principle of love, like that described by Plato, a transcendent power which lures our hearts away from passing sensible beauty and focuses them instead on the eternal truth? Even more, does not love unite lover and beloved? As the indwelling of divine love, the Breath binds us together in one communion of faith and service. Might She not then be understood as the bond of love uniting Father and Son within the Godhead?[65]

In Augustinian trinitarian theology, therefore, wisdom and intelligence are associated with the Son, while love is linked to the divine Breath. That love is God's supreme gift to us. Without it other gifts and charismatic graces are profitless (On The Trinity, XV, xiv, 23-xviii, 32).[66]

Medieval trinitarian speculation offers an extended footnote to Augustine's De Trinitate. But it was perhaps Thomas Aquinas (c. 1225-1274) who brought Augustine's conception of the trinity to its most systematic expression. For while Aquinas was attracted to the philosophical vision of Aristotle, in matters trinitarian he remained a systematizing Augustinian.

With Aristotle, Aquinas held that the human soul is the form of the body. But he also defended its spirituality and immortality. He held for the presence in the soul of two spiritual powers: the intellect and the will. Spiritual beings live. Accordingly, Aquinas concluded that if God is both spiritual and alive, He must also possess in some transcendent sense both an intellect and a will. He then argued that the presence of two and only two spiritual powers in God explains why there can be two and only two divine processions. The procession of the Word is an immanent act of the divine intellect; the procession of the Breath, an immanent act of the divine will. For the Son is eternal wisdom; the Breath eternal, divine love (Summa Theologiae, I, xxvii).

We are seeking an integrated theological perception of God's Holy Breath. But the possibility of integrating biblical pneumatology with the Platonized vision of the trinity which resulted from the identification of the Johannine Logos with the divine intelligence remains speculatively remote. In this specific Platonization of the Christian God (there were others), one can continue to speak of the Holy Breath as the source of divine love. Here Platonizing theologians and the biblical witness agree. But the Son, rather than the Breath, has become the source of gracious enlightenment; the Son, rather than the Breath, is the mind of God. On these last two points, the Platonic tradition we have examined and biblical pneumatology diverge.

But in rejecting this particular conception of the Trinity as inadequate, we are not suggesting that the contemporary Christian is forced to choose between the Bible and tradition. For Christian tradition offers other conceptions of the triune God, conceptions which better accord with the biblical witness. One theological alternative is hinted at in the writings of Irenaeus of Lyons (c. 130-c. 200).

For Irenaeus soteriology offers the key to pneumatology. He believed that the economy of salvation expresses the divine monarchy (**monarchia**). The term "monarchy" means single sway. It implied that one and the same God both creates and redeems. And because there is only one God there is finally only one path of salvation.[67]

But the Christian God is three-in-one. The triune life of the deity serves, therefore, as a principle of order within the one redemptive economy. The Son reveals to us the Father. The divine Breath leads us to the Son. Within salvation history, therefore, Son and Breath function as "the two hands of God" (Against the Heresies, III, xxiv, 1, Iv, xx, 5-9).[68]

Irenaeus' concern to integrate the activity of the Holy Breath into a single economy provides the key to his pneumatology. The Father remains unknown, transcendent, mysterious until He is historically revealed by the Son. The Father acts efficaciously through the Son to save us. The Son can be recognized in faith as the revelation of the Father only through the illumination of the divine **Pneuma.** For She is transcendent divine wisdom. The Son executes the Father's commands; the Breath nourishes, increases, and illumines (Against the Heresies, IV, xx, 4, V, viii, 1, xiii, 4; Demonstration of the Apostolic Preaching, V, VII).[69]

A similar trinitarian scheme emerges in the writings of Gaius Marius Victorinus. Victorinus was a noted rhetorician in Rome. In his old age he astonished the Roman intelligentsia by converting to Christianity (c. 354). Moreover, shortly after his baptism he rose to the defence of his newfound creed by publishing a series of anti-Arian tracts. His theological achievement was overshadowed by that of Augustine. But his conception of the trinity offers an interesting alternative to that defended by the bishop of Hippo.

Like Augustine, Victorinus espoused a devout Neo-Platonism. But he put his philosophy to very different theological uses. For Victorinus, the Son is the action (**agere**) of the Father. And for that very reason, He is one in being (**homoousios**) with the Father. For a living God cannot be without acting. Nor can the divine activity be other than the God who acts. The Father precedes the Son as being precedes action. The Son reveals the Father, Who otherwise dwells in inaccessible light (Against Arius, I, 2. 1-4).

But if the Son is the Father's activity, the divine **Spiritus** is His mind. She is the living thought of God, as inseparable from the Father and Son as thought is from activity and life. For She is the subsistent, living act

64

of divine self-understanding (Against Arius, I, 51.19-52.9). Through the Son the divine being and vitality of the Father is channeled outward and downward into matter. Through the Breath it is channeled inward and upward to grace and glory. The Son is divine creative energy; the Breath, divine intelligence Whose enlightenment leads us back to the Father. For the divine Breath is "the first movement toward interiority (**intus**), the Father's conception (**excogitatio patrica**), that is, His self knowledge" (Against Arius, II, 1.57. 28-29).

The pneumatology of Irenaeus and of Victorinus suggests a different conception of the trinity from that defended by Augustine and Aquinas. In confessing Jesus to be the divine Word, the eternal **Logos**, one need not conceive of Him in the manner of some Christian Platonists as the eternal conception of the divine intellect. He is indeed the Word of God. He is God's spoken word because through Him God acts and speaks efficaciously to save us. The spoken Word of God also expresses the divine mind and wisdom. If, then, with Paul the Apostle we confess Jesus Christ to be the wisdom of God, by that we mean that through Him we come to know not only the face of the Father, but the divine mind who is the Holy Breath. This is a fundamental point; and we shall return to it in other contexts.

Let us once again take stock of the progress of our argument. We are seeking an integrated theological perception of God's Holy Breath. We are approaching pneumatology experientially. Having in the preceding chapter examined the dynamic structure of human experience, we have in the present chapter begun to examine the way the divine Breath enters human experience and graciously transforms it. But we concern ourselves here less with the graced convert and more with what the gracing of experience tells us about the Breath Herself.

We have accepted the Bible as the normative expression of the way the Holy Breath of God ought to be perceived in faith. We have found a remarkable convergence in both Old and New Testament pneumatology. In both, the Breath of God is experienced as a divine principle of gracious illumination. In Hebrew pneumatology this is taken to be revelatory of the fact that She is subsistent divine wisdom. In the New Testament the Breath illumines and guides Jesus in His obedient accomplishment of the mission given Him by the Father. The Breath therefore stands revealed to Christian faith as the cognitive link between the Son and the Father, as the mind of God and of Christ.

We have also examined two divergent strains in post-biblical pneumatology. In the first, several influential theologians came to perceive the Son rather than the Breath as the mind of God. They did so as a direct consequence of their artificial Platonization of the Johannine **Logos**. We have suggested that if the Bible provides us with a normative insight into the reality of the Christian God, then this particular strain in post-biblical pneumatology ought to be abandoned as a theological aberration. For it distorts a fundamental aspect of the biblical witness.

But we have also examined a second strain in Christian trinitarian speculation, one that remains closer to the biblical witness. This second strain understands the Son not as the conception of the divine mind so much as the one through whom the Father speaks and acts. He can therefore be legitimately conceived as the spoken Word of God who reveals to us simultaneously both the reality of the Father and His mind, who is the Holy Breath.

One final task remains in the present chapter. We must show that we experience the enlightenment of the Holy Breath as Her historical mission. This final stage of our argument will advance in two parts. First, we will examine what the biblical witness has to say about the Breath's eschatological mission to the Church. Second, we will attempt to identify the experiences that lie at the basis of the biblical descriptions of the Breath's mission. In the process we will be forced to elaborate an experiential account of the historical missions of both Son and Breath.

The New Testament accounts of the Breath's eschatological mission display both convergence and contrast. In his surviving letters Paul the apostle never discusses Her mission as such, although he may have done so elsewhere. But he does speak of Her as the Breath of God and of Christ. That She comes from Them is revealed by the fact that She leads us to Them in conscious faith. For She is certainly and manifestly present whenever anyone confesses the Lordship of Jesus and the Fatherhood of God (1 Th 4:1-8; 2 Th 2:13; Phil 1:19; 1 Co 2:12, 14, 3:16-17, 6:9-20, 15:42-50; 2 Co 3:1-3, 7-18; Rm 5:1-5, 8:7-17).[70]

Both Matthew and Mark confess Jesus to be the Breath baptiser. Both promise that She will teach the disciples of Jesus what to say under persecution. But neither evangelist offers us an account of the arrival of the Breath in the Christian community. Instead, Matthew's gospel closes with the promise of the risen Christ that He will abide with His Church as an immediate personal presence:

> All authority in heaven and on earth has been
> given to me. Go therefore and make disciples of
> all nations, baptizing them in the name of the
> Father and of the Son and of the Holy Breath,
> teaching them to observe all that I have
> commanded you. And, lo, I am with you always,
> to the close of the age (Mt 28:18-20).

Presumably, for Matthew baptism in the triune name fulfills the prophecy of John the Baptist that Jesus would be the Breath baptiser. The formula also implicitly asserts that Son and Breath enjoy a divinity on a par with the Father.

But if among the synoptic evangelists Matthew and Mark remained reticent concerning the actual arrival of the Holy Breath, Luke describes the event in considerable detail. In Acts She comes to the assembled disciples under the double sign of wind and of fire. The same signs had accompanied the ascension of Elijah into heaven; and the vision had revealed to the prophet's disciple Elisha that he would receive a double portion of his master's prophetic **Ruah** (2 Kgs 2:9-15).[71] But now the Breath of Elijah has become the Breath of Jesus Christ, and instead of descending on a single individual She comes to fulfill Joel's prophecy that She would one day be poured out on "all flesh," men and women alike (Ac 2:15-21; Jl. 2:28-29).[72]

The Pentecostal fire also recalls the prophecy of the Baptist that the Breath would be poured out in purification and in judgment (Lk 3:16-17).[73] But the Breath arrives under the sign of "tongues like fire" (Ac 2:3).[73] The fire of purification and of judgment will then burn in the disciples' proclamation of Jesus even to the ends of the earth. And that event is foreshadowed in the eruption of glossolalic speech among those gathered in the upper room (Ac 2:4). The appearance of glossolalia among the disciples is interpreted as a sign of the gathering of the new Israel from the four corners of the earth (Ac 2:5-13), an event that portends the outpouring of the Breath on all humankind (Ac 2:14-21).

In linking Joel's prophecy to the phenomenon of glossolalia Luke may also have intended to portray the arrival of the Breath as a reversal of Babel. At Babel Yahweh had confounded tongues as a sign of the universal sinfulness of humankind (Gn 11:1-9). Now He does so anew as a portent of universal salvation.

The arrival of the Pentecostal Breath is followed by a diffusion of charismatic gifts throughout the community of disciples: there are tongues and prophecy, cures and exorcisms, preaching, and works of mercy. And the apostolic witness is especially confirmed by signs and wonders (Ac 2:1ff, 3:12, 4:32-37, 5:12, 21:10).

Moreover, the initial proclamation of Jesus is confirmed by the "little pentecost" narrated in Acts 4:23-31. Warned by the Jewish leaders to stop proclaiming Christ, the apostles, joined by the entire community lift up their voices to God in prayer. They recall how Jesus' own innocent death at the hands of His persecutors only fulfilled an ancient prophecy. Threatened now by the same powers, they appeal to their servant status in God's eyes; for they follow a servant messiah. They pray for boldness in proclaimiing Jesus in defiance of His and their enemies and for confirming signs and wonders, like those worked at the first exodus. But these signs are to be worked now in the name of Jesus. Their prayer is answered immediately. The house in which they are praying is rocked. They are filled anew with the divine Breath. And, as on the first Pentecost, they are immediately impelled out into the streets to proclaim the gospel with renewed boldness.

The passage interweaves rich Lukan themes. The divine **Pneuma** will not be coveted. She comes to impel the disciples of Jesus to proclaim His name to others. She forces the servants of a suffering messiah into defiant conflict with the same dark powers as sought His life. She works in them a boldness that strengthens them to do and say things they could not left to their own fearful devices. And She comes to effect a new exodus and thereby to complete and to transcend Mosaic religion.

At the beginning of Acts, the risen Christ had promised that the good news would be preached first to Israel, then to the Samaritans (Ac 1:7-8). Philip the deacon instructs the Samaritans and baptises them. His ministry is accompanied by signs and wonders. But there is a puzzling absence of charismatic manifestations of the Breath among his converts. Peter and John come down from Jerusalem to pray over the newly baptised, possibly because in the confusion of persecution Philip's Samaritan mission had not been officially commissioned by the Jerusalem community. The two apostles lay hands on the baptised converts. "And they received the Holy Breath" (Ac 4:32-5:11).[74]

This story has been theologically abused. Both Roman Catholics and Protestant Pentecostals have used it as a proof text: the former to establish the existence of confirmation as a separate ritual in the apostolic church; the latter to prove the inefficacy of water baptism and its distinction from Spirit baptism.

In describing the Pentecost of the Samaritans, Luke remained, however, quite oblivious of the post-Reformation debates concerning the efficacy of sacramental worship. He seems to suggest that the quality of the first faith of the Samaritans was suspect. He notes excessive fascination with the miraculous in the Samaritan Simon. The story climaxes in Simon's attempt to purchase from the apostles the power to confer the divine **Pneuma** on others. He is roundly denounced by Peter, who informs him that he is "trapped in the bitterness of gall and the chains of sin." And Simon thus judged seems to repent (Ac 8:14-23).

Luke's central point in telling the story is, however, clear. The divine **Pneuma** can never be bought or sold. Indeed, the freedom with which the Breath is divinely dispensed stands as an abiding rebuke both to human avarice and to the proud and superstititous desire to control Her activity. To such as Simon, the Breath comes in judgment.

In Acts, the "Pentecost" of the Samaritans is soon followed by the "Pentecost" of the gentiles. Before Peter goes to the home of the pagan Cornelius, he is instructed three times in a vision not to consider profane what God has purified. He then preaches to Cornelius and his household, telling them how Jesus was anointed by the divine Breath, crucified, and how He rose from the dead. The meaning of Peter's earlier vision becomes plain when the Breath descends upon the listening pagans with charismatic manifestations similar to those which accompanied Her descent on

Pentecost. Peter orders the gentiles baptised without circumcision and then justifies his action to the Jerusalem church by insisting that he performed it in manifest obedience to God (Ac 10:1-11:18).

Clearly, for Luke Pentecost did not occur once and for all in the history of the Church. It keeps happening. The Holy Breath given on the first Pentecost continues to be breathed into the world whenever there is human openness to the good news about Jesus. Her coming in Acts follows the movement of the gospel. She is portrayed as a divine force that follows the path of least resistance. Her arrival is revealed in a visible transformation of those who believe, by their confession of Jesus in faith and by their reception of charismatic gifts. Father and Son send Her from on high. Her arrival prolongs the historical mission of Jesus by ensuring that He is proclaimed to Jews and gentiles alike.

Several of these Lukan themes find an echo in the Paraclete pneumatology of the fourth gospel. The Paraclete proceeds simultaneously from both Father and Son (Jn 14:26, 16:7). She will be sent by the Father at Jesus' intercession and in Jesus' name (Jn 14:16, 26). But Jesus Himself will also effect Her coming (Jn 4:7, 16:7). Moreover, that the Father and Son are co-senders of the Paraclete manifests their intimate vital union with one another (Jn 10:30).

But John's descriptive account of the mission of the Breath differs in a number of its details from Luke's. In the fourth gospel Jesus' prophecy of the coming of the Paraclete is fulfilled on Easter morning. The risen Savior appears to His startled disciples, breathes on them, and says: "Receive a Holy Breath. Those whose sin you shall forgive are forgiven them, those whose sins you shall retain are retained." (Jn 20:20-23).[75]

Omitting the Greek article before the phrase "Holy Breath," John's Jesus says, "Receive **a** Holy Breath," not "Receive **the** Holy Breath." We are perhaps dealing here with a biblical inclusion. The fourth gospel began with the promise of the Baptist that Jesus would baptise His disciples with "a Holy Breath" (Jn. 3:1-21). But the omission of the article may also have a deeper intent. Had the evangelist chosen to use the article, he would have called attention to the noun it modifies. Jesus' words would have implied "Receive the Holy Breath, that same divine Breath whose coming has been foretold." By omitting the article, however, the evangelist calls grammatical attention not to the noun **Pneuma** but to its accompanying adjective. It is the holiness of the Breath that is at this point the special focus of the evangelist's theological concern. Jesus is equivalently saying: "Receive a Breath that sanctifies."

Such an interpretation is reenforced by the fact that the Breath comes to effect the forgiveness of sins. She will work forgiveness through Her witness in the disciples. For Her mission to them coincides with their sending forth into the world. Their witness will, then, reveal Her divine holiness.

69

But as in Luke and Matthew, the Breath comes not in forgiveness only, but in judgment. By the retention of sins, the Breath that sanctifies the faithful disciples of Jesus carries out her forensic mission of judgment, convicting unbelievers of their malice before God (Jn 4:34, 5:30, 6:38-40, 17:4, 19:30).

In both Luke and John, therefore, the mission of the Breath cannot be separated from the Church's efficacious commissioning by the risen Christ to bear wtiness to the good news. Christians come to an awareness of Her mission by being themselves sent forth to live and proclaim the gospel. Because the Breath that impels them is the same that dwelt in Jesus and because She keeps them faithful to Him, Her mission in them prolongs Jesus' own historical mission. Moreover, in both Luke and John She comes to purify and sanctify those who believe and to effect the conviction and judgment of unbelievers.

A Johannine and a Lukan account of the Breath's arrival differ most obviously in their timing. Of course, neither author is attempting to write a newspaper account of this important event in the life of the Church. But both may in fact be telling us a literal truth about the way the divine Breath was communicated to the first disciples. It seems likely that the encounter with the risen Christ would have effected a religious enlightenment and that that illumination would have been experienced as the work of the Breath of God present in the risen Savior. Very likely too the illumination in question would, as the evangelists tell us, have included a commissioning to bear witness to the divine forgiveness revealed in Jesus' resurrection. But neither experience would preclude the kind of communal outpouring of the Holy Breath which Luke describes in Acts. Nor does it contradict the Johannine tradition to say that this communal experience occurred after the apparitions of the risen Christ had ceased. In other words the mission of the Breath, being an historical process, could well have happened in stages.

But even if one chooses to insist on the contrasts between a Johannnine and a Lukan account of the sending of the Breath of Christ, those accounts differ more dramatically than doctrinally. One finds, to be sure, differences of emphasis. Luke, for example, insists more on the charismatic manifestations that reveal the Breath's arrival than John does. But John's gospel does testify to the prayer, the prophetic illumination, the teaching, and the visible witness that the Advocate will inspire. The disciples are promised that they will do greater works than Jesus Himself. In other words, without insisting on the charismatic manifestations of the Breath, the fourth gospel points to their presence in the Johannine community. In portraying the coming of the Breath as an Easter event John links it with greater dramatic unity to Jesus' death and glorification. It is a moment within His "hour." Although Luke postpones Her coming until Jesus has ascended, he insists that the risen Christ sends the Pentecostal Breath. The two accounts are then theologically convergent even though they differ in their dramatic details.

We would, however, misinterpret the biblical witness were we to imagine that the saving activity of the Holy Breath is confined to Her Pentecostal illumination of confessing Christians. The Bible insists that She was present and active in Jesus Himself and that She also prepared His coming by inspiring all the great charismatic leaders of the Old Testament. In other words, even though we have as Christians learned to speak of a mission of the Holy Breath through Her missioning activity in Jesus and in the Christian community, we can with perfect theological justification speak of a gracious sending of the Breath every time human experience is illumined by Her in faith.

These reflections cast light on the way in which the historical missions of the divine persons have come to be experienced. The incarnation is the historical mission of the Son of God. The ongoing Pentecost of the Church and the eschatological mission of the Holy Breath also coincide. The incarnation inaugurates the last age of salvation. What distinguishes the mission of the Breath during the end time from Her other historical missions is therefore that it is mediated by the incarnation. As a consequence, in Her eschatological mission She is experienced not merely as the Breath of God, but explicitly as the Breath of the Son and of the Father Who sent HIm. She is experienced in faith as being sent by both. In our response to Her illumination She prolongs Jesus' mission by teaching us to confess Him as the Breath-baptiser sent us by the Father.

Constitutive of both historical missions is a human experience of being divinely sent. Jesus claims to be sent by the Father. The Church claims to be sent most immediately by the risen Christ but ultimately by the Father who sent Him. Both claim to exercise their missions in the illuminating power of the Divine Breath. Our **awareness of being sent** is, therefore, our human experience of Her historical mission. And the mission is historical because our human experience, which Her coming graciously transforms, is, as we saw in the last chapter, spatio-temporal in its structure.

In experiencing the historical mission of a divine person, a divine reality is perceived. Realities, as we also saw in the last chapter, are perceived affectively and inferentially within experience. The human experience of the mission of a divine person is as a consequence an interpreted event. It has, therefore, an evaluative form capable of description in its own right. Its form is fiducial. For the mission of a divine person coincides with that person's historical self-revelation. We can experience the free self-revelation of a divine person only on terms that are divinely set. When we respond to God on terms divinely set, we consent to Him in faith. Through faith experience begins to take on a graced character. We can therefore acknowledge that the mission of a divine person has taken place only through the gracious transformation of our human experience in faith.

One must distinguish two gracious transformations of experience. The first reveals the divine person being sent; the second allows the believer to recognize the first transformation for what it is. In the course of the historical mission of Son and Breath the two transformations are dynamically interrelated. Let us reflect on the character of that relationship.

To be more specific, Jesus was revealed to us as Son of God through the gracious transformation of His human experience in obedience to the Father's missioning commands and the Breath's illuminations. Jesus could not then be fully revealed to us as God until the gracious transformation of His human experience was achieved totally. We call total transformation in God "resurrection."

But if the mission of the Son was revealed to us through the gracious transformation of His human experience, the Breath of God is historically revealed in every human consent to God in faith. She is historically revealed as the Breath of Christ in every human consent to Jesus as Lord, savior, and incarnate Son of God.

The gracious transformation of Jesus' human experience in the incarnation and the Christian community's graced testimony to Him are, therfore, both revelatory events. They reveal the historical mission of Son and Breath. But the revelation remains incomplete until it is made to someone. Both events must be acknowledged in faith for what they are if they are to be experienced as the historical mission of a divine person. As revelatory events they have saving significance. But only faith can endow that significance with personal meaning for the believer. We may, then, discern a subtle interplay between faith and revelation in our experience of the divine missions of Son and Breath. The mission of Jesus begins the revelation of God in the end time. It invites faith. The mission of the Breath effects faith in the believer. It also prolongs the revelation begun in Jesus. For when I consent to Him in faith I reveal the illuminating presence of His Breath in my life. That illumination is Her historical mission, for it incorporates me into the Son's own mission to the world.

Both Son and Breath are efficaciously sent into the world. The Son is sent by the Father; the Breath, by both Father and Son. Both missions are interpreted events. In both sendings, therefore, we must distinguish efficacious and interpretative elements. The efficacious element in the mission of the Son has two components: There is (1) the commissioning command of the Father to the Son, and (2) the Son's obedient submission to it. The interpretative element in the Son's mission is His illumination by the Holy Breath.

The efficacious element in the mission of the Breath has three components. There is (1) the Son's command in obedience to the Father to witness to His resurrection and to the message of salvation He had proclaimed, (2) the efficacious sending of the Breath by the Father and Son to be the source and inspiration of the Church's witness, and (3) the Church's decisive response to the mission of Christ and to the Breath's illumination. The interpretative element in the Pentecostal mission of the Breath is Her illumination of the Christian community. That illumination proceeds both individually and collectively. Individual illumination bears fruit in every personal profession of faith in the risen Christ. Collective illumination results from the sharing of faith and of the charisms in the eucharistic community that is created by Christian initiation.

In both the efficacious and interpretative phases of the historical mission of a divine person, we find of necessity the copresence of divine and human elements. The Father's sending of the Son and their joint sending of the Breath are divine acts. Jesus' acts are simultaneously divine and human; for His decisions are the human decisions of God. The Breath's activities are divine. Her illumination of Jesus graciously transforms His human mind. And the Church which She transforms in faith is all too human.

Because the missioning of a divine person demands the simultaneous experience of the divine and of the human, it is a sacramental event. A sacramental revelation both reveals and conceals the reality of God. God is sacramentally revealed in the gracious transformation of something that is not God. Because the transformed reality is not God, to some extent it conceals Him. But because it is transformed by and in God, it reveals Him.

How then do we experience the historical mission of a divine person? It is experienced as a **gracious transformation of human experience in God which reveals sacramentally the reality of the person sent, the character of the relation of that person to the other divine person(s) who function in the sending, and the conditions which must be met if the historical mission of the divine person is to be experienced as such.**

Moreover, our examination of biblical pneumatology allows us to characterize the historical mission of the Breath more specifically. In it we are at one and the same time graciously illumined and divinely commissioned to bear witness to God and to His Christ. In Her eschatological mission, the Holy Breath comes to fulfill God's desire to ·save all people by summoning them to faith in the incarnate Word. The mission of the Breath of Christ is historically manifest in Her charismatic transformation of those who are baptised in Jesus' name. The Holy Breath comes in both purification and in judgment. She comes in purification because She testifies to the forgiveness of sins proclaimed by Jesus and accomplished in His death and glorification. She comes in judgment because She inspires His disciples to bear witness against those forces which nailed the Lord of glory to a cross. Because She frees us in Christ from the bondage of sin and death, the mission of the Holy Breath is also experienced as a liberation, as a new exodus. Her coming is a sovereign act of divine grace. It is pure gift. It cannot be controlled by any creature. Her mission is also experienced as an atonement. For it effects the reconciliation of all people in the one church of Jesus Christ. Only those who refuse the divine forgiveness stand by their own choice outside that community. They also by their own choice stand under the divine judgment. Finally, the mission of the Holy Breath is also experienced as sanctifying. It consecrates us to God by conforming us to the Breath baptiser, to Jesus, Who in His perfect obedience to the Father reveals to us the meaning of holiness.

The historical missions of Son and Breath are those events that reveal to us the way in which the divine persons relate to one another within the Godhead. They reveal to us the very reality of God because both Son and Breath are sent to us as divine realities. For the Son to be sent by the Father is for Him to stand in a relationship to the Father. For the Breath to be sent simultaneously by both Father and Son is for Her to stand in a simultaneous relationship to both. That both Son and Breath are sent to us as divine means that the relationships revealed in Their missions are divine relationships. In other words the procession of the Son from the Father within the Godhead is historically revealed in the efficacious mission of the Son into the world by the Father. The simultaneous procession of the Breath from both Father and Son is historically revealed in Her efficacious mission into the world by both.

Not only are the relationships of the divine persons to one another within the Godhead revealed to us in the divine missions; but the missions are also the **only** place where the relationship of the divine persons to one another is revealed to us. The inner life of God, as a result, stands fully revealed only in the last age of salvation. For apart from the divine missions we simply have no information about the existence of a multiplicity of persons within God or how those persons relate to one another within the Godhead.

We close these reflections with two historical observations. Perhaps the most significant contribution of Karl Rahner (1904-1984) to contemporary trinitarian speculation has been his repudiation of any attempt to separate the "immanent" from the "economic" Trinity. The immanent Trinity, it will be recalled, is God in His inner triune life. The economic Trinity is that same divine reality in its historical revelation. Rahner has correctly insisted that God's self-communication to us in Jesus and the Holy Breath is itself the historical revelation of the inner life of the Godhead. And he has constructed a complex metaphysics of symbol to explain how this is possible. [76] The preceding reflections suggest, however, that the rift between the economic and immanent Trinity is best closed experientially by a theology of the divine missions.

Secondly, we observe that the preceding account of the divine missions attempts to transpose a Thomistic explanation of their significance into the language of experience. Every mission, Aquinas held, expresses a relationship between a sender and the one sent. He recognized that the sending of the divine persons seeks the gracing of human experience. And he believed that the missions revealed the relation of origin of the divine persons within the Godhead, i.e., their eternal processions.[77]

In the preceding chapter we attempted to establish an experiential context for approaching the Christian God. We explored identifiable realms of human experience and reflected on some of the more obvious traits of spatio-temporal experience. In the present chapter we began to examine the ways in which the Breath of God impinges on human experience. We have argued that because the Holy Breath is experienced in Her historical mission as a divine source of gracious illumination and as the cognitive link between the Father and the Son, She ought to be perceived in faith as the mind of the triune God. In the chapter which follows, we will attempt to explore further some of the consequences of this insight. In the course of that exploration we will attempt to decide whether the construct of experience elaborated in Chapter II can interpret the reality of the Christian God. If it can, then we will be justified in calling God an experience, as process theory suggests we should, even though our conception of God and construct of experience diverges in significant respects from those popularly invoked in process circles. Having argued for the legitimacy of understanding the God of revelation as an experience, we will then begin to explore the analogies between divine and human interpersonal experience.

1.   In Hebrew the word **"nishmat"** is roughly synonymous with the more familiar term **"ruah."** Unless otherwise indicated citations from the Bible are adapted from the R.S.V. However, for the sake of stylistic uniformity, I have substituted the term "Breath" for "Spirit" or else have left it untranslated.

2.   Cf. The Jerome Biblical Commentary, edited by Raymond E. Brown, S.S., Joseph A. Fitzmeyer, S.J., and Roland Murphy, O. Carm. (Englewood Cliffs, N.J.: Prentice Hall, 1968), 34:12, 34:120. Hereafter this edition will be abbreviated as JBC.

3.   Cf. George T. Montague, S.M., The Holy Spirit: Growth of a Biblical Tradition (New York: Paulist, 1976), pp. 3-8; JBC, 2:22-23; Gerhard von Rad, Old Testament Theology, trans. by D.M.G. Stalker (New York: Harper and Row, 1957), I, pp. 133-139; John L. McKenzie, The Two Edged Sword (New York: Bruce, 1957), pp. 90-106; Dale Moody, Spirit of the Living God (Philadelphia: Westminster, 1952), pp. 11-14.

4.   Montague, op. cit., pp. 9-11; JBC, 2:37; Lloyd Neve, The Spirit of God in the Old Testament (Tokyo: Seibunsha, 1972), pp. 5-13.

5.   JBC, 34:203; von Rad, op. cit, I, pp. 152-153; Montague, op. cit., pp. 9-16, 70, 101-102.

6. Montague, op. cit, pp. 11-12; JBC, 5:46; von Rad, op. cit, II, pp. 33-49; Moody, op. cit., pp. 14-19; Neve, op. cit., pp. 14-32.

7. Cf. John L. McKenzie, A Theology of the New Testament (New York: Doubleday, 1974), pp. 212-213.

8. Montague, op. cit., pp. 13-18, 31.

9. Ibid., pp. 20-23.

10. JBC, 9:26, 28; Montague, op. cit., pp. 21-23.

11. Montague, op. cit., pp. 34-45; JBC, 15:25.

12. Neve, op.cit., pp. 32-57.

13. Montague, op. cit., p. 45.

14. Montague, op. cit., p. 45; JBC, 21:15-16.

15. Montague, op. cit., pp. 45-46; von Rad, op. cit., II, pp. 223-224; W. Vogles, "Les recits des vocation des prophetes," Nouvelle Revue Theologique (Jan. 1973), XCV, pp. 3-24.

16. For a discussion of some of the exegetical complexities of this passage, see Montague, op. cit., pp. 54-58; JBC, 22:63.

17. Montague, op. cit., pp. 64-68; von Rad, op. cit., I, pp. 139-153; McKenzie, The Two Edged Sword, pp. 772-789; Moody, op. cit., pp. 27-32; JBC, 2:16.

18. Montague, op. cit., p. 71; JBC, 35:120.

19. Montague, op. cit., pp. 72-73; JBC, 35:155.

20. Montague, op. cit., pp. 95-97; JBC, 29:11, 31:111, 33:14.

21. Montague, op. cit., pp. 13-16, 106-111; JBC, 5:26, 34:24-25; von Rad, Old Testament Theology, I, pp. 289-296.

22. Montague, op. cit., pp. 93-95.

23. Ibid., pp. 48-51; cf. Krister Stendahl, Paul Among Jews and Gentiles (Philadelphia: Fortress, 1978), pp. 7-23; Lucien Cerfaux, The Christian in the Theology of St. Paul, trans. by Lilian Soyron (New York: Herder and Herder, 1967), pp. 37-107.

24. Montague, op. cit., pp. 127, 135-136; JBC, 48:14; James Dunn, Baptism in the Holy Spirit (Naperville, Ill.: Allenson, 1970), pp. 105-113; Cerfaux,

op. cit., pp. 69-106; I. Hermann, Kyrios und Pneuma: Studien zur Christologie der paulinischen Haupbriefe (München: Kosen Verlag, 1961), pp. 99-104; R. Birch Hoyle, The Holy Spirit in St. Paul (New York: Doubleday, 1929), pp. 32-48.

25. Cerfaux, op. cit., pp. 109-128. James Dunn has attempted to portray the apostolate in terms that seem to me to reflect better his own reticence concerning the advantages of institutional religion than the Pauline witness. [Cf. James Dunn, Jesus and the Spirit (Philadelphia: Westminster, 1975), pp. 357-361.] Dunn opposes the apostolate to the charismatic action of the Holy Breath. And he defines the sources of apostolic authority in a way that ensures the withering away of institutional authority in the post-apostolic church (Ibid., pp. 271-280). He is correct to endow the term "charisma" with immediate experiential content. But his attempt to restrict its meaning to what amounts to an actual grace lacks textual foundation in the writings of Paul. Paul asserts nowhere Dunn's thesis that charisma is "the experience of grace and power in a particular instance and only for that instance" (Ibid., p. 254). Moreover, such a reading of Paul cannot finally be reconciled with Paul's discussion of the charism of celibacy. Paul compares and contrasts celibacy with marriage. He recognizes marriage as a permanent state of life and speaks of celibacy as an alternative to marriage. He argues specifically that as a state of life it offers advantages for an active apostle like himself. Paul is also concerned to rebuke those who would renounce the use of sex for the wrong reasons. His own renunciation is charismatic because it is undertaken for the sake of facilitating the proclamation of the good news. And he speaks of those who are called to marital union as enjoying a different charisma than his own. The apostle writes: "I wish that all were as I myself am [i.e,. celibate]. But each has his own special charism from God, one of one kind and one of another" (1 Co 7:7). Not only, then does the term "charisma" in Paul include permanent vocational calls; but among those calls is the call to enter into institutional marriage. He regards the call to celibacy as a similar call. It is significant, then that Dunn can offer no textual support in Paul for his own definition of celibacy as the ability to deny sexual impulses one at a time. Nor does the apostle share Dunn's concern to deny the apostolate charismatic basis. On the contrary, Paul lists it as the chief of the charisms. Moreover, it holds the primacy not simply in the local church founded by the apostle, but in the church as a whole (cf. 1 Co. 12:28). Finally, Dunn's thesis that the apostolate is not a charism is finally irreconcilable with Paul's own insistence that his apostolic witness is sustained and confirmed by the action of the Holy Breath (1 Th. 1:4-6; 1 Co. 2:4-6).

26. Montague, op. cit., pp. 127-128, 131-132, 138, 156-157, 187-188; JBC, 48:14, 23, 51:21, 23, 26; Hermann, op. cit., pp. 60-65, 97-99, 120; Cerfaux, op. cit., pp. 129-152.

27. Montague, op. cit., pp. 193-194; Dunn, Baptism in the Holy Spirit, pp. 106-108; JBC, 49:20.

28. Montague, op. cit., pp. 145-147; Hermann, op. cit., pp. 102-104.

29. Montague, op. cit., pp. 139-140; JBC, 51:29-32.

30. Stendahl, op. cit., pp. 23-40.

31. Montague, op. cit., pp. 194-196.

32. Kurt Stadler, Das Werk des Geistes in der Heilung bei Paulus (Zurich: EVZ-Verlag, 1962), pp. 183-185, 317-359; Dunn, Baptism in the Holy Spirit, pp. 112-115; Cerfaux, op. cit., pp. 373-445; John L. McKenzie, "Justice and Justification," The Way, XIII (July, 1973), pp. 198-206; G.B. Caird, Principalities and Powers (Oxford: Oxford at Clarendon, 1956); Hoyle, op. cit., pp. 77ff.; Gunther Bornkamm, Paul, trans. by D.M.G. Stalker (New York: Harper and Row, 1969), pp. 141-154.

33. Montague, op. cit., pp. 156-159; JBC, 51:77-78, 52:48; Rudolf Schnackenburg, Baptism in the Thought of St. Paul, trans. by G.R. Beasley-Murray (New York: Herder and Herder, 1964); Dunn, Baptism in the Holy Spirit, pp. 116-130; Cerfaux, op. cit., pp. 137-138; Oscar Cullmann, Baptism in the New Testament (London: SCM Press, 1950), pp. 10-12, 39-40; Hermann, op. cit., pp. 78-83.

34. Montague, op. cit., pp. 128-129, 131, 139-140.

35. JBC, 53:84.

36. Montague, op. cit., pp. 188-190; JBC, 49:29-30, 53:50, 80-83, 52:14; Ignace de la Potterie, S.J. and Stanislaus Lyonnet, S.J., The Christian Lives by the Spirit, trans. by John Morries (Staten Island: Alba, 1970), pp. 146-174.

37. Montague, op. cit., p. 148; JBC, 51:76-77; Dunn, Jesus and the Spirit, pp. 201, 209; Hoyle, op. cit., pp. 52ff.

38. Montague, op. cit., pp. 145-184, 213-214; Dunn, Jesus and the Spirit, pp. 209-265; JBC, 51:75-81, 53:118; Gotthold Hasenhüttl, Charisma: Ordnungsprinzip der Kirche (Freiburg: Herder, 1969); Stadler, op. cit., pp. 87-92; Gabriel Murphy, Charisma and Church Renewal (Rome: Catholic Book Agency, 1965); Cerfaux, op. cit., pp. 239-311.

39. C.K. Barrett, The Holy Spirit and the Gospel Tradition (London: S.P.C.K., 1947).

40. JBC, 42:78.

41. Haenchen, op. cit., pp. 166 ff.

42. Dunn, Jesus and the Spirit, pp. 49-53; Montague, op. cit., pp. 244-248.

43. JBC, 63:77.

44. Raymond Brown, S.S., The Gospel According to John (New York: Doubleday, 1970), I, pp. 181-182; Montague, op. cit., pp. 346-347; JBC, 63:77.

45. Brown, The Gospel According to John (New York: Doubleday, 1970), I, pp. 293-303; Montague, op. cit., pp. 346-347; JBC, 63:77.

46. Porsch, op. cit., pp. 161-212.

47. Raymond E. Brown, "The Paraclete in the Fourth Gospel," New Testament Studies, XIII (1966), pp. 113-132; de la Potterie and Lyonnet, The Christian Lives by the Spirit, pp. 57-76.

48. Brown, The Gospel According to John, II, pp. 637-648.

49. Montague, op. cit., pp. 350-352.

50. William J. Fulco, S.J., Maranatha: Reflections on the Mystical Theology of John the Evangelist (New York: Paulist, 1973), pp. 55-64.

51. Porsch, op. cit., pp. 257-273, 290-303.

52. Brown, The Gospel According to John, II, pp. 702-717.

53. Hermann, op. cit., p. 19.

54. Montague, op. cit., pp. 188-191; Hermann, op. cit., pp. 57-58, 60-61, N.Q. Hamilton, The Holy Spirit and Eschatology in Paul (Edinburgh: Oliver and Boyd, 1957), pp. 3-16.

55. Montague, op. cit., pp. 141-144; Hermann, op. cit., pp. 60-61, 120; JBC, 51:86, 52:17; J. Massingberd Ford, "The Holy Spirit in the New Testament," Commonweal, LXXXIX (November, 1968), pp. 173-179.

56. Montague, op. cit., pp. 141-144, 206-209.

57. Ibid., pp. 135-138; JBC, 51:18-20.

58. Cerfaux, op. cit., pp. 196-197, 208-213.

59. Edmund J. Fortman, The Triune God (Philadelphia: Westminster, 1972), pp. 37-43; Henry Barclay Swete, The Holy Spirit in the Ancient Church (London: Macmillan, 1912), pp. 11-31.

60. Swete, op. cit., pp. 33-38; L.W. Barnard, Justin Martyr (New York: Cambridge, 1967), pp. 95-99.

61. Salvatore C. Lilla, Clement of Alexandria: A Study in Christian Platonism and Gnosticism (New York: Oxford, 1971), pp. 41-42.

62. Alois Grillmeier, S.J., Christ in the Christian Tradition, trans. by John Bowden (Atlanta: John Knox Press, 1975), pp. 139-140.

63. Oliver du Roy, L'intelligence de la foi en la Trinite selon S. Augustin: Genese de sa theologie trinitaire jusqu'en 391 (Paris: Etudes Augustiniennes, 1966), pp. 37-95.

64. Fortman, op. cit., pp. 322-338.

65. John Edward Sullivan, The Image of God: The Doctrine of St. Augustine and its Influence (Dubuque: Priory, 1963), pp. 48-66.

66. Swete, op. cit., pp. 322-338.

67. J.T. Nielsen, Adam and Christ in the Theology of Irenaeus of Lyons, trans. by G.E. van Baaren-Pape (Bronigen: Van Gorcum, 1968), pp. 66-67.

68. John Lawson, The Biblical Theology of St. Irenaeus (London: Epworth, 1948), pp. 125-128; Albert Houssiau, La christologie de S. Irenee (Louvain: Publications Universitaires de Louvain, 1955), pp. 92-93; J. Ochagavia, Visibile Patris Filius: A Study of Irenaeus' Teaching on Revelation and Tradition. (Rome: Gregorian, 1964), pp. 129-134.

69. Houssiau, op. cit., pp. 72-78, 92-93; John Lawson, The Biblical Theology of Saint Irenaeus (London: Epworth, 1948), pp. 123-124.

70. Montague, op. cit., pp. 128-129, 131-132, 140-147, 187-191, 196-198, 204-209.

71. Ibid., pp. 27-29; Haenchen, op. cit., pp. 166-175.

72. Haenchen, op. cit., pp. 176-189; George Montague, S.M., "Baptism in the Holy Spirit and Speaking in Tongues," Theology Digest, XXI (Winter, 1973), pp. 342-361.

73. Luke does not say "tongues of fire"; the Greek phrase is **glossai hosei pyros.**"

74. Montague, op. cit., pp. 291-292; Haenchen, op. cit., pp. 230-241.

75. Montague, op. cit., pp. 362-365; Brown, The Gospel According to John, II, pp. 1018-1045; JBC, 63:177.

76. For Rahner, the concept "symbol" implies multiplicity. In any symbolic relationship one thing expresses or interprets another. But a "real

symbolic" relationship combines multiplicity and unity. A real symbol comes into existence when one reality posits within itself another reality in some way distinct from itself but in another way one with itself. As a consequence the posited reality expresses the very being of the reality which posits it. For example, actions are real symbolic expressions of the one who performs them. I am all my actions, but I am much more than any one of them. They are one with me, yet distinct from the whole of me. Therefore, they express symbolically who I am. Rahner uses the notion of a "real symbol" to explain why the immanent and economic Trinities cannot be separated. In generating the Son from all eternity, the Father posits within Himself a reality distinct from Himself who nevertheless shares with Him the same divine life. The Son is therefore a real symbolic expression of the Father within the Godhead. Similarly, in spirating the divine Breath, Father and Son posit within themselves a reality which is distinct from themselves but which shares with them an identity of life. The Breath is then a real symbolic expression of both Father and Son and of their relationship to one another. When the Word, however, becomes flesh He posits within Himself a human nature distinct from His person and yet one with it. His human nature is then a real symbol in space and time of the person of the Son. Similarly, Pentecost transforms the Church into a real symbolic expression of the Holy Breath. The mysteries of the Christian faith are, then, fundamentally three: the mystery of God's inner Triune life, the mystery of the incarnation, and the mystery of divine grace and of the Church, effected by the mission of the Advocate [Karl Rahner, "The Theology of Symbol," Theological Investigations, IV, pp. 222-245; "The Concept of Mystery in Catholic Theology," Theological Investigations IV, pp. 60-73; Donald L. Gelpi, S.J., Life and Light: A Guide to the Theology of Karl Rahner (New York: Sheed and Ward, 1966), pp. 8, 281-290].

Rahner's pneumatology remains relatively undeveloped, largely because he has preferred the medieval language of created and uncreated grace to biblical terminology, which speaks of the Breath, Her gifts, and Her activity. But he has insisted quite correctly that the charisms of the Holy Breath are a perennial endowment of the Church [Karl Rahner, S.J., The Dynamic Element in the Church (New York: Herder and Herder, 1964); Gelpi, op. cit., pp. 243-246]. Rahner describes the Holy Breath as a self-communication of God which "divinizes us in the innermost center of the existence of the individual person." She effects justification and Her present illumination anticipates the beatific vision. We therefore experience Her as "the finalization of human existence toward the immediacy of God through God's self-communication." That gracious redirection of experience effects a conscious participation in the resurrection of Christ. The risen Christ is, therefore, present in and through the action of His Breath; hence, wherever She is present She orients human experience to the incarnation, cross, and resurrection of the Son of God. She creates the Church and animates both the proclamation of the Word and the sacramental life of the Christian community. She inspires the Scriptures and preserves the Church in truth [Karl Rahner, S.J., Foundations of Christian Faith, translated by William Dych, S.J. (New

81

York:Seabury, 1978), pp. 116-121, 136, 240, 274, 316-318, 339-340, 355, 374, 385].

77. Aquinas realized that the divine persons stand historically revealed in their temporal missions. To establish a link between what we now call the immanent and economic Trinities, one need then only clarify what it means to say that a divine person is historically sent into the world. The term "mission" he observed, implies relationship. In every mission a sender sends the missionary to some third party. The missionary therefore "goes forth" from the sender. The missions of the Son and Breath are, however, distinct from their eternal processions. Their processions are immanent acts within the Godhead. In their missions, Son and Breath are always sent to a person or persons existing in space and time. Their missions have a saving purpose: the gracing of an individual or of a community. But while the mission of a divine person is not the eternal procession of that person, the two are intimately linked. We know that the Son proceeds from the Father because He was sent into the world by the Father. We know that the Breath proceeds from Father and Son because She is sent by both. The Father, who proceeds from none, cannot be sent. There is then a new sending of the Holy Breath every time someone is graciously transformed by Her. Moreover, like the theologians of his time, Aquinas spoke of the "visible" and "invisible" missions of the Breath. Her invisible mission is real, although its effects are not always sensibly perceptible. The "invisible mission" of the Breath encompasses Her indwelling in the heart of believers as well as Her "surprises (innovationes)," the charismatic impulses by which She gives new hope and direction to human history. Her visible missions occurred at the baptism of Jesus and at Pentecost, when She arrived under the visible signs of the descending dove and of wind and fire (Summa Theologiae, I. xliii).

82

CHAPTER IV:

IS GOD AN EXPERIENCE?

We become what we worship; for we worship that to which we aspire absolutely and ultimately. The attempt to name God is then freighted with important personal and practical consequences. For unless the divine names we use actually interpret God's own self-revelation to us, we run the serious risk of worshiping and therefore of becoming a foolish idol of our own creation.

We are attempting to test the legitimacy of calling the God Christians adore an experience, in the manner of contemporary process theologians. We are doing so in the hope that if we can in fact understand the Trinity on an analogy with human social experience, trinitarian doctrine will thereby acquire new immediacy and freshness as human experience yields an insight into the divine experience and as the divine experience endows human experience with ultimate meaning, purpose, and significance.

Our argument has so far advanced in two stages. First, we have attempted to clarify descriptively the meaning of the term "experience." We have found it triadic, not dipolar, in its dynamic structure. Second, we have reflected on the Christian experience of the Holy Breath. For that experience gives us access to the reality of the triune God. We have concluded that the converted Christian ought to perceive the reality of the Holy Breath as noetic. She illumines us graciously. She enlightened Jesus concerning the saving purpose and scope of the mission He had received from the Father. She functions therefore as the interpretative link between Father and Son, as the mind of God and of Christ. Moreover, we have reflected on the historical missions of Son and Breath and found in them the unique and privileged source of whatever information we possess concerning the inner life of God.

This last insight provides us with an important methodological key to answering the question which faces us. For we will be justified in calling God "an experience" if the category "experience" as we have defined it interprets the divine reality revealed to us in the missions. We have defined experience as a process made up of relational elements called feelings. In human, personal experience we have discovered three kinds of feelings: qualities, facts, and laws. In the present chapter we will attempt to show that experience so conceived does in fact apply analogously to the triune God. In the process we will begin to reflect on the ways in which the divine experience both resembles and differs from spatio-temporal experiences.

That the God Christians adore stands historically revealed as triadic cannot be seriously questioned. Already in the Old Testament the Breath enjoys divinity. The Son in His resurrection confronts us as Lord and God.

The distinction of Son and Breath from the Father and from one another has been revealed in Their distinct missions. The Father initiates the work of salvation by sending the Son to redeem us. As the originating source of Jesus' efficacious intervention in human history, the Father, therefore, stands historically revealed as a principle of creative, aboriginal efficacy within the Godhead. Jesus reveals the Father to us because whatever He says and does is done in obedience to the missioning will of the Father. The Son therefore confronts us in His mission as a divine principle of obediential efficacy through whom the Father acts to save us. The two redeem us through the Son's perfect obedience. They act with one will. Moreover, because the Son is sent to us from the Father, He confronts us in His incarnation as proceeding from the Father. The Son in obedience to the Father's saving plan baptises us in the Holy Breath. Because She is sent efficaciously to us by both Son and Father She stands historically revealed as proceeding from both. And because within the economy of salvation She links the Son consciously and cognitively to the Father, She stands self-disclosed as Their mind.

A mind is a law, in the technical sense in which we have defined that term. It is a general tendency to respond evaluatively. To understand the reality of the Breath as a law even has some scriptural warrant. Paul speaks of Her explicitly as the law which governs Christian conduct; and Johannine imagery links Breath and Torah (Rm 8:2, Jn 4:14, 7:37-39; cf. Pr 9:5, Si 24:1, Is 55:1).

At this point I would, for the sake of clarity, like to introduce a technical term borrowed from the philosophy of Charles Sanders Peirce: namely, the term "interpretant." Let us call a mind an interpretant.

Peirce offered several different descriptions and definitions of the term "interpretant." At one point he called it "the proper significant outcome of a sign." In other words, it is the intelligent response any sign seeks to elicit.[1] The term not only calls attention to the symbolic character of evaluative responses but also allows one to discriminate three kinds of interpretants corresponding to three different kinds of signs. Some signs, artistic or literary ones, for example, appeal most directly to affectivity. Their interpretants Peirce called "emotional." They could also be called "affective interpretants." Other signs, like practical directions or commands, seek to evoke intelligent decisions. These Peirce called "energetic." They could also be called "decisive interpretants." Still other signs evoke abstract thought. These Peirce called "logical interpretants."[2]

Interpretants are, then, cognitive habits. They are habitual tendencies to elicit specific kinds of evaluative response. All interpretants, including energetic ones, should then be distinguished from habits of decision. An energetic interpretant is not a tendency to respond decisively. It is the ability to understand an order or a practical direction. Having understood, one may or may not choose to follow it. Similarly affective interpretants yield the ability to sense the emotional connotations of words, gestures, art objects. Logical interpretants, the ability to follow an argument.

Every interpretant has, therefore, two components: one immediate, the other, dynamic. An "immediate interpretant" is the meaning of an interpreted sign. A "dynamic interpretant" is the habit which evokes the immediate interpretant.[3]

Peirce also spoke of a "final interpretant." But he did so in vague and conflicting ways. He defined a "final interpretant" most clearly as the true and ultimate interpretation of any reality.[4] The final interpretant too is therefore composed of an immediate and a dynamic interpretant. It consists of those same interpretants in a state of perfection.

These distinctions allow us to state with a bit more precision what it means to speak of the divine Breath as the mind of God and of Christ. Human minds need words to communicate because they are embodied. But we need not suppose that Father, Son, and Breath need spoken words in order to communicate within the Godhead. Until the Son became incarnate, no divine person was under constraint to speak as humans do. But because God stands historically revealed as minded, we may legitimately speak of a tendency within God to respond cognitively and evaluatively. To that extent we may discern within God the presence of an immediate and of a dynamic interpretant. The immediate interpretant in God is the meaning of the divine evaluative responses, the ideas and attitudes shared by all three divine persons. The dynamic interpretant is the Holy Breath. She is the law, the habitual, autonomous source of the deity's knowledge and evaluation of Himself and of creation. She is also the final interpretant of any reality, for in God any reality is comprehended without the blemish of ignorance or error. Let us reflect in a bit more detail on the implications of these insights.

The New Testament ascribes a variety of evaluative responses to God. God knows the world and the needs of all creatures that dwell in it (Mt 6:9, 33, 10:29, Lk 12:31-34, Rm 4:6, 1 Co 8:3, 2 Co 5:11, 11:12, 12:2, Ga 3:11, 2 Tm 2:19, 1 Jn 3:21). The Father and Son know one another in a privileged and intimate way (Mt 11:25-27, Lk 10:21-22). With some persons God is especially pleased (Lk 1:31, 2:40, Phil 3:18). At the sight of others He is filled with compassion (Lk 6:36, Phil 2:27). But He is angered at human sinfulness (Rm 1:18ff, 5:19, 9:22, Col 3:6, Ep 5:20, 1 Jn 3:11, Rv 5:11). For He not only knows what we do, but He also reads even the secrets of our hearts (Lk 16:15, Ac 15:8, 23:1, 27:29, 1 Th 2:10). God also knows what He purposes to accomplish in the world and why He decrees certain things to happen (Ac 3:36, 18-21). He knows with an infathomable wisdom (Rm 8:33-36, 1 Co 1:21-31, 2:7-16, 3:18-23, Lk 12:49).

For the converted Christian these biblical affirmations about God's knowledge do not result from a metaphysical insight into the spiritual essence of God. Rather, they are rooted in the confession of the Lordship

85

of Jesus. Because He is Lord, He incarnates God's attitudes toward His creation. In His goodpleasure and compassion, in His anger, in His vision of human conduct and salvation, in His comprehension of the human heart, God's evaluative reponse to His creation stands normatively and historically revealed. For the Son incarnates not only the will of the Father but a divine self-awareness that is worked in Him by the Holy Breath. For She is the divine interpretant, the law that rules every divine evaluative response.

When we speak of the Holy Breath as a "law," as a divine self, as the divine interpretant, we use philosophical categories to interpret the biblical witness to Her reality. A philosophical category interprets the bibilical witness when it applies to the biblical witness in the sense in which it was originally defined. As the **mind** of the Father and Son, the divine interpretant stands historically self-disclosed as the source within God of **omniscient divine wisdom.** As the personal ground of divine evaluative response She puts preferential order into God's envisagement of the totality of possibility. She thus establishes the purposes that guide the divine activity.

God, moreover, is experienced in faith as ultimately and absolutely valuable. No creature can surpass in desirability a supremely good and loving God. Under no conceivable circumstance could God be less than supremely loveable. The purposes which shape the divine activity participate in God's loveability. They are ultimately and absolutely desirable. The divine wisdom functions, therefore, as Augustine saw, as **the uncreated measure of created value, integrity, and righteousness.**

As the final interpretant, the Holy Breath also measures the truth and authenticity of every gracious enlightenment ascribed to Her. Through faith, hope, and love She seals God's righteous covenant in our hearts. Through Her prophetic inspiration She rebukes our sinfulness. By teaching us God's purposes, She leads us to personal holiness. Through Her charismatic inspirations She creates the Church, the new Israel. She inspires its worship. Moreover, in this last age of salvation Her charisms are democratically available to all. We experience Her therefore as a **divine matrix of life** in which the Christian community is graciously and charismatically transformed.

The Holy Breath also functions as **a principle of continuity within salvation history.** She inspires all authentic religious enlightenment. Laws endow experience with continuity. As a personal, legal element in an eternal, non-spatio-temporal process, the divine interpretant endures with a continuity of life that spans the centuries. They transpire in Her even as She encompasses and transcends them.

As the final interpretant of truth and falsity, of good and evil, of authenticity and inauthenticity, the Holy Breath is also **the living law** to which Christian conduct must conform. The law of the new covenant is not therefore written on stones or in books. It is engraved on human hearts by a divine person.

The biblical witness also presents the Holy Breath as a **source of salvation.** The saved stand in a lifegiving relationship with God through faith. The Holy Breath saves us by conceiving the Word of life which the Father speaks to us in Jesus. Through Her enlightenment we are brought to the faith which saves. And when we know the Word made flesh by the faith She inspires, we begin to glimpse the full scope of God's saving intentions. We then come alive in new ways.

But if within the Godhead the Holy Breath functions as the legal ground of divine evaluation rather than of divine decision, why is it that we can perceive Her presence in efficacious impulses of grace? As we shall see in greater detail below, the three divine persons in all their operations on realities other than themselves act as one. As a consequence, when we are touched by God in efficacious ways, we experience that impulse as coming not simply from Father and Son but also from the divine Breath as well. But because She functions within God and the divine interpretant, we perceive Her **inferentially** and **in faith** as the personal, legal ground within God of the divine intentions that give meaning to every efficacious impulse of grace. At the same time and for similar reasons, in faith we perceive the Father inferentially as the personal, legal ground of the spontaneous, creative efficacy of gracious impulses and the Son as the personal, legal ground of their obediential, redemptive efficacy.

Finally, laws are dynamic forces. And the laws which shape personal growth are living laws. For real persons live. When predicated of the divine Breath, the term "law" connotes, therefore, supreme vitality. As a legal entity, a self, the divine Breath is experienced by believers as a **life force.** And as -co-creator, co-redeemer, and co-sanctifier with Father and Son, She is also perceived in faith as a **life source.**

We may therefore conclude that in applying the category "law" to the third person of the Trinity we interpret rather than distort fundamental themes in biblical pneumatology. We may also conclude that there is an evaluative component within the Christian Godhead and that its source is the Holy Breath. We may also safely affirm the legitimacy of understanding Her as a divine self, as an autonomous source of divine cognitive activity, as a divine law, as the divine interpretant.

But the New Testament ascribes other activities to the Christian God that must be characterized as decisions rather than as evaluations. God chooses freely (Ac 1:7, Rm 8:11, Ga 1:15, Ep 1:3-4, Col 12:13, 1 Th 1:4, 2 Th 2:13-14, Jm 2:5, Tit 1:1), speaks (Mt 4:1-4, 10:33, 17:5, Mk 1:12-13, 9:7-8, Lk 3:2, 4:1-13, 9:16, Jn 3:34, 5:28, 8:18, 9:3, 10:25, Hb 1:1, 5-14, 3:8, 12, 11:7), legislates the norms of human conduct (Mk 7:8-13, 12:28-34, 5:36-37, Mt 22:34-40, Lk 2:25-28, 1 Th 4:1-8), wills the salvation of all (Mt 18:114, 35, Ac 28:28 1 Tm 2:4), loves (Jn 3:15-16, 5:9, 13:49-50, Rm 5:5, Col 3:12-13, 2 Th 2:13-14, Rv 20:9), decides the course of events (1 Pt 3:17). God's decisions are, to be sure, shaped by His wisdom and by His knowledge of the world. But in judging the world God does more than respond to it evaluatively. He also executes His judgments decisively. He rewards the good and gives to sinners their just deserts (Mt 6:1, 4, 6, 18, 10:28, Lk 12:5-6, 16:15, Ac 23:3, Rm 2:2, 8, 3:6, 19-20, 8:34, 1 Co 4:5, 5:13, 2 Th 1:1-2, 8:2, 2 Tm 4:1, Rv 14:17, 16:17). He responds to prayer and to good works, forgives our sins, and reveals His mercy (Mt 18:19-20, Lk 1:78, Ac 10:4, 27:24, Mk 2:7-12, 6:14-15, 12:25, Jn 9:45, Rm 12:7). He actively guides the course of history according to a plan of salvation (Lk 8:7, Ac 1:7, 13:36, 3:18-21, 28:20, Jn 11:52-53, 2 Co 5:18, Ep 1:3-14, 1 Tm 1:4, 2 Tm 2:4, 4:10, 1 Pt 1:15, 3:17). He makes promises and keeps them (Tit 1:1, Hb 6:13).

Moreover, the New Testament characterizes the relationship of the Father to the Son in images that connote decisive efficacy. Father and Son are said to speak to one another in heaven (Mt 10:33, Lk 12:8, Rm 8:33). The Father entrusts everything to the Son; the Son returns everything to the Father (Mt 11:25-27, 13:43, Lk 1:32, 10:21-22, 22:28-30). The Son imitates the Father's actions, says and does only what the Father says (Jn 5:19, 10:38, 14:10-11, 12). These images need not be interpreted with a fundamentalistic literalism. But they do tell us something important about the way that the writers of the New Testament consistently perceived the relationship of Son and Father.

In the New Testament witness the decisions of the Son are uniformly characterized as obediential. The decisions of the Father are, by contrast, always aboriginal, creative, and spontaneous. But the decisions of Father and Son are the same divine decision, such is the perfection of the Son's obedience. In other words, through the Lord Jesus' perfect and sinless obedience to His heavenly Father the first Christians came to perceive and to understand that They enjoy not only the same mind but the same will (Lk 1:26, 3:8, 5:21-25, 19:44, Phil 2:1-11). Let us examine this pattern in the New Testament witness in greater detail.

The Father emerges in the pages of the New Testament as the one who inaugurates each new saving impulse that advances salvation history. It was He who gave the law to Moses (Rm 3:21, 7:24, 8:7; Mt 15:3-4, Ac 7:1-53, 22:14, 24:14-15). The Father proclaims Jesus as Son and commissions Him as messiah and suffering servant (Mt 9:8, Mk 1:11, Lk 3:22, Ac 2:22). The Father raises Jesus from the dead and exalts Him to His right hand where the Son reigns in power (Mt 23:22, 29-33, Mk 12:24-27, Lk 22:44-45, Ac 2:23, 32, 3:15, 5:31-33, 13:30, 34, 17:31, 26:8, Rm 6:4, Ph 2:9-10, 1 Pt 1:21). In exalting the Son the Father creator establishes Him as head of a new creation (Mk 10:6-9, 13:19, Ga 6:15, Ep 1:3-14, 2:10, 1 Co 15:21, 45, Rm 1:20, 15:13, 6:14, Ac 17:24-29, Hb 2:10, 3:4).

The Father and the Son act together in redeeming us. Through the words and deeds of the Son the Father's reign is established on earth (Mt 12:28, 13:43, Lk 7:13, 18:39, 19:42-44, Jn 3:10). The Father acts in the Son to effect the signs and wonders that testify to the truth of the words the Son speaks in the Father's name (Jn 3:34, 5:20, 10:17, 13:49-50, 14:10-11,

20, 15:9, Hb 2:4). Together They send the Breath. (Lk 11:13; Ac 2:33-34, 5:32, 10:38, 11:23, 15:9, 14, 19; Jn 6:23, 14:6, 26, 20:21; Rm 8:3; 1 Co 1:4, 3:10, 7:7, 12:6; Ga 3:5, Ep 4:13; 1 Pt 4:6-11). The Son therefore confronts His disciples as the efficacious presence of the Father (Jn 14:8-9, Hb 9:24).

But the Son does not act mechanically. He relates to the Father in free and autonomous obedience (Mk 4:1-11, 26:36, Lk 4:1-13, 21-25, Mk 8:33, 12:11, 14:37). Even as a young man Jesus is already busy in the things of His Father (Lk 3:50). His submission to God is manifest in His prayer (Lk 6:12, 7:48-49). To do the will of the Father is His food and drink (Jn 4:34, 14:31, Mt 4:1-3, Lk 4:1-4). He always acts and speaks in submission to the Father and in faithful imitation of the Father's own activity (Jn 5:19, 30, 10:38). And He passes the supreme test of His obedience by submitting humbly to death on a cross (Mt 26:36-46; Mk 14:32-42, Lk 22:40-46, Jn 10:18, 29; Hb 2:8, Rm 3:25, 8:11, Ep 2:16-17, Ph 2:6-11, 1 Pt 3:18).

Moreover, those who live as the children of God in Jesus' image are called to practice the same kind of obedience as He (Mt 13:50, Mk 3:31-35, Lk 8:19-21, Jn 8:47, Col 4:11, Hb 11:13, 1 Pt 4:2). Indeed, Jesus' death teaches us the full extent of the obedience to which we are called in faith (1 Pt 3:18, Ph 2:6-11, Hb 2:8). In summoning and empowering us to imitate His own obedience to the Father the Son establishes God's own reign among us (Mt 5:17-19, Ac 4:20, 5:5, Lk 11:2, Mt 6:7-13, Jn 8:19, Ac 18:17, Rm 1:8, 7:24, 8:20-27, 15:7-9, 1 Co 1:30, Ep 5:21-22, Tit 8:8, Ph 1:6, 2:13). And the disciples' obedient witness of faith reveals the efficacious indwelling of both Father and Son (Jn 15:10, 1 Jn 2:3, 5:3-4).

The association of the Father with spontaneous creative efficacy and of the Son with divine obediential efficacy flows inevitably from the Christian confession of the Lordship of Jesus. Efficaciously sent into the world by the Father He had proclaimed, the only Son of God had accomplished His mission in an obedience that led even to death, death on a cross. His submission had been free but total. The divine reality encountered in Christian conversion possesses then three autonomous centers of activity. The Father functions as a center of spontaneous, creative efficacy. The Son functions as a center of submissive, obediential efficacy. The Breath functions as the mind of God and of Christ. Each is a tendency to respond in a specific way. Each is a self. Because Father and Son are autonomous centers of efficacious divine activity, They contribute to the deity's inner life a dynamic factual component. Not that They are mere facts. Rather, They are two divine selves who function as the legal, causal ground of the divine decisions. The Father is their habitual initiating cause, the Son their habitual obediential cause.

We find no activity ascribed to God in the biblical witness that cannot be characterized as a decision, as an evaluation, or as some combination of evaluation and decision. In The New Testament evaluation and decision are ascribed to three distinct divine selves. Qualitative evaluation is associated with the Breath, creative and redemptive efficacy with Father and Son. We have, therefore, identified the presence in the Christian God of some analogue to the three generic variables that constitute human experience. We find quality because the Deity responds evaluatively. We find fact because the Deity acts decisively. And we find law because there are in God three distinct divine selves: Father, Son, and Breath. If we can also affirm that these three variables are dynamically integrated in God, then we shall have initial warranty for speaking of the triune God as an experience analogous to our own.

The integration of quality, fact, and law in God is demanded by the fact that in the New Testament witness, Father, Son, and Breath share an identity of life. When one acts, the others are present in that activity. The Breath does not communicate with Father and Son in the way that two humans communicate. Instead, She is their mind. The Son does not merely tell us something about the Father; He incarnates the Father's will: to see Him is to see the Father (Jn 6:57-58, 8:19, 5:3-4, 1 Co 2:14-16). The integration of the three experiential variables in God is then demanded by the fact that God is both one and living. We experience God as living because through the twofold mission of Son and Breath, He communicates to us His very own life (Lk 21:35-38, Ac 2:33-34, 5:32, 10:38, 14:15, Jn 1:12-13, 3:5-21, 6:44-58, Rm 8:33-36, 12:1-15, 6; Ph 2:1-18, Ep 5:1-33, 1 Pt 1:3).

Clearly, then, the New Testament witness to Christ provides warranty for affirming that the God Christians worship is an experience analogous to human experiences. We should not underestimate the novelty or the importance of this conclusion. Its novelty flows from the fact that to the best of my knowledge no one in the history of trinitarian theology has ever attempted to think the reality of God under the rubric of experience, even though theologians have in the past recognized the need to ground trinitarian faith in recognizable human experiences. Our conclusion enjoys importance because the language we use to speak about God stands within religious experience and shapes in significant ways the manner in which we relate to God, to the world, to one another, to ourselves. Our conclusions are, of course, at this point extremely tentative. At best we have established only the initial plausibility of a foundational trinitarian hypothesis. What then are its implications?

Our foundational approach to God follows the way of analogy. Having said that God is an experience, we must immediately deny that God is an experience in exactly the same way that His creatures are. The divine experience transcends spatio-temporal experiences. God confronts us as the supreme exemplification of experience. Creatures copy the divine experience in finite and imperfect ways. Let us begin to reflect on why this is so and what it implies.

Human experience, as we have seen, begins to take on a religious character as soon as it is tinged with ultimacy. It becomes so tinged as soon as one acknowledges values and realities not only worth living but worth dying for. Religious experience becomes theistic when the reality worth living and dying for is identified as God. Theistic religious experience becomes Christian when God is encountered in the historical missions of the Son and of His Breath. Authentic theistic religion affirms that every other entity is subordinate to God in reality and worth. As a consequence no reality can be truthfully conceived as greater than God. If therefore the religious mind is to conceive God at all, He must be conceived as the supreme exemplification of reality, value, beauty, goodness, and truth. For nothing greater than God can be conceived. As the supreme exemplification of experience God cannot, then, be an experience like any other. How then do experiences differ from one another?

In Chapter II we reflected on how experiences resemble and differ from one another. They resemble one another to the extent that the same generic kinds of variables function within them. To be a human experience a process must integrate three variables: qualities, facts, and laws. Experiences differ because in the concrete what is experienced and the way that it is experienced differ from one experience to the next. We know that this is true from personal reflection. No two human experiences are identical. They incarnate different histories. Both experience facts but not the same facts. The wandering bedouin and the city sophisticate must deal with different kinds of environments. Their beliefs and attitudes will differ in significant ways. Even when our histories overlap, we find ourselves viewing the same facts and realities from different perspectives and in different ways.

Because experiences both resemble one another and differ, they are analogous. The analogy of experience explains the uniqueness of each self. Every self is an experience. But because experiences are only generically alike, no two selves are specifically the same. I cannot assume that you have experienced what I have, or that you are habitually inclined to value the same things that I do, or that you will automatically concur in all my decisions. Yet both of us are selves, both are experiences.

But if we can extrapolate in the concrete from one human experience to another only with difficulty, how much more difficult must it be to extrapolate from my own experience to God's. For while the biblical witness sanctions naming God as an experience, it warns us that no human can comprehend God. It warns too that sinners think different thoughts from God's (Mk 8:33, 1 Co 2:17).

Nevertheless, if we are to understand the divine experience in any way, it must be by analogy with experience as we know it. But in reflecting on the divine experience, we must be careful to deny of God any experiential trait irreconcilable with the divine supremacy and with God's self-revelation to us in Jesus and the Holy Breath. How therefore must we qualify the notion of experience so as to make it applicable to the transcendent reality of God?

91

We can make a certain number of immediate and preliminary quali-fications. The supremacy of the divine experience demands that it be (a) unrivaled in perfection, (b) unique, (c) desirable beyond all else, (d) un-derived from any cause, (e) eternal, (f) ontologically prior to any finite, created experience that comes into existence, (g) omniscient, and (h) omni-potent. Let us consider each of these distinguishing characteristics in order.

(a) **unrivaled in perfection:** As the supreme exemplification of experience, God can lack no conceivable good. For if the divine experience lacked any perfection it might conceivably have, it would forfeit its supre-macy and cease to be divine. The divine experience must then possess every perfection it is better to have than not to have.

(b) **unique:** Every experience enjoys uniqueness. For every experi-ence constitutes a unique perspective on the universe. It encompasses a particular set of facts, evaluates them in a specific manner, and reacts or responds in specific ways. Every experience harmonizes the feelings that constitute it in a manner proper to itself. The uniqueness of each exper-ience thus individualizes it. But the divine experience's uniqueness lies in its supremacy. God experiences everything that could conceivably be experienced. The divine experience encompasses all other experiences and surpasses them. God does not view reality from a finite, spatio-temporal perspective. Rather the experiences that make up space and time transpire within the divine experience.

(c) **desirable beyond all else:** We desire the good, the true, the beautiful whenever we aspire to what is virtuous and lifegiving. The beautiful expands our hearts; the true nourishes our minds; the good yields vital satisfaction. We discover the good, the true, and the beautiful by interacting with other experiences. As the supreme exemplification of experience, God blends every good in supreme satisfaction, grasps all truth in an integrated insight, and unifies all perfection in a harmonious beauty. A supremely good, true, and beautiful reality also enjoys supreme desirability. Union with the divine experience merits, then, both living and dying for.

(d) **underived from any cause:** Effects derive their reality from their causes. Causal dependence implies subordination. But an experience that encompasses every conceivable perfection can be subordinate to none. Neither, therefore, can it depend on any other reality or stand toward it as its effect.

(e) **eternal:** If the divine experience does not derive its reality from anything else, it enjoys self-existence. It cannot not exist. It does not, therefore, like spatio-temporal experiences, come into being or perish. It is therefore eternal. Its eternity need not, however, be understood as static unchangeability. As we shall see, the triune God is an eternal process coexistent with every other process.

92

(f) **ontologically prior to any finite, created experience that comes into existence:** The beginning of any spatio-temporal process finds the divine experience already existing. For being unique in supremacy, underived, and eternal, God stands as the source of every created, spatio-temporal reality.

(g) **omniscient:** No fact, no truth, no possibility can be concealed from the divine experience, for it encompasses every conceivable perfection. No event escapes the divine ken. No truth eludes its attention. No frame of reference surpasses the divine capacity to understand. God experiences the truth and falsity of every judgment and grasps why it is true or false. And the divine wisdom knows and orders every conceivable possibility. For were God less than omniscient, the divine experience would lose all claim to supremacy.

(h) **omnipotent:** God's power to act must also reflect the supreme perfection of the divine experience. Our power to change ourselves and our world stands circumscribed by our individual histories. We can do whatever we have learned to do in the course of our individual development. But the divine experience, being eternal, suffers no such historical circumscription. God can do anything compatible with His reality and supremacy. And in this sense the divine experience enjoys omnipotence.

We can contrast the divine experience with spatio-temporal experiences in other ways as well. In reflecting on spatio-temporal experiences we have found them finite, relational, symbolic, and transactional. We found that they incarnate real rather than clock time. And we found them mutually inexistent. How many of these traits are transferrable in some transcendent sense to the divine experience? We can anticipate that not all of them will be applicable to God. For the divine experience is eternal rather than spatio-temporal. And He is the supreme exemplification of experience.

The finitude of experience flows necessarily from its spatio-temporal character. For finite experiences are bounded by other experiences with which they must interact in order to become the kinds of experiences they prove to be. Being both supreme and eternal, the divine experience suffers no such limitation. Everything is encompassed by an experience of all that could conceivably be experienced. The divine experience is therefore bounded by nothing. It is therefore **infinite** in the sense that it contains all things and is contained by none.

Because qualities, facts, and laws are relational elements within experience, the divine experience should also be conceived as **relational.** But in speaking of the triune God we must distinguish the relationships that constitute the divine experience in its eternal transcendence from God's relationship to His creatures. The relationships which constitute the Divine Experience order the divine persons to one another. In His active relationship to the world God manifests supreme creativity. As the experience of all that is experienceable, He is supremely receptive.

Because the divine experience is symbolic in its structure, it **enjoys communicable significance.** It is not only intelligible but supremely so. The intelligible can be revealed. A revealable experience can be felt and perceived. We perceive the divine experience either directly or sacramentally. We perceive God directly when He touches us without created intermediaries. In moments of solitude, for example, the human heart can expand to a sense of the divine presence. When that happens we may be moved to use images derived from creation to describe what we felt. But we are attempting to give voice to a perception of being touched by a transcendent, divine reality. We perceive God sacramentally when He touches us in the words and deeds of persons he has graciously transformed. In listening to the faith witness of another, or in shared, Breath-filled prayer, whether spontaneous or eucharistic, I may sense the presence of the divine. At such moments I know that I am in communion with a reality that encompasses and transcends the humans whose faith witness it inspires.

The transactional character of experience follows from its dynamic, relational structure. We must distinguish two sorts of transactions performed by the Divine Experiencer. First, the divine persons have transactions among themselves. The shape of these transactions has been revealed in the historical missions of the Son and of the Breath. But the relationships among the persons historically revealed in the divine missions are abiding, eternal, and perfectly coexistent, not developmental and successive.

Besides the transactions of the divine persons among themselves, God has transactions with His creatures. As finite experiences grow in complexity, their transactions increase in consciousness, freedom, and adaptabililty. Consciousness, freedom, and flexibility describe aspects of the evaluative shape of an experience. Any divine transaction inspired by the divine interpretant enjoys **supreme consciousness, freedom, and adaptability.**

We have spoken of the divine experience as eternal. But we should not confuse eternity with the static immobility of abstract essences. Eternal processes neither begin nor end. They coexist with one another and with every spatio-temporal event. God's interventions in history can, of course, be dated. But they reveal to us a divine reality that always was and always will be. The divine eternity, however, includes much more than contemporary process philosophy suggests. It includes God's evaluative grasp of the totality of possibility. On this point process theory is quite correct. But the eternity of God also includes the processions of the divine persons, their abiding integration into a single divine experience, and their interpersonal transactions with one another. The inclusion of divine processions and transactions within the eternity of God entails that we conceive eternity as a non-spatio-temporal process, an eternal and spontaneous welling up of divine life. That eternal process measures spatio-temporal processes, for it exists simultaneously with all of them. It is measured by none of them, because in comprehending all of them the supreme experience is comprehended by none. Such an all comprehending experience enjoys infinity; for the infinite, viewed existentially, comprehends every reality but eludes comprehension itself.

Finally, because both God and creatures are experiences, both can be correctly described as **mutually inexistent.** Whatever is experienced stands within experience and makes it to be the kind of experience it is. God is the supreme experience, the experience of all that could conceivably be experienced. God experiences the world. The world therefore stands within the divine experience. It exists in God. This is not to say that the world is God or the body of God. The world is simply what God experiences. It is not the only thing He experiences. For God also experiences Himself. But a world experienced by God exists in God.

If therefore God is an experience, His relationship to the world **must be understood in pantheistic terms.** One is not likely these days to hear panentheism preached from Christian pulpits, although it has been. The term is likely to sound strange to contemporary Christian ears, and probably a bit suspect. It sounds vaguely like pantheism. And hasn't pantehism been condemned? Pantheism has indeed been condemned and correctly so. But a panentheistic interpretation of God's relationship to the world has not been condemned. It enjoys, moreover, the sanction of scripture and the blessing of tradition.

We note with some interest that since the days of Jonathan Edwards American thinkers have been attracted to a panentheistic vision of God and the world. Panentheism, we repeat, differs doctrinally from pantheism. The latter asserts that everything is God. Panentheism, however, asserts that God and the world are distinct realities but that everything that is not God exists in God. The idea surfaces in the writings of American thinkers like Jonathan Edwards, Ethan Allen, Ralph Waldo Emerson, Francis Ellingwood Abbot, Josiah Royce, and William James.[5] It ranks as an important theme in contemporary process speculation.

But Jonathan Edwards was not the first Christian thinker to defend panentheism. Pauline theology, Luke, and John the evangelist all interpreted the relationship of God and the world in panentheistic terms (Ac 17:28, Jn 14:1-11, 16-17, 20, Ep 4:5-6, Col 1:16-17, 3:11). A significant number of the fathers of the Church endorsed panentheism, not the least of them being Augustine.[6] His panentheism finds an echo in the writings of medieval scholastics.[7] And modern Christian theology has tended to view the idea with sympathy.[8]

But we must distinguish different schools of panentheism. Contemporary process philosophy espouses a naturalistic version of the doctrine. In process theory everything exists in God. But God's relationship to the world would seem to be best understood as one of enlightened self-interest. The process God needs the world in order to become God. In such a reading of the relationship between God and creation, little apparent room remains for the gratuitous working of divine grace.

A sound panentheism must interpret the self-revelation of God which we have received in Jesus and in the Pentecostal Breath. Christian panentheism ought to subscribe to the following assertions: (1) All things exist in the triune God in the way that they are. (2) Realities which exist in God are relationally distinct from Him and from one another. (3) Humans may exist in God naturally, graciously, or sinfully; but everything else exists in God only naturally. (4) The way that we humans exist in God makes a difference to God. (5) The way we humans exist in God makes a difference to the way God exists in us. Let us begin to explore some of the implications of each of these propositions.

(1) **All things exist in the triune God in the way that they are.** If God stands as the supreme exemplification of experience, He can only know the world truthfully. Error blemishes the face of experience. The erroneous judgment fails to grasp reality as it is. Any erroneous experience could, then, conceivably be more perfect than it actually is. But the Supreme Experiencer can never be less perfect than He might conceivably be without forfeiting His divinity. God therefore experiences the world at any point exactly as it is, without the least blemish of error. Because God knows us as we are, we exist in His experience exactly as we are and are understood for what we are. And to the extent that we can reach a true judgment about the way that we exist, to that extent we can know how God experiences us.

Does this imply that when we are in error the things we experience do not exist in our experience in the way in which they really are? The answer of course is that they both do and do not. They are physically present within experience in the way in which they are, for they have a significant structure and impinge efficaciously upon experience. But they are not present in our experience in the way in which they are to the extent that there is a discrepancy between what they signify and the meaning I attach to them.

(2) **Realities which exist in God are relationally distinct from Him and from one another.** The God of the old and new covenants confronts us as a transcendent, personal reality who freely chooses to enter into a graced relationship with His creatures. Related realities confront one another as relationally distinct.

God's relational distinction from humans also follows from the fact that both we and God are experiences. Both divine and human experience consists, as we have seen, of relational elements called feelings. Experienced relations are (1) conceptual and qualitative, (2) factual and efficacious, or (3) habitual and legal. Because both divine and human experience are structured from the same kinds of relational elements, they confront one another as relationally distinct.

96

But here we confront a perplexing problem. For if our existence in God and our relational distinction from Him follow from the fact that both of us are experiences, in order to show that subhuman realities exist in God as relationally distinct from Him we must justify calling them experiences as well. In Whiteheadian theory the extension of the term "experience" to subhuman realities is justified in part by the belief that every process, including the most primitive physical process, possesses an evaluative component. This thesis can be questioned. But even its denial would not preclude using the language of experience to talk about any experienceable process. Human experience assumes two different forms: causal efficacy and presentational immediacy. Experience in the mode of causal efficacy takes the form of physical interaction. Experience in the mode of presentational immediacy creates the realm of value. Our evaluative responses enjoy degrees of differentiation and of consciousness. Some occur unconsciously. Nevertheless, both causal efficacy and presentational immediacy constitute identifiable forms of experience. Even were we to prove that subhuman processes lack any trace of presentational immediacy, they could still experience one another in the mode of causal efficacy. And they would enjoy mutual inexistence and relational distinction from one another and from every other finite experience. And the Supreme Experiencer would know them as well. They would therefore exist in God as relationally distinct from Him and from every other experience.

(3) **Humans may exist in God naturally, graciously, or sinfully.** No created experience can transcend the divine experience. For God's experience encompasses everything. My experience has a datable beginning. My physical death will also be datable. But since I am destined for life with Christ in the world to come, my life will finally have no datable end. Every human perspective on reality, though finite, can expand and when healthy is actually expanding. But because my perspective on the world has a datable origin, it remains always finite. It consists entirely of the sum total of the evaluative and decisive habits I have acquired since conception.

A finite perspective on reality may or may not include God. Those, then, who proclaim that the human mind enjoys an essential orientation to God preach a gospel of complacency. Humans can ignore God; and when they do they experience no innate drive toward the divine. Or they may acknowledge the reality of God but ignore His acts of historical self-revelation. Or they may fail to take either God or revelation seriously because those who speak of both do so in ways that are trivial and contradictory. Or self-styled believers' professions of faith may be belied by the way they live. Similarly, I may affirm God's reality as a reasonable propositional truth without knowing that I am called to respond to Him graciously and in faith. Or having encountered and assented to God in faith, I may forget to integrate Him or the assent of faith into this or that concrete activity. Finally, having assented to the God of revelation, I may also choose to oppose Him sinfully. For when all is said and done, our religious orientation expresses no Teutonic **a priori** dynamism present in every human mind. It remains as idiosyncratic as our personal religious history.

When I grow in ways that prescind inculpably from God's historical self-revelation, I develop naturally. That is to say, I develop ways of responding exclusively to the values and realities of this world. I may do so virtuously or viciously. If virtuously, my behavior is motivated by a legitimate appreciation of created truth, beauty, and goodness. If viciously, my development is motivated either by the wanton destruction or by the perverse prevention of created goodness, beauty, and truth. Analogues to naturally virtuous or vicious behavior occur in subhuman activity. The shark devouring the swimming child destroys life wantonly. The thrush blesses me with its liquid call all unknowingly. But natural behavior, whether destructive or creative, becomes virtuous or vicious when it achieves reflective self-awareness of its character and consequences. When I respond to creation with natural virtue, I exist in God naturally and virtuously. When with vicious malice, then I exist in God naturally and maliciously.

But if I can exist in God naturally, I can also exist in Him either graciously or sinfully. I may experience God's self-revelation either in the privacy of my heart or through His presence in the faith witness of others. When I respond positively to that encounter in hope, faith, and love, I grow graciously. When, however, I cling to natural realities as an alternative to faith in a self-revealing God, I develop in sinful ways. In either case I exist in God the way I choose to be, for that is also how God experiences me.

We know, then, three ways in which humans can exist in God: either naturally, graciously, or sinfully. And natural human existence in God may be either virtuous or vicious. But selves incapable of either a moral or a gracious act can exist in God only naturally. For that is the only way they can respond; and the way they respond constitutes them to be what they are.

(4) **The way that we humans exist in God makes a difference to God.** If God reacts evaluatively to things the way that they are, then He prizes whatever is genuinely valuable and recognizes what is vicious, cheap, or trival for exactly what it is. He is pleased with any legitimate natural satisfaction. The nobler the satisfaction, the more He is pleased with it. God is then especially pleased with naturally virtuous behavior, for it creates new value, new goodness, new beauty. He is displeased with naturally vicious behavior because it needlessly and wantonly destroys what is naturally good and satisfying.

Gracious human satisfactions, however, please God most of all, because they are the noblest satisfactions of which we are capable. By the same token, sinful acts displease God the most; for they are the deliberate frustration of His free and gracious desire to draw us into loving communion with Himself.

If, however, our decisions have the capacity to either please or displease God, then the way we exist in God makes a difference to Him.

We can prevent, dishonor, and destroy what God loves and values. We can please Him by creating new value, truth, and beauty. And we can cooperate with His desire to make us one with Him.

(5) **The way we humans exist in God makes a difference to the way God exists in us.** We exist in God only naturally when we function within the divine experience without responding to His historical acts of self-revelation. Gracious consent to God does not, however, abolish what I have become naturally. It transvalues natural values and realities by demanding that they be appreciated and understood in the light of God's saving deeds. Gracious consent also transmutes my own experience by introducing into it a new element that has the capacity to bring the satisfactions I experience to a new and heightened form of integration. The variable in question is faith. When faith transmutes and transvalues human experience, God begins to function within it in new and hitherto unknown ways. Human hope expands to the vision of a world recreated in the risen Christ. The human mind begins under the divine breathing to take on the mind of Christ. Then human actions become the loving expression of the charismatic indwelling of God. Faith therefore causes me to exist in God in a different way. But because it introduces me to a new knowledge and experience of God, through faith God functions in my experience in a new way. He therefore exists in me in new ways. Through the response of faith, therefore, we and God begin to experience each other and therefore to exist in one another differently.

The same is tragically true when I sin. For sin is always done before God. I cannot sin without experiencing God and recognizing His claims upon me. Because sin transforms the way that God and the sinner experience one another, it also changes the way in which they exist in one another. The tragedy of sin is the tragedy of both. God's tragedy, the tragedy revealed as Jesus hung on the cross on Calvary, is the tragedy of a selfless, creative love thwarted and abused. The sinner's tragedy is one of needless self-diminishment through failure to appreciate and love what is supremely loveable. It is the tragedy of every Judas.[9]

In the present chapter we have attempted to do two things. First, we have attempted to establish the initial plausibility of speaking of the God of revelation as a divine experience. Second, we have begun to reflect on how the divine experience differs from created, spatio-temporal experiences and on how it resembles them. But at this point, the full implications of speaking of God in the language of experience remain vague. For there are a number of questions raised by both pneumatology and by Christology that remain unanswered. We have, for example, been speaking of the members of the divine triad as persons. The legitimacy of so speaking is, however, seriously questioned by some responsible theologians. Can we then describe the divine experience as tripersonal? And if we can, then how are we to understand the unity of the three divine persons in one and the same divine experience? We have also spoken of Jesus' relationship to the Holy Breath. But how specifically is that relationship to be understood? And what does it tell us about our own relationship to God? We have also spoken of the presence of the Holy Breath in the Christian community. How is that presence to be interpreted experientially? We have then constructed only a preliminary frame of reference for interpreting the God of revelation. Until we have answered a series of challenging theological questions, its implications will remain of necessity vague.

1. Charles Sanders Peirce, Collected Papers, ed. by Charles Hartshorne and Paul Weiss (8 vols.; Cambridge: Harvard, 1931-1958) 5:474.

2. Ibid., 5:475-476, 481, 491, 7:527.

3. Ibid. 4:536.

4. Ibid., 8:184.

5. Cf. Leon Howard, ed., "The Mind" of Jonathan Edwards (Berkeley: University of California, 1963), pp. 139-140; Douglas Elwood, The Philosophical Theology of Jonathan Edwards (New York: Columbia, 1960), pp. 12-21; Ethan Allen "An Essay on the Universal Plentitude of Being and on the Nature and Immortality of the Human Soul and its Agency," in Reason the Only Oracle of Man (Bennington, Vt.: Haswell and Russell, 1884), pp. 29-31; Jonathan Bishop, Emerson on the Soul (Cambridge: Harvard, 1964); Sherman Paul, Emerson's Angle of Vision (Cambridge: Harvard, 1952); Stephen E. Whicher, Freedom and Fate: An Inner Life of Ralph Waldo Emerson (New York: Barnes, 1961); Francis Ellingwood Abbot, Scientific Theism (Boston: Little, Brown, and Co., 1885); The Syllogistic Philosophy, (2 vols.; Boston: Little, Brown, and Co., 1906); Josiah Royce, The World and the Individual: Second Series, (2 vols.; New York: Dover, 1959), p. 417; William James, Pluralistic Universe (New York: Longmans, Green, 1909), Chs. IV and V; Alfred North Whitehead, Process and Reality, (New York: Free Press, 1978) pp. 337-351; Charles Hartshorne, The Divine Relativity (New Haven: Yale, 1948).

6. Hermas, The Shepherd, Mandate 1.1; Origen, Against Celsus, IV, 5; Cyril of Alexandria, On the Gospel of John, XI, 9; Athanasius of Alexandria, Letter on the Decrees of the Council of Nicea, 11, Letters to Serapion, I, 26; Gregory of Nazianzus, Theological Orations, I, 1; Hilary of Poitiers, On the Trinity, I, 8, II, 6, 19, IV, 8; Ambrose of Milan, On the Holy Spirit, I, vii, 86-87, II, iv, 29-31. For a lucid analysis of Augustine's doctrine on this point see: Stanislaus J. Grabowski, The All Present God (St. Louis: Herder, 1954).

7. John Scotus Erigena, On the Division of Nature, III, 1; Anselm of Canterbury, Monologium, XIV, XX; Thomas Aquinas, Summa Theologiae I, viii, i, ad 1.

8.   Karl Barth, Church Dogmatics, translated by T.H.L. Parker, W.B. Johnson, H. Knight, and J.L.M. Haire (New York: Scribners, 1957), I-I, p. 532, II-I, pp. 149-150, 300; Heribert Mühlen, Una Mystica Persona: Eine Person in Vielen Personen (Munich: Verlag Ferdinand Schonigh, 1968); Jürgen Moltmann, The Trinity and the Kingdom (San Francisco: Harper and Row, 1981).

9. The panentheism defended in these pages differs from that proposed by Jürgen Moltmann in several respects, even though it concurs with his overall suggestion that the relationship of God and the world should be conceived in panentheistic terms. The position here defended invokes the category "experience" conceived and used transcendentally to make the mutual inexistence of God and creation thinkable. While Moltmann invokes the concept of panentheism, he leaves the reader bereft of a clear rubric under which to think of it. Moreover, the position taken here does not necessarily commit one to the dialectical understanding of creation which Moltmann defends. Finally, the panentheism proposed here takes pains to differentiate itself explicitly from the naturalistic panentheism defended by process philosophy. [Cf. Jürgen Moltmann, The Trinity and the Kingdom, 105-114; Alfred North Whitehead, Process and Reality. edited by David Ray Griffin and Donald W. Sherburne (New York: Free Press, 1978) 337-351.]

101

CHAPTER V:

IS THE HOLY BREATH A DIVINE PERSON?

Not every advance in Christian pneumatology has resulted from exclusive preoccupation with the Holy Breath. To the extent that the Father and the Son resemble the Advocate, theological insight into who They are throws light on Her reality as well. The development of trinitarian speculation about the divine persons illustrates the kind of pneumatological advance of which we speak. In the fourth century Arianism forced the fathers of the Church to create a technical language for speaking about the unity and trinity of God. The Greek fathers distinguished three entities (**hypostaseis**) in God called Father, Son, and Breath. And they came to recognize that all three are one in being (**homoousios**). But they regarded the divine being (**ousia**) as mysterious and ineffable and offered only vague definitions of the term "hypostasis," the term ultimately adopted to designate each member of the divine triad.

"Hypostasis" was translated in the west by the Latin term **"persona."** And during the middle ages "person (**persona**)" underwent a series of clarifying definitions which suggested an analogy between divine and human persons. The result enriched Christian pneumatology, for it allowed Christians to think of the Holy Breath as a divine person. But this new, personal conception had not resulted from a narrow concern with the Breath as such. Rather it marked an advance in a trinitarian theology of the divine persons which had consequences for Christian pneumatology.

In our own century, however, both Karl Rahner and Karl Barth have expressed reservations about conceiving Father, Son, and Breath as divine persons. They find the idea theologically misleading. Barth fears that the idea of a tripersonal God will lead to the false assumption that there are three distinct personalities in the Godhead. Rahner fears that the same idea will lead to tritheism. On the other hand, Heribert Mühlen has vigorously defended the personalism of medieval trinitarians. And he has drawn on the existential philosophy of Martin Buber to construct a social understanding of the Christian deity very much in the tradition of the great medieval scholastics. Jürgen Moltmann espouses a similar position.

The modern dispute over the advisability of applying the term "person" to the members of the divine triad raises then an important question for Christian pneumatology, a question to which we now turn. Our argument will advance in three steps. First, we will examine human personal experience in order to see if we can derive from it a definition of the term "person" that might be applicable to the members of the divine triad. Finally, we will examine the missions of the Son and of the Breath to see whether they lend warranty to the application of personal language to Father, Son, and Breath.

103

The history of trinitarian theology testifies to the fact that the tendency to speak of Father, Son, and Breath as divine persons evolved gradually. The argument over their personal character advances in identifiable stages: (1) Tertullian introduces the Latin term **"persona (person)"** as a technical trinitarian concept and offers a preliminary definition of it. (2) The Arian controversy forces the Greek fathers to work out their own technical vocabulary for speaking of the Christian God as triune. (3) In the assimilation of the results of the Arian controversy in the east by the Latin church in the west the term "person" came to be accepted as the proper designation of Father, Son, and Breath and linked to the idea of relationship. (4) As medieval theology advanced a person was first conceived as a thinking substance, then as not only relational and conscious but as ecstatic and social as well. (5) Insights from existential philosophy were then used to further develop the results of a medieval theology of the divine persons. (6) A countersuggestion emerges to replace the term "person" by the term "mode" in any reference to Father, Son, and Breath. (7) The attempt is then made to repudiate this countersuggestion as a form of modalism and to return to the more traditional term "person." Let us examine this centuries-old debate for what it has to teach us about the experience of being a person and about the reality of the divine Breath.

Among major Christian theologians, Tertullian (c. 160-c. 220) first applied the term **"persona (person)"** to the three members of the divine triad. In his early writings he restricted the term to Father and Son. But later, during his Montanist period, he came to apply it to the Holy Breath as well (<u>Against Praxeas</u>, VIII).[1] He was, moreover, the first major theologian to offer us something like a definition of what it means to be a divine person. For Tertullian conceived a "person" as a communicating subject. Moreover, in his trinitarian speculations Tertullian associated the concept "person" with the idea of a "relationship of origin" (<u>Against Praxeas</u>, IX).[2]

The Greek equivalent of **"persona"** was **"prosopon."** Both words signified the mask worn by actors in Greek and Roman drama. But in the east **"prosopon"** was not favored as a designation for Father, Son, and Breath. In Greek theological ears **"prosopon"** suggested that the Son and the Breath were only masks, only deceptive historical disguises of the sole subsisting reality of the Father. They recognized such a notion as the heresy called modalism. As a consequence, when the Greek fathers were faced with the need to find a technical term for the members of the Trinity, they chose the vaguer term **"hypostasis."** It meant "entity."

The context within which fourth-century Greek trinitarian theology developed was defined by the heresiarch Arius (d. 336). Arius was a presbyter of Alexandria. He espoused a straightforward subordinationism. God, he taught, is uncreated, unbegotten, unoriginated. The Son, who is originated and begotten, cannot therefore be God. For a God who is by nature one and immutable cannot communicate His substance to another without ceasing to be one and undergoing change. The Son is, therefore, a creature, albeit a perfect, spiritual creature whom God created before He made anything else. This creature, whom Christians call the Son of God, is also the agent of human salvation. He became incarnate in order to teach sinful humans how to live. This he accomplished through the perfection of his obedience. The one God also created a second spiritual creature less perfect than the Son called the Holy Breath.[3]

In the year 313 the pagan emperor Constantine had recognized Christianity as one of the official religions of the empire. As the Arian controversy threatened to divide the Church, the emperor feared its possible political consequences. In 325 a.d. he therefore summoned the bishops to Nicea to settle the Arian question once and for all. The council did not silence the Arians, but it did lend decisive shape to the Christian creed.

It soon became apparent in the debates at Nicea that the Arians could accept the wording of the traditional baptismal creed while tacitly reinterpreting its meaning to suit their own purposes. They affirmed, for example, all the traditional titles of Jesus. They confessed that He is "God from God" and "light from light." But they held tacitly that Jesus is divine by grace, not by nature and that His light is a created reflection of the divine light. They also confessed publicly that He is Son of God and savior, while tacitly denying His divinity.

Most of the bishops at Nicea never doubted that Arius should be condemned. Many of them still bore in their flesh the scars of Roman torture, and they were not about to abandon to some Alexandrian intellectual a faith for which they had bled and others had died.

Nevertheless, the more conservative wing of the anti-Arian forces resisted at first the introduction of novel theological terms into the baptismal formula, especially terms of pagan, philosophical origin. But at Nicea the Arians stuck at the term **"homoousios."** They would not confess that the Son is "one in being" with the Father. The term was accordingly inserted into the creed sanctioned by the council. The new creed read:

> We believe in one God, the Almighty Father, Creator of all things both visible and invisible. And in one Lord Jesus Christ, the Son of God, the only begotten, born of the Father, that is, of the being (**ousia**) of the Father; God from God, light from light, true God from true God, begotten, not created, one in being (**homoousios**) with the Father; through Him all things were made, those in heaven and those on earth.

Arius had denied the divinity of the Holy Breath. But on that subject Nicea remained laconic. It asserted only: "And we believe in the Holy Breath" (DS 150).[4]

But the insertion of the term **"homoousios"** roused opposition enough. It was denounced as non-biblical. It was attacked as vague and contradictory. At first the opponents of Nicea outnumbered its supporters. Some of the opposition felt that the new creed smacked of modalism and threatened the distinction of Father, Son, and Breath. Others felt that it compromised the unity of the divine governance of the world. Alternatives to the term **"homoousios"** were suggested. The semi-Arians defended the legitimacy of **"homoiousios** (similar in being)."

Among the defenders of Nicea Athanasius of Alexandria (c. 296-c. 373) first recognized that if Arianism was to be extirpated root and branch, the term **"homoousios"** would have to be extended to the divine Breath as well. And in his Letters to Serapion, written during his third exile, he argued the point at some length.

With hints from other Platonizing theologians, Athanasius at first ascribed the gracious illumination of believers to the Word of God rather than to the divine Breath. But he was eventually forced through controversy to acknowledge the illegitimacy of ascribing any divine activity exclusively to any one member of the Trinity. In his first letter to Serapion he observed:

> The Father does all things through the Word and in the Holy Breath....The gifts which the Breath divides to each are bestowed from the Father through the Word....For there is nothing that is not originated and actuated through the Word and in the Breath (Letters to Serapion, I, 28).

The Breath acts, then, as co-creator and co-sanctifier with Father and Son. She is the actualization (**energeia**) of the divine power present in the Son, the very reality and power of God Himself (Letters to Serapion, I, 22-27).

The term **"ousia"** had already been canonized at Nicea. But the jibes of the Arians forced Athanasius to grope also for technical terms to characterize the production of the Son and of the Breath within the Godhead. "Generation (**gennesis**)" seemed apt for the production of the divine Son from the eternal Father. It too enjoyed official blessing. But it displeased the Arians. They objected that if the Holy Breath is also a divine hypostasis, then She must also be "generated" and therefore be either the brother of the Son or the grandson of the Father. Athanasius dismissed the argument as devoid of biblical proof. He spoke of the procession (**ekporeusis**) of the divine Breath, rather than of Her generation.[5]

Athanasius vindicated the divinity of the Breath forthrightly and unambiguously. But his achievement exacted its speculative price. In portraying Father, Son, and Breath as equally co-active in creation and in the divinization of each believer, he ran the risk of downplaying the specific function of each **hypostasis** within the economy of salvation.[6]

Athanasius found strong theological and political support for his defence both of Nicea and of the Breath's divinity in the writings of Basil of Caesarea (c. 330-379). But Basil insisted more explicitly than Athanasius had on the noetic character of the divine Breath. He regarded Her as an intelligent reality (**noera ousia**), incorporeal, unlimited in power, greatness, and duration.[7]

Basil rejected outright the notion that the Breath is a creature (**ktisma**). That She is a source of sanctification proved to him that she is divine, for only God can sanctify. She makes us children of God, dispenses the charisms, acts with divine authority, knows the deepest things of God, makes us partake of divine life. Such actions surpass the power of a mere creature (<u>Letter</u> 125:3, 159:2).[8]

Basil distinguished more clearly than Athanasius had between the term "ousia" and "hypostasis." The latter he used to designate Father, Son, and Breath as distinct, particular. The former he reserved for the divine nature common to the three **hypostaseis.** Accordingly, he defined the term "**hypostasis**" as a particular mode of existence. But since he regarded the divine **ousia** as ineffable, he was forced finally to describe the **hypostaseis** as "modes of ineffable existence." Subsequent thinkers would, understandably enough, find such a definition somewhat vague (<u>On The Holy Spirit,</u> 46).[9]

Basil died prematurely at the age of fifty, exhausted by his labors. But his fallen banner was immediately raised by his friend Gregory of Nazianzus (c. 330-389). And Gregory's efforts were soon seconded by those of Basil's brother, Gregory of Nyssa (c. 330-395). Both defended the theological legitimacy of speaking of one **ousia** and of three **hypostaseis** in God. Gregory of Nyssa, like Athanasius, spoke of the **hypostaseis** as dynamic actualizations (**energeiai**) of the Godhead but believed that the reality of the **hypostaseis** remained shrouded in the ineffable mystery of God. He could discover no analogy between a divine **hypostasis** and a human person (Gregory of Nazianzus, <u>Theological Orations,</u> XXX, 17, 20, XXXI, 6, XXXIII, 9-11; Gregory of Nyssa, <u>Against Eunomius,</u> I, 32).[10]

The reader may surmise even from the preceding thumbnail sketch of some of the issues raised by the Arian controversy that when the Greek fathers applied the term "**hypostasis**" to Father, Son, and Breath, they meant by it something quite different from what is normally connoted today by the term "person." When we speak of persons in a contemporary context we do not mean to refer to a particular mode of an ineffable existence. And none but the most metaphysical of minds would even be remotely inclined to define a "person" as the actualization of an essence. Even were such a definition tendered, its adequacy could be legitimately challenged. If truth be told, just what the Greek fathers meant by the term

"hypostasis" remained obscure. But in the west the term **"hypostasis"** was destined to be translated by Tertullian's term **"persona."** And as Latin trinitarian speculation developed, theologians of a more logical and less rhetorical or mystical bent would attempt to define the meaning of **persona** with greater precision.

Augustine set the parameters for a medieval theology of the divine persons. In his De Trinitate he underscored their relational character. As the source within God of those activities common to Father, Son, and Breath, the divine substance is, Augustine argued, a subject of predication in its own right. So are the divine persons. He concluded then that two kinds of predicates can be applied to God. Predications common to all three persons envisage the divine substantial essence. Other predicates envisage the persons themselves. The latter are relational predicates. After Augustine we find, then, a solid theological consensus in the west that the divine persons are relational realities (On the Trinity, V, v, 1-xiv, 17).

Ancius Manlius Severinus Boethius (c. 474-524) wrote in the twilight of the Roman empire. But his love of logic endowed his theology with a rationalistic cast that foreshadowed the systematizing tendencies of the great medieval scholastics. But in his reflections on the divine persons, Boethius remained baffled. He described them as scarcely comprehensible relational realities in the Godhead (De Trinitate, V, 33-40). Nevertheless, he bequeathed to western theology a working definition of the term "person (persona)." He did so, not in his De Trinitate, but in a short treatise on Christology.

The term "person," Boethius argued, can be properly said only of a substance. Substances are, however, either universal predicates (like "man," "rock," "tree") or particular individuals (like "this man, "this rock," "this tree"). Persons, however, are always individual substances; and they differ from other individual substances by their ability to think rationally. He therefore defined a "person" as "the individual substance of a rational nature (**naturae rationabilis individua substantia**)" (Against Eutyches, II, 1-5, 28-37). After Boethius persons were conceived of as intelligent.

In the twelfth century Richard of St. Victor subjected Boethius's definition of a"person" to a creative and systematic critique. Richard held that there can be only one divine **substantia:** namely, the divine essence (De Trinitate, I, xi). The persons are three "someones (**aliquos**)" (Ibid., IV, viii, ix), who possess one and the same divine substance. But they cannot be called substances in their own right. For if the divine persons were substances, they would have to differ from one another as substances differ, that is to say, qualitatively. But if the divine persons differ in the kind of reality they are, how can they be equally divine? (De Trinitate, IV, xiii-xv).

As a replacement for Boethius's term "**substantia**," Richard suggested "**existentia**." It seemed apt for three reasons. First, it called attention to the relational character of the persons, that they subsist (**sistere**) from (**ex**), or out of, one another. Second as a relational term "**existentia**" lacked any connotation of qualitative difference. Third, as existences the divine persons could be conceived as ecstatic, social realities and their relationship with one another could be conceived on an analogy with human social experience (De Trinitate, IV, x).

Following Anselm of Canterbury, Richard imagined the divine reality as the supreme exemplification of all perfection, including the perfections of goodness, happiness, and love. These three divine perfections, he believed, imply one another and illumine the way in which the divine persons relate to one another. A supremely good God would long to share His goodness perfectly with another. To share the divine goodness perfectly, that other would have to be the divine goodness itself. That is to say, He would have to enjoy the divine nature. For God is His own goodness. The sharing of divine goodness is a supreme act of love. And the loving communion among the divine persons constitutes supreme happiness. In God, therefore, goodness, happiness, and love imply one another and are inseparable (De Trinitate, III, ii-vi).

The supreme happiness of God also demands that the love of the divine persons be reciprocal. For happiness in love involves both giving and receiving. Moreover, the reciprocity of the love between Father and Son gives rise to the divine Breath. For two supremely good, mutually loving persons would not be perfectly happy unless they could share their love with a friend (De Trinitate, III, vii, xi-xv).

Finally, Richard conceived the divine persons as individuals. And he regarded the individuality of each person as incommunicable. He therefore defined a divine person as "an incommunicable existence of the divine nature" (De Trinitate, IV, xvi-xvii, xxi).

Clearly, Richard advanced theological understanding of personal experience in a number of significant ways. He saw that persons are not only relational and intelligent but ecstatic and social. They live in and through communion with one another. They are unique, for each person enjoys a particularity that is incommunicable.

In the thirteenth century Thomas Aquinas (c. 1225-1274) would also defend the relational character of the divine persons. But he was less concerned than Richard had been to critique Boethius's definition of person. He spoke instead of the divine persons as subsistent relations (Summa Theologiae, I, xxix, 4). In the thirteenth century the idea of a subsistent relation was something of an anomaly. For relations are accidents, and only substances subsist. As we shall see, however, in an experiential understanding of person the notion of subsistent relations becomes eminently thinkable.

Among twentieth century theologians, Heribert Mühlen has attempted to build constructively on the work of Richard of St. Victor and of Aquinas. He has argued that their understanding of person is finally convergent. And he has further suggested that the social relationship of Father, Son, and Breath within the Godhead can be accurately interpreted in categories derived from Martin Buber's existential phenomenology of interpersonal relationship. With Buber, Mühlen argues that persons enjoy two irreducible kinds of relationships: either "I-Thou" or "We-Thou" relationships. He defines an interpersonal relationship as one that engages both knowing and willing.[11]

The relation of Father to Son within the Trinity must, Mühlen argues, be characterized as an "I-Thou" relationship. The Father as source and origin of the Son and Breath stands as the primordial "I" within the Trinity. He is constituted as person through His knowing, loving relationship to the Son. That is to say, He actively generates the Son. In being passively generated by the Father, the Son stands toward the Father as a "Thou." Because his relation of filiation is both knowing and loving, it too is personal.[12]

The relationship of Father and Son to the Divine Breath is a "We-Thou" relationship. In actively spirating the Breath, Father and Son stand toward Her in a knowing, loving, personal relationship. She in being spirated stands in the same kind of relationship to Them.[13]

The Breath is sent to Jesus and to the Christian community. Both missions reveal the "We" character of Her relationship to the other divine persons. She comes to Jesus as the head of the mystical body, as the one divinely appointed by the Father to begin a new Israel. Her coming to Jesus effects the graced transformation of His human nature. But that transformation has as its purpose His mediation of the Breath to the Christian community after the resurrection.[14] In communicating Herself to Jesus and the church the Breath makes them into a single "We," into the community we call the mystical body of Christ. For by participation in the Breath, Christians live in communion with one another and with Christ their head. But our union with the Breath differs from the Son's hypostatic union with His humanity. Our relationship to the Breath is not hypostatic but interpersonal.[15]

Her coming is, moreoever, an instance of personal causality. Personal causality effects an interpersonal relationship. In it one person affects another but in such a way as to evoke from the other the capacity for free, conscious self-donation in the mutuality of love.[16]

Clearly, Mühlen's theology of the divine persons builds constructively on the foundation laid by Richard of St. Victor and Aquinas. It distinguishes more clearly than they did, however, between personal and impersonal relationships and between personal and impersonal causality. Mühlen discovers a difference between the interpersonal "I-

Thou" relationship of Father and Son and the communal "We-Thou" relationship that is the work of the Breath. And he insists more explicitly than the medievals had that the way the divine persons function in the economy of salvation reveals to us the character of their relationship to one another within the Godhead.

But, as we have already seen, not every twentieth-century theologian rejoices at the prospect of interpreting the relation of Father, Son, and Breath in interpersonal categories. Both Karl Barth and Karl Rahner hesitate to apply personal language to the divine hypostases. Instead, they recommend a return to the vaguer patristic term "mode" in speaking of the three members of the divine triad.

But while Karl Barth (1886-1968) has preferred the term "mode" to the term "person," he claimed to mean by "mode" what "person" has traditionally meant in trinitarian speculation: namely, a special, distinct, absolutely individual, relational way of existing. He objected to the term "person" because in a modern context it connotes "personality." And he denied the existence of three distinct personalities in God. Nevertheless, the three divine modes constitute for Barth three really distinct expressions of the divine reality.[17]

Karl Rahner shares Barth's reluctance to apply the term "person" to Father, Son, and Breath. But his motives differ. Because he conceives of God as infinite and absolutely mysterious, he hesitates to predicate the same term of God and of creatures without considerable qualification. Though he looks on God as "personal," he prefers, with Gregory of Nyssa, to leave the meaning of the term "divine person" shrouded in "the ineffable darkness of the holy mystery." Moreover, because he defines "person" as a "free center of consciousness and free activity which disposes of itself and differentiates itself from others," he fears that if we conceive of the divine persons as three free and autonomous centers of consciousness we jeopardize the unity of the divine essence.[18]

Jürgen Moltmann has, however, criticised the modalism of both Barth and Rahner for imagining that some sort of divine subjectivity lurks "behind" the three divine persons. Instead of beginning with a principle of divine unity which becomes manifest in three modes of revelation, Moltmann believes that trinitarian theology should begin historically with the three divine persons and then attempt to explain how the three are one. We will succeed in this enterprise, he believes, if the reality of the persons is so conceived that it demands "God's at-oneness." But he offers no detailed discussion of the meaning of personal existence and remains content to appeal to the mutual inexistence of the divine persons as the explanation of their unity.[19]

We are examining the legitimacy of applying the term "person" to the three members of the Trinity. As a first step in our argument, we have reviewed the state of the question. We must now advance to our second step: we must clarify the meaning of the term "person." Only then will we be able to determine whether it can interpret the biblical witness to God's self-revelation in Jesus and the Breath.

We will not, however, find a direct answer to the question which confronts us in the pages of the Bible. For while some of the biblical terms used to describe the Breath have personal connotations, sacred scripture contains no technical discussion of the meaning of the term "person." Nor does it apply this term as such to the members of the Trinity.

Two speculative tasks face us. First, we must clarify the meaning of the term "person" by reflecting on human personal experience. Second, we must examine the historical missions of the Son and of the Breath in order to assess the legitimacy of extending the term analogously to Them and to the Father. We therefore face the following question: what are the typical, diagnostic traits of personal, human experience?

We humans experience the fact that we are persons with a certain immediacy. But personal experience is complex. And any attempt to characterize it should reverence its complexity. The very fact, however, that we can ask ourselves what it means for us to be human persons entails that human persons are **self-aware.**

Human self-awareness is developing, not static. It grows because humans are growing, living realities. As we go through life we acquire new habits, new skills, new capacities to react and to respond evaluatively and decisively. The more complex I become as a human personal experience, the more about me there is to understand. And the more I comprehend my own history, the more differentiated my personal self-awareness becomes.

But though I develop as a person, I always remain myself. Though sleep interrupts my conscious life, the self who awakens each morning lives in developmental continuity with the self who went to sleep. The self I am today stands in continuity with the self I was one year, three years, ten years ago. And that self stands in continuity with the self I was at my conception and birth. **Real continuity** constitutes then a second diagnostic trait of human personal experience.

Personal continuity needs interpretation. In the experiential frame of reference proposed in Chapter II, a person is a self; and the real, individual continuity of every self is interpreted descriptively by the category "law." Let us recall some of the important implications of this description.

We have defined experience as a process made up of feelings. Three kinds of feelings structure human experience: qualities, facts, and laws. Because all feelings are relational, they all endow experience with some kind of felt continuity. Qualities, being evaluative, endow experience with conceptual continuity. Facts, being instances of interaction, endow

112

experience with social continuity. But laws, being the dynamic relationship between an individual past and its future, endow human experience with individual and personal continuity.

Our evaluative responses are qualitative. As experience grows and develops, qualitative, conceptual responses take on, as we have seen, the character of an evaluative continuum. Sense data disclose factual interactions. But sense qualities are already emotionally charged. They therefore develop in conceptual continuity with more complex emotive responses like love, sympathy, compassion, fear, rage, guilt. Our affective responses are shaped in turn by images. And images of universal import form an evaluative bridge between emotive responses and abstract thought. Both affective connotations and logical implications link evaluation into an experienced continuum. Affective and inferential perceptions of myself and of my world disclose to me the selves that people it. But while the evaluative continuum presents to us the social and individual continuities that shape experience, it does not create them.

Social continuity results from interaction. It is factual in character and therefore utterly determinate and actual. What I said and did at ten o'clock this morning remains eternally the concrete word and act it was. Human social relationships are also ephemeral. When I speak to you and you hear and respond, our conversation links us. But that bond ceases as soon as I leave the room. Because the social continuities that shape human personal experience are disjunctive and ephemeral, factual relationships cannot explain individual, personal continuity. Instead individual, personal continuity explains facts by linking them together in significant patterns of habitual behavior.

Laws, being habits, orient human experience toward the future. Because they provide the dynamic link between an individual past and the future it is in process of becoming, laws endow experience with individual and personal continuity. They constitute the developing selves whose reality I perceive when I respond affectively or inferentially to my world. They unite disjunctive facts into a personal history. But because human experience is a process, laws endow it with individual, personal continuity **within development.** Continuity within development occurs when new habits are acquired and integrated more or less successfully into the other habitual patterns of reaction and response that constitute the self.

The fact that personal continuity is grounded in the realm of law tells us something else important about what it means to be a person. For laws endow experience with individual and personal **autonomy.** Autonomy is the capacity to initiate reaction and response. As we have seen, autonomy may be suppressed through change, as it is in the digestive assimilation of food or in the transformation of two elements into a single compound with new properties. But while it may be suppressed, autonomy can never be transferred. It remains incommunicable. It is, indeed, the incommunicable particularity that Richard of St. Victor discovered in each individual, personal self. Autonomy makes a self an "I." When autonomy vanishes, so does the "I," and with it every claim to being a self, a person. We shall return to this important point later in another context.

Every personal, human self is also a **relational** reality. Each human person links an individual past dynamically to an individual future. Each human self also stands dynamically engaged with its body and with the body's impinging environment. It is present to itself and its world both consciously and unconsciously. To be a person means, therefore, to stand in an autonomous, self-conscious, responsive relationship with some reality other than oneself. When those realities are other persons, personal experience ceases to be merely relational and transactional and becomes **social.**

Because human experience grows and develops, not all human persons have achieved self-awareness to the same degree. Propriosensation is the most primitive form of self-awareness. We share it with the animals. Animals, however, are not persons. Persons then enjoy a special kind of self-awareness. To understand what distinguishes personal self-awareness, we must examine it in its most heightened form. We humans come of age as persons when we assume **conscious responsibility** for our own future growth and development and for the consequences of our own decisions. As we have seen in Chapter II, the decision by which we do so is called conversion. We can identify four kinds of personal conversion: affective, intellectual, moral, and religious. We must then also distinguish four corresponding kinds of personal responsibility and irresponsibility.

But I can make decisions whose consequences affect not only my own personal growth but that of others as well. Fully responsible behavior responds to other persons as persons by inviting them to assume responsibility for their own lives and decisions. It respects their freedom and autonomy. For activity which springs from personal conversion also invites it in others. I call the decision to assume responsibility for summoning others to responsible behavior socio-political conversion.

Responsible behavior differs from knee-jerk reactions. Mere retaliations, the latter lack evaluative differentiation. Because unreflective, they are better characterized as pre-responsible rather than as irresponsible; for they precede critical insight into oneself, one's motives, or the impact of one's decisions upon others. When, for example, a boorish cretin affronts and insults me, I may **react** to the individual with spontaneous rage, even though I **respond** responsibly and sensitively. Instead of matching boorishness with vengeful retaliation, I try to understand why my adversary lacks the most basic social graces and how I can help rather than harm him.

We may on the basis of all the preceding reflections formulate a diagnostic definition of the term "person." **A person is a dynamic relational reality, not only subsistent in its own right (that is to say, as an autonomous** center of responsive evaluation and decision), but also imbued with vital continuity and with the capacity for responsible self-understanding, for decisions that flow from that same self-understanding, and for entering into responsible social relationships with entities like itself.

The preceding definition incorporates the valid insights of the other definitions of "person" we have examined. It allows us with Tertullian to think of persons as **communicating subjects.** The Greek fathers insisted that those hypostatic realities we now call persons are **particular.** And Richard of St. Victor found their particularity to be **incommunicable.** Our definition allows us to identify what makes each person particular and why personal particularity is indeed incommunicable. Each person becomes an "I," a particular self through the exercise of **autonomy.** Autonomy not only establishes the particularity of each person, but it resists communication. Our definition sanctions the attempts of western theologians to think of persons as **relational, social realities;** and it understands personal relationships as legal and habitual. It characterizes the personal **"rationality"** of which Boethius spoke as the kind of **responsible self-awareness** that results from conversion. Our definition refuses with Richard of St. Victor to call persons substances and conceives them instead as **autonomous, relational selves.** It discovers the **"I-Thou"** and **"We-Thou"** **relationships** of which Mühlen speaks in **responsive** (as opposed to merely reactive) **behavior.** And among human interpersonal responses, it recognizes in the summons to initial and ongoing conversion the highest form of what Mühlen calls "personal causality."

Our experiential definition of what it means to be a person gives some evidence, then, of being fairly comprehensive. But can we apply it to Father, Son, and Breath? Before we can answer that question we must examine more closely how They relate to one another within the Godhead. And since no one has seen God face to face in this life, we must search for our answer in those historical events that reveal to us the inner triune life of God, namely, the historical missions of the Son and of the Holy Breath.

That the historical Jesus experienced God as Father (**Abba**) cannot be questioned. Moreover, the New Testament suggests that Jesus' **Abba** experience was integral to His own personal self-awareness. He spoke consistently in ways that indicate that He regarded His own filial relationship to the Father as of a different order than that of His disciples. Jesus invited His disciples to live as the children of **Abba.** But though He spoke of "My heavenly Father" and of "your heavenly Father" and though He taught His disciples to pray "Our Father in heaven," nowhere in the New Testament does he join His disciples in saying "our Father." In other words, while He regarded His own relationship to the Father as paradigmatic of what the relationship of His disciples ought to be, He seems to have experienced His own relationship to the Father as something distinctive and as normative in its uniqueness.[20]

115

His relationship to the Father was not only self-conscious, it was also morally responsible. Human persons come to moral responsibility through conversion. The New Testament never speaks of Jesus as having been converted to God from a life of sin. His Jordan experience is better characterized as a messianic commissioning than as a conversion. Nevertheless, Jesus models perfect, responsible, loving submission to the will of the Father (Jn 4:34, 5:30, 6:38-40, 19:30, Mt 26:39, Mk 14:36, Lk 22:42, Hb 5:7-10).

In other words, the relationship of the incarnate Son to the Father gives every evidence of having enjoyed all the diagnostic traits we have discovered in human interpersonal relationships. It was a responsive, responsible, self-conscious relationship between two autonomous selves. It was also therefore in some real sense a "social" relationship.

In naming God "**Abba**" Jesus used innovative language. The name invokes parental and therefore explicitly personal imagery. In speaking about the divine Breath, however, He seems to have adhered to more traditional terms. In the Old Testament, however, the Holy Breath had not been conceived as a distinct person within God. As a consequence, in the New Testament Jesus' statements about Her sound less clearly personal in intent than His proclamation of the Father.

Jesus comes closest to speaking of the Holy Breath in personal terms in His promise of the Paraclete. As we have seen, He assured His disciples that when the Breath would come She would be "another Advocate" like Jesus Himself. Presumably, therefore, She would, like Him, be a personal divine presence. Moreover, the actions She will perform--teaching, reminding, instructing, revealing--are all personal acts.

The Paraclete theology of the fourth gospel is, however, distinctively Johannine, although it echoes and develops pneumatological themes present in the synoptics. But some exegetes, because of its peculiarly Johannine flavor, question whether it qualifies as "authentic Jesus" or as a doctrinal embellishment of the evangelist.

In the synoptic gospels, Jesus, as we have also seen, speaks of the divine Breath only occasionally. Indeed we can scarcely avoid the impression in reading all four gospels that Jesus spoke much more about the Father than about the Breath. In the synoptics, Jesus warns His disciples against blaspheming the Breath. And He parallels Breath blasphemy with speaking against the Son of Man. One might argue from the parallelism that for Jesus the Breath would seem to be as personal a reality as the Son of Man. But the personal character of the Breath is not finally the point of Jesus' remark. Jesus in the synoptics also invokes the Holy Breath as the source and inspiration of His exorcisms. But His words as they are recorded in Matthew and in Mark offer no clear indication that He perceived Her as a person. The same obscurity attends His promise that the Holy Breath will speak in the testimony of His persecuted disciples.

116

In other words, while the New Testament gives solid evidence that Jesus experienced an interpersonal relationship with the Father, we are harder pressed to establish from the New Testament texts the interpersonal character of His experience of the Holy Breath. On the other hand, neither does the New Testament offer clear evidence that He did not experience the Holy Breath as a person. And some texts suggest that He did.

What the New Testament does assert quite clearly is that Jesus' **Abba** experience was the work of the divine Breath within Him (Mk 1:9-13, Mt 3:13-14, Lk 3:21-4:13, 10:21-22). And that fact is significant. For it provides a solid basis for arguing that the integrally converted Christian ought to perceive the Holy Breath as a divine person. That the Holy Breath subsists in God as a divine reality distinct from Father and Son is historically revealed in the fact that She is sent to us by both to do things that only God can do: to grace us, to save us, to fill us with divine life. She is also the cognitive link between Father and Son and inspires in Them an awareness that is inter-personal. A distinct divine principle of interpersonal awareness cannot, however, be less than a divine person. For the character of any reality is revealed by the way it acts.

To put the matter somewhat differently, in the mission of the Son the divine experience is revealed as consciously interpersonal. Through the distinct missions of Son and Breath it is also revealed to be triadic in its structure. The members of the divine triad are three autonomous selves, for each contributes something distinctive to the divine experience. The Father is the autonomous source of creative efficacy. The Son, the autonomous source of obediential efficacy. The Breath, the autonomous source of divine self-awareness. The presence in God of three autonomous selves endowed with personal self-awareness means that the divine experience must be characterized as tripersonal.

One can also argue to the tripersonal character of the divine experience from the co-equality of the divine persons. If there are three autonomous divine selves, they must enjoy perfect co-equality. For if one lacked something the other two have, the deficient person would be less than supreme in perfection and therefore less than divine. The Holy Breath stands historically revealed as the divine interpretant and therefore as an autonomous divine self. If then the Father and Son can be called divine persons in virtue of the quality of the self-consciousness the Holy Breath inspires in Them, She must be a self no less personal than They in virtue of Her divine co-equality with Them.

Another argument for the personal character of the Holy Breath can be derived from the way in which She functions in both divine and human experience. She functions in both as a personalizing principle distinct from Father and Son. An autonomous personalizing principle exercises personal causality in Heribert Mühlen's sense of that term, for it creates in another the capacity to respond personally. A distinct, autonomous divine self who functions as a personalizing principle cannot be less than person. Let us reflect on what this means and why it is so.

117

Experience becomes personal when it becomes responsibly and socially self-aware. The divine experience is historically revealed as possessing three distinct, autonomous, functioning centers of activity. The Father and the Son are autonomous centers of efficacy. For the Father in sending the Son into the world is revealed as His efficacious source within the Godhead. And as co-sender of the Holy Breath, Father and Son stand revealed as Her efficacious co-principle within the Godhead. Because the Son sends the Breath in obedience to the Father, He is an efficacious obediential principle of divine activity. The Holy Breath in Her historical self-revelation stands disclosed not as a missioning principle endowed with divine efficacy but as a missioned principle of divine illumination. She is the wisdom that descends from on high, the cognitive link between the Father and the Son, the divine interpretant, the mind of God and of Christ. A divine principle of illumination is the source, not of causal efficacy, but of presentational immediacy. For it grounds the divine evaluative response. Through evaluative response, an experience becomes present to itself and to its world. The divine interpretant is, therefore, historically revealed as the source of divine self-awareness.

Father, Son, and Breath are all divine and therefore all equally co-eternal. There never was a moment in which They were ever separate from one another. Nor could one exist without the others, for that would compromise their perfect co-equality. But if **per absurdum** the Breath were to be separated from Father and Son, They of Themselves would be able to act only efficaciously. For without the divine interpretant to be Their mind, They would simply be divine principles of causal efficacy. In other words, without the Holy Breath, they could react efficaciously and automatically but not respond self-consciously and responsibly as persons do. As the source of divine responsiveness and responsibility, the Holy Breath personalizes the divine experience by endowing the Father and Son with a self-awareness which enables them not only to react efficaciously but to respond to one another as persons.

The divine interpretant performs a similar function in human experience. As we saw in Chapter II, human experience becomes fully responsible through conversion. Affective, intellectual, moral, and socio-political conversion can occur only naturally: they may result from human initiative alone exercised in the normal course of becoming an adult. In natural conversion one responds correctly to created values. But in authentic religious conversion, one always responds to some gracious act of divine self-revelation. In religious conversion the initiative always lies with God, whose free self-disclosure always demands a response of faith.

When through the gracious illumination of the Holy Breath the naturally converted person begins to become aware of what God has said and done within human history, a new kind of consciousness dawns. Religious conversion introduces one into a novel frame of reference that encompasses and fulfills any insight available to the mere natural convert. It transforms affective conversion into religious hope, intellectual assent into faith, and moral commitment into religious love.

118

Humans achieve full stature as persons through conversion. For until one has assumed responsibility for one's own growth, one remains personally immature. But one achieves full stature as a convert through religious conversion, since religious conversion perfects and fulfills mere natural conversion. Religious conversion is worked in us by the illumination of the divine Breath, Who is the source of all gracious enlightenment. As the source of that experience by which we achieve perfect stature as human persons, the Breath stands within human experience as its ultimate personalizing principle. [21]

A personalizing principle engages in personal causality. Personal causality establishes an interpersonal relationship between two self-conscious, responsible, responsive selves. Only persons engage in personal causality. As the ultimate personalizing principle and agent of personal causality, the Holy Breath confronts us in Her historical self-revelation as a divine person.

But if we can legitimately speak of three divine persons in God, we must not hastily assume that the members of the Trinity are persons in exactly the same way that humans are. For one thing, if the term "person" applies to Father, Son, and Breath, **They,** not human persons, constitute the supreme exemplification of personal existence. For if God is not only an experience but the supreme experiencer, Father, Son, and Breath must also subsist as the supreme exemplification of personal experience. Were we to demand that divine personhood exemplify all the traits possessed by finite, human persons, we would be betrayed into blasphemy. The divine persons cannot, for example, achieve moral responsibility in exactly the same way that human persons do. Humans come of age morally through conversion, by the conscious decision to assume responsibility for the character and consequences of personal decisions. As converts human persons need to be called to responsibility from personal irresponsibility. The divine experience, however, betrays not the slightest trace of irresponsibility. As the supremely responsible experiencer, God exemplifies the kind of personal responsibility to which human persons are summoned by conversion. But by that very fact God never needs conversion. For one needs conversion when one could assume personal responsibility for one's life but refuses to do so.

We must, then, anticipate that in consequence of the analogy of experience and in virtue of the divine supremacy, divine and human persons while similar in some respects will differ in others. In the chapter which follows we will attempt to identify some of those differences.

1. Edmund J. Fortman, The Triune God (Philadelphia: Fortress, 1972), pp. 113-114; Wolfgang Bender, Die Lehre über den Heiligen Geist bei Tertullian (Munich: Hueber, 1961), p. 2; Jean Danielou, The Origins of Latin Christianity, translated by David Smith and J.A. Baker (Philadelphia: Westminster, 1977), pp. 343-362.

2. Bender, op. cit., pp. 49-61, 80, 92-98.

3. Robert C. Gragg and Dennis E. Groh, Early Arianism: A View of Salvation (Philadelphia: Fortress, 1981); Fortman, op. cit., pp. 63-65; Grillmeier, op. cit., pp. 219-248; H.B. Swete, The Holy Spirit in the Ancient Church (London: Macmillan, 1912), pp. 249-273.

4. DS 150; Grillmeier, op. cit., pp. 249-273.

5. C.R.B. Shapland, ed. and trans., Letters of Saint Athanasius Concerning the Holy Spirit (New York: Philosophical Library, 1951), pp. 43, 97-99, 158-160; Fortman, op. cit., pp. 72-75.

6. J. Rolandus, Le Christ et l'homme dans la theologie d'Athanase d'Alexandrie (Leiden: Brill, 1968), pp. 239-249.

7. Hans Denhard, Das Problem des Abhänigkeit des Basilius von Plotin (Berlin: Gruyer, 1964), p. 69.

8. Hermann Dorries, De Spiritu Sancto: Der Beitrag des Basilius zum Abschluss des trinitarischen Dogmas (Göttigen: Vanderhoeck und Ruprecht, 1956), pp. 8-12.

9. Fortman, op. cit., p. 61; Swete, op. cit., pp. 199-200.

10. Edward P. Hardy and Cyril C. Richardson, The Christology of the Later Fathers (Philadelphia: Westminster, 1954), pp. 147, 191, 199-200; Jean Danielou, Platonism et théologie mystique: doctrine spirituelle de Gregoire de Nysse (Aubiers: Editions Montagne, 1944), pp. 152-161; Roger Leys, S.J., Image de Dieu chez S. Gregoire de Nysse (Paris: Desclée, 1951), pp. 30-33; Werner Jaeger, Gregor von Nyssas Lehre von Heiligen Geist (Leiden: Brill, 1966), pp. 12-14; Swete, op. cit., pp. 247-251.

11. Heribert Mühlen, Der Heilige Geist als Person (Münster: Westfalen, 1963), 3.10-3.26.

12. Ibid., 5.103.

13. Ibid.

14. Ibid., 7.49; Una Mystica Persona: Eine Person in Vielen Personen (Munich: Verlag Ferdinand Schoningh, 1968), 6.16, 39, 52.

15. Mühlen, Der Heilige Geist als Person, 7.15-29, 63.

16. Ibid., 8. 75; Una Mystica Persona, 9. 21.

17. Karl Barth, Church Dogmatics, I-I, pp. 405-418. Barth's trinitarian doctrine and pneumatology are thoroughly orthodox. He formulated the doctrine of the Trinity in the following terms:

> We mean by the doctrine of the Trinity, in a general and preliminary way, the proposition that He whom the Christian Church calls God and proclaims as God, therefore, the God who has revealed Himself according to the witness of Scripture, is the same in unimpaired unity, yet also the same in unimpaired variety thrice in a different way. Or in the phraseology of the dogma of the Trinity in the Church, the Father, the Son, and the Holy Spirit in the Bible's witness to revelation are in the unity of their reality the one God; and the one God is in the variety of His persons, the Father, the Son, and the Holy Spirit (Ibid., p. 253).

The doctrine of the Trinity, Barth realized, had been created by the Church. But he discovered in it a sound interpretation and exposition of the biblical witness. And he regarded the biblical witness as an accurate expression of God's own historical self-revelation. In other words, the dogma of the Trinity is God's self-revelation correctly interpreted (Ibid., pp. 353-357).

Barth discovered three elements in God's historical self-disclosure: an element of form, an element of hiddenness, and an element of impartation. The Father is the veiled hiddenness of God; the Son, God's unveiled form; the Breath, God's historical self-impartation (Ibid., pp. 368-382). These three elements each explicitate a different facet of the divine name "Yahweh-Kyrios."   They are ways in which the Godhead stands revealed to us. The three divine persons are then three distinct "modes of being in God" (Ibid., pp. 403-407).

Barth also endorsed the doctrine of **perichoresis**. The three modes of God are "involuted (**Ineinander**)" and "convoluted (**Miteinander**)." And he held with John Damascene that the mutual inexistence of the divine persons grounds their perfect unity in being and in operation (Ibid., pp. 426-430, 454-455).

Barth's reluctance to admit natural analogues to God left him critical of Augustine's search for vestiges of the Trinity within the human psyche. But in other respects his trinitarian theology echoes the Augustinian tradition. This is particularly so of his pneumatology.

In the incarnation and resurrection of the Word, he taught, the Father Creator stands objectively and historically revealed. Through the mission of His Son, the divine Reconciler, the Father reconciles us to Himself. The mission of the Son reveals His generation by the Father from all eternity. And the Son's eternal generation negates the personal self-sufficiency of the Father within the Godhead (Ibid., pp. 441-500, 553).

The Holy Breath is "God in His freedom to be present to the creature and so to create this relation [to Himself], and thereby to be the life of the creature." She is not the Son, for Her historical mission follows upon His death and glorification. Moreover, the Holy Breath guides and instructs us in ways that transcend mere human understanding and insight. The Breath is divine for She accomplishes works that only God can do; creation, salvation, sanctification. She is the third mode of divine being. She is "the act in which the Father is the Father of the Son, or Speaker of the Word, and the Son is the Son of the Father, the Word of the Speaker" (Ibid., pp. 516-539).

She is also, as Augustine had suggested, the bond of love uniting Father and Son. For She proceeds from both by spiration (Ibid., pp. 537-543). In his defense of the **Filioque**, Barth argued cogently that if the Breath proceeded from the Father alone, She would come to us as a divine agent of creation, but not of reconcilication. For even though the three divine persons are perfectly co-active in dealing with creation, the Son reveals to us the reality of God as Reconciler. Moreover, the co-spiration of the Breath by Father and Son manifests the perfect communion in reality, action, and love which unites them. And the eternal spiration of the Holy Breath negates all loneliness in God, just as the generation of the Son negates self-sufficiency in the Father (Ibid., pp. 548-550, 553).

The Breath of God comes to us as the "subjective reality" of divine revelation. That subjective reality becomes visible in the Church. The divine reality thus revealed is only "subjective" because there is no hypostatic union between the Church and the Breath. Moreover, as a subjective reality, the Breath focuses the faith-consciousness of believers on the objective element in divine revelation, namely, on the incarnation of the divine Word (Ibid., I-II, pp. 204-223, 235).

The subjective reception of God's revelation has itself four components: (1) the coherence of those elevated above fleshy existence by the Son's incarnation; (2) the lordship of His grace over their lives; (3) the unity of those who cohere through the ruling word of God; (4) the visible manifestation of their unity in those acts of God which extend and renew the Church in space and time. The divine reality thus made visible in the faith response of the Christian community is the person of the Holy Breath (Ibid., pp. 220-221, 223).

18. Karl Rahner, S.J., Foundations of Christian Faith, translated by William Dych, S.J. (New York: Seabury, 1978), pp. 71-75.

19. Jürgen Moltmann, The Trinity and the Kingdom, pp. 139-150.

20. James Dunn, Jesus and the Spirit (Philadelphia: Westminster, 1975), pp. 71-75.

21. There is a hint of this insight in the trinitarian theology of Hilary of Poitiers (310-367). Like Tertullian, Hilary employed the term **"spiritus"** as

a name for the third member of the Trinity; but at times he also used it to designate the essence common to all three persons. Indeed, he seems to have felt that Father and Son are "spirit" in consequence of their union with the divine **Spiritus**. He discovered an analogous process in the gracing of human nature. The divinity of the Breath appears precisely in this: that through Her presence within us we share in the indestructible life of the Godhead. We are "spiritualized" (De Trinitate, I, 36, II, 29-31, VIII, 23-26). If one takes "spirit" in the Pauline sense of conscious self-awareness, then Hilary's point is very well taken.

CHAPTER VI

IS THE DIVINE EXPERIENCE TRIUNE?

The time has come to pause once again and take stock of the progress of our argument. We are attempting a foundational pneumatology. We are exploring the question: how ought the Holy Breath of God to be perceived by an integrally converted Christian? We are approaching this question experientially in a double sense: we are attempting to understand the kinds of experiences which ought to lie at the basis of doctrinal affirmations about the divine Breath. At the same time we are attempting to test the legitimacy of perceiving Her as a facet of the divine experience.

We first clarified descriptively the meaning of the term "experience." We defined it as a process composed of relational elements called feelings. We discovered three generic types of feelings in human experience: qualities, facts, and laws. We then reflected on some of the describable traits of spatio-temporal experiences.

Next we tried to understand how human experience is transformed through the gracious illumination of the Holy Breath. We found Her revealed as a divine principle of enlightenment, as the wisdom that descends from on high, as the cognitive link between Father and Son, as the mind of God and of Christ. And we identified the divine missions as the events which reveal to us both the transcendent reality of God and the way in which the divine persons relate to one another within the Godhead.

A closer examination of the missions of Son and Breath allowed us to distinguish three distinct and autonomous centers of activity within the Christian deity. Two of them, the Father and the Son, function efficaciously as principles of mission and of procession. For the historical missions reveal the eternal processions. The Father stands as the aboriginal, creative source of the Son He efficaciously generates and sends into the world. The Son in His mission is historically revealed as a divine principle of obediential efficacy. Father and Son function, moreover, as the efficacious co-principles within the Godhead of the Holy Breath Whom they send jointly into the World. We found one autonomous source of evaluative response in God: the Holy Breath, the divine interpretant.

We concluded that the biblical witness allows us to identify in God the same kinds of generic variables as function within human experience. We found qualitative, evaluative responses; efficacious acts of causality, or divine facts; and three divine selves, which function as habitual, legal entities, in the technical philosophical sense of "law" we have suggested. Taken together these two conclusions pointed to the legitimacy of speaking of the Christian God as a divine experience.

But because we are approaching God by way of analogy, we were immediately forced to contrast the perfection of the divine experience with that of spatio-temporal experiences. We found God exists as the supreme exemplification of experience, as an eternal divine process at one and the same time supremely creative and supremely receptive.

Contemporary debate over the advisability of speaking of Father, Son, and Breath as divine persons forced us to examine the history of the controversy. Our historical survey yielded a number of insights into the meaning of personal existence. But we were forced finally to reflect on the human experience of personal existence in order to derive from it a diagnostic definition of the term "person." Further reflection on the divine missions convinced us that the divine Breath inspires in the Father and Son a kind of consciousness that can only be characterized as interpersonal. And we were then forced to confess that a distinct, autonomous source of interpersonal consciousness in God cannot be less than a distinct divine person. We concluded therefore that the divine experience stands revealed as the supreme exemplification of social self-awareness.

But having asserted the legitimacy of speaking of Father, Son, and Breath as divine persons, we were immediately faced with the fact that They both resemble and differ from human persons. Moreover, only divine persons, not human ones, exemplify perfectly personal existence. And we recognized our need to explore more fully how the divine experience of being a person differs from a human one.

Human persons seem at first to be sundered from one another by the very reality that makes them persons: namely, by their autonomy. Only an autonomous self can say "I," and only those autonomous selves capable of saying "I" with responsive and responsible self-awareness can claim to be persons. Because you and I are human persons, our actions and evaluations will never coincide perfectly. What you say and do proceeds from your own autonomy. What I say and do proceeds from mine.

But in their historical dealings with us, things stand somewhat differently with the divine persons. When one of Them acts and speaks, the others act and speak as well. John's gospel assures us that when we see and hear the Son we see and hear the Father. Similarly, the Holy Breath is not merely present to us; She is the presence of the Son and of the Father. Moreover, in Johannine theology, the members of the Johannine Trinity all share an identity of divine life called pneuma. In Pauline theology, the glorified Son is not only related to the Holy Breath; He is a life giving Pneuma. Despite Their distinction from one another, Their identity with one another remains not only functional but ontological and vital. Similarly, the Father creates and saves the world in and through the Son.

To speak of the vital identity of the three divine persons raises the question of the unity of a tripersonal God. How then should that unity be understood? Here we stand face to face with the central mystery of our

126

Christian faith. But a mystery should not be mistaken for a contradiction or a conundrum. Rather its full intelligibili y exceeds and therefore baffles our finite minds. We should not then confuse its theological contemplation with obfuscation or obscurantism. Let us therefore attempt to advance as far as we can in a positive understanding of the divine unity.

Like the last chapter the present one falls into three parts. In the first we will examine six different explanations of the unity of the Christian God. In the second, we will examine the dynamic structure of human social experience for the light it may have to offer concerning the unification of the divine experience. In the third we will examine the divine missions in order to discover what they reveal to us concerning the union of Father, Son, and Breath.

In the history of theology one may discover six different theological explanations of the unity of the Christian God: modalism, reduction to mystery, substantial unity, dynamic vitalism, mutual inexistence, and tritheism. Let us reflect briefly on the implications of each of these explanations.

(1) **Modalism:** Modalism unifies the Christian deity by collapsing the realities of Son and Breath into that of the Father. The modalist denies that Son and Breath enjoy distinct subsistence within the Godhead. They are portrayed instead as masks (**prosopa**) which the Father wore in His historical manifestations. They are, then, ways, or modes in which the Father has appeared to us, not distinct facets of the Godhead.[1]

(2) **Reduction to Mystery:** We have noted in another context the existence of an esoteric strain in patristic trinitarian theology. Three fonts nourished this esoteric impulse: the personal mysticism of the fathers, gnosticism, and neo-platonism. Eventually, it produced a kind of explanation of the divine unity: namely, that the unity of a tripersonal God is a mystery that exceeds any human powers of understanding.

At first patristic theologians restricted their esoteric rhetoric to the Father. He was characterized as invisible, ineffable, incomprehensible, mysterious.[2] Rhetorical insistence on the incomprehensibility and remoteness of the Father enabled the first Christian thinkers to insist with equal rhetorical skill that this same remote and mysterious Father had been concretely and intimately revealed in the historical missions of the Son and of the Breath. But in the course of the Arian controversy, the Son and Breath came to share the Father's remoteness and mystery.

One can trace their theological absorption into the transcendent mystery of the Father in the writings of the Cappadocians. Basil of Caesarea, like other theologians before him restricted his esoteric rhetoric to the Father: invisible and mysterious, He is best approached with wordless reverence and contemplative awe. The Son and Breath by Their saving activity draw us prayerfully into the transcendent mystery of the

127

Father. For Gregory of Nazianzus, however, not just the Father but the entire Godhead in its unity and trinity confronts us as a mystery beyond human comprehension. And as members of the Trinity Son and Breath share in its mystery. Gregory of Nyssa not only agreed but insisted that the three divine persons dwell in a heaven that lies beyond even the Platonic realm of ideas. The realm of ideas is rational, intelligible; but the inner life of the triune God is ineffable, incomprehensible, mysterious. When viewed as an explanation of the unity and trinity of God, reduction to mystery maintains, therefore, that there can in principle be no explanation of a divine reality that lies absolutely and utterly beyond human comprehension.[3]

One can scarcely deny that the human encounter with God remains mysterious. But much depends on how one explains its mysterious character. Here the speculative theologian faces a fundamental option. In its most radical formulation, esoteric theology conceived the divine reality as wholly other, as totally different from any created reality, as inconceivable, unimaginable, inexpressable in finite created symbols.

But even within Christianity one discovers varieties of mystical experience. Christian mystics agree that in contemplative union one knows God with an intimacy that transcends both conceptual and imaginative representation. Some Christian mystics have explained that transcendence in terms borrowed from radical esoteric theology. But a more temperate rhetorical strain in Christian mystical literature characterizes unitive contemplative awareness as a knowing which is loving. When the love of God intensifies until it becomes one's primary way of knowing the divine, it supercedes both abstract and imaginative representations of the deity because they may or may not be loving and therefore may or may not unite us to God. To cling to images and concepts of God as an alternative to a loving, unitive knowledge of Him transforms concepts and images into idols.

In this second, more temperate rhetorical strain within Christian mystical literature, the abandonment of concepts and images for contemplative forms of knowing need not imply that the reality of God is essentially unintelligible but only that unitive knowledge of the deity surpasses knowledge that may or may not be unitive. This moderate strain within Christian mysticism remains open to an analogical approach to the divine mystery. It conceives God not as unintelligible but as supremely intelligible. It cheerfully concedes that the all-encompassing reality of God can never be itself encompassed in any finite image or concept. But it maintains nevertheless that images and concepts can reveal to us some truth about God, even though they do not guarantee that our perception of that truth will be a loving one. When, for example, the demons know the holiness of God and tremble, they live in no illusion. They grasp the reality of God truly but without loving it. Still, imaginative and rational insight into the supreme intelligibility of God need not lack all love. And when both true and loving, such insights become a charismatic propaedeutic to unitive contemplative awareness.

We must, then, conclude that a sound foundational approach to the triune God will follow the path of moderate Christian mysticism. For the divine experience does resemble analogically the finite experiences it has created. Were we to conceive the triune God as wholly other in the manner of radical mysticism, we would misconceive Him. We must, of course, eventually reduce any theological construct of God back to the divine mystery. But we must do so, not because the reality of God is unintelligible, but because it is all-encompassing and supremely intelligible, more intelligible than any finite construct of it.

(3) **Substantial Identity.** One important and influential attempt to understand the vital identity of the divine persons in rational terms was suggested by Augustine of Hippo. He maintained that Father, Son, and Breath enjoy an identity of life because they all possess one and the same divine substance. Augustine characterized the divine substance as invisible, unchangeable, and eternal (On the Trinity, III, xi, 21-22, IV, xix, 24). Because it subsists eternally, it differs essentially from mutable, created substances (Ibid., V. iii, 3-iv, 5). More to the present point, however, the divine substance functions as a principle of operation common to all three divine persons (Ibid., I, xii, 25). It grounds those vital traits all three possess. The divine substance is, for example, intelligent, volitional, eternal, immutable, immaterial. Shared divine characteristics are then predicated of the divine substance, while relational predicates refer to the divine persons (Ibid., III, xi, 21-22, IV, xviii, 21-23, V, v,1-xiv, 17, XV, i, 1-xiv, 23).

Much medieval trinitarian theology systematically reworks basic Augustinian insights. The Augustianian tradition provides as a result a useful historical laboratory for testing a particular trinitarian hypothesis. History suggests, however, that serious problems attend any speculative attempt to conceive the vital identity of the divine persons as their substantial identity.

For example, like the fathers of the church, medieval trinitarian theologians characterized the divine essence as simple.[4] Often enough the simplicity of God was merely asserted rather than argued. But belief in the divine simplicity rested on a number of identifiable philosophical presuppositions. With the Greek and Roman thinkers who inspired them, medieval theologians equated reality with immutability. Whatever changes they believed, is to that extent imperfect and unreal. Change was also assumed to result from internal complexity. As the supreme being, God had to be unchangeable. And the divine immutability seemed to preclude the possibility of internal complexity within God. The divine substance was, as a consequence, characterized as absolutely and essentially simple.

Unfortunately, however, essential simplicity would seem to preclude the presence of any kind of multiplicity in God including a multiplicity of divine persons. The problem arises because God's substantial characteristics express His nature or essence. An essentially simple reality lacks all internal distinction. It would seem to follow, therefore, that in a meta-physically simple God there cannot subsist three really distinct divine persons.

But if God is an experience rather than a substance, the need to conceive of Him as absolutely simple vanishes. The equation of experience and reality reverses many of the presuppositions of classical Greco-Roman philosophy. Experiences are processes. In a world of experiences, therefore, something enjoys reality to the extent that it is in process. Even the divine experience is a process, though not a spatio-temporal one. In a universe composed of processes, flexibility, the ability to change and adapt, cease to betray imperfection and become instead signs of vitality. The living God is supremely alive and therefore supremely flexible. Finally, in a world of experiences, complexity too ceases to betray imperfection. Quite the contrary, we measure the perfection of any experience by the extent to which it balances unity and complexity. As the experience of everything experiencable God enjoys supreme complexity. And the perfection of the divine experience demands that it be supremely integrated as well.

The Augustinian attempt to explain the vital identity of the divine persons as their substantial identity raises other problems besides that of reconciling the divine simplicity with the trinitarian character of the Christian God. The divine substance functions as a spiritual principle of operation common to all three divine persons. The divine substance possesses an intellect and a will which endow God with freedom and self-awareness. But an intelligent, volitional, free, and self-aware substance sounds remarkably like a fourth divine person. Augustine himself did not, of course, hold for a quaternity of divine persons. But the spectre of quaternity did haunt the attempt of his disciples to explain how a tripersonal God could be one.[5]

A third difficulty with a theory of substantial identity arises from the need to provide a causal explanation of the divine processions. The divine substance being a principle of activity common to all three divine persons explains those actions which the three perform simultaneously. Since the time of Athanasius theologians have agreed that the co-equality of the divine persons demands that in Their impact on creation, They all act simultaneously. An Augustinian substance could then conceivably explain divine activity directed toward some reality other than God.

But we must posit other activities in God. The Father alone generates the Son. Only Father and Son spirate the Holy Breath. In generation the Son and Breath do not act. And the Breath has no active part in Her efficacious spiration by Father and Son. A theory of substantial identity must then explain how a substantial principle of activity equally and perfectly possessed by all three divine persons can also explain activities performed exclusively by a single person or by only two persons acting in conjunction. For the substance provides the only principle of activity in the Augustinian Trinity. But to this problem the Augustinian tradition offers no satisfactory solution.[6]

There are, however, two further reasons why an Augustinian account of the divine unity remains unacceptable in the present context. We have conceived the divine reality as an experience. And in an experiential frame of reference the term "substance" in its classical definition simply does not function. Moreover, in an experiential frame of reference the closest analogue to the idea of "substance" is that of "self." The category "self," however, interprets not the vital identity of the divine persons but three distinct and autonomous divine realities whose vital identity with one another needs explanation.

(4) **Dynamic vitalism:** Christian trinitarian theology offers, however, speculative alternatives to a theory of substantial identity. One such alternative was formulated by Gaius Marius Victorinus. Victorinus began his theological career by replying to an Arian named Candidus. From the time of Justin Martyr, it had been theologically assumed but never proven that God's eternity meant that He can in no way change. Candidus used this assumption to discredit the possibility of generation within the Christian God. Generation is change, mutation, he argued. Since God is immutable and unbegotten, what is begotten and mutable is other than God. If, then, the Son is begotten He is a creature.[7]

Victorinus' replied directly: while we must exclude from the deity any notion that implies imperfection, the God whom Christians worship is not some static essence. He is powerfully, transcendentally alive. In such a deity there can indeed be a kind of motion. Not indeed the generation proper to creatures but an abiding, indestructible, welling up of divine life. Accordingly, in his explanation of the divine unity Victorinus avoids any mention of a substance common to the divine persons. He speaks instead of their vital identity. The Son is the activity (agere) of the Father; the Breath is the Father's conception, or mind (excogitatio patrica) (To Candidus, VII, 1-X, 37; Against Arius, I, 2. 1-4, 51. 19-52. 9, II, 1.57. 28-29).

Victorinus's dynamic vitalism is suggestive for two reasons. First, it avoids the problems raised by an Augustinian theory of substantial identity by refusing to interpret the **ousia** common to the divine persons as a substantial principle of activity. Second, in describing the union of Father, Son, and Breath as a vital identity, Victorinus's theological construct of the Trinity converges at a number of points with the biblical witness. In the New Testament, Father, Son, and Breath enjoy not an identity of substance but an identity of life. Moreover, in describing the Holy Breath as the conception of the Father, Victorinus seems to have grasped more clearly than Augustine that She is a noetic reality. And in associating the Son with the Father's activity, Victorinus seems to have grasped as well that Jesus is the one in whom and through whom the Father speaks and acts.

131

The limitations of his position Victorinus shared with most of the fathers of the Church. He endorsed the term **"hypostasis"**; but he failed finally to provide an adequate definition of what it means. As a consequence, his characterization of the Son as the Father's activity and the Breath as His conception falls short of full personhood. In the incarnation the Son confronts us as more than a divine activity. He is an autonomous, divine self who stands in an interpersonal, obediential relationship to the Father who sends Him and the Breath who illumines Him. Similarly, the Holy Breath is not just the conception of the Father. She is the divine interpretant, the autonomous source of divine evaluative response, a divine person in Her own right, and the ultimate personalizing principle in the Godhead.

But Victorinus points the way toward a defensible, foundational account of the divine unity. In order to explain how a tripersonal God can also be triune, one must show, not how it is possible for them to possess identically the same substance, but how three divine selves come to share not just vital similarity but an identity of divine life.

(5) **Mutual inexistence:** The Christian tradition offers a fifth account of the divine unity which is not only foundationally suggestive but enjoys a conciliar sanction (DS 1331). The theory in question also complements that of Victorinus and offers a hint of how the vital identity of the divine persons might be conceived. The position to which we refer was defended by John of Damascus (c. 675-c. 749). As we have already seen, John explained the unity of the divine persons as their mutual inexistence, their perfect and total compenetration within the Godhead, their **perichoresis**.

In his trinitarian use of the term **"perichoresis"** John seems to have regarded the coinherence of the divine persons not as the consequence but as the equivalent of their unity. **"Perichoresis"** signifies then the mutual indwelling (**hydrysis**) of the **hypostaseis**. They find in one another a mutual abode (**mone**).[8]

While the positions of Victorinus and of the Damascene suggest complementary and potentially fruitful lines of speculation, both need further elaboration if they are to provide a plausible account of the unity of a tripersonal God. But before we pursue their insights further, a sixth attempt to characterize the unity of the Christian God deserves our attention.

(6) **Tritheism:** As we have already seen, Richard of St. Victor espoused a social conception of the Trinity. He characterized Father, Son, and Breath as persons. And he attempted to understand Their relationship to one another on an analogy with human friendship. Richard, however, followed Augustine when it came to explaining the divine unity. The divine persons, he held, possessed identically the same substantial essence. His position remained, therefore, within the parameters of orthodoxy.

132

Joachim of Flora, who also lived in the twelfth century, spoke of the Trinity in similar social terms. But in contrast to Richard, Joachim believed that the divine persons differ substantially. He also held that they resemble one another the way that substances do: namely, that they are only similar. The unity of the divine persons was then for Joachim that of a collectivity. His position came to be known as tritheism and was quite correctly condemned at the Fourth Lateran Council (DS 803-808; Psalter of Ten Choirs, I, d.1; Commentary on The Apocalypse, Introduction, c.12).

Joachim's tritheism offers an heretical antithesis to modalism. Modalism sacrifices the multiplicity of the divine persons to Their unity. Tritheism sacrifices their vital identity to their multiplicity. Clearly, the truth about the divine unity lies somewhere between these two heretical extremes.

Our survey of constructs of the Trinity has, moreover, identified a certain number of speculative dead ends. We must avoid the extremes of radical esoteric mysticism. We must approach the divine mystery prayerfully and contemplatively. But we must seek to advance as far as we can in an inferential and imaginative interpretation of the revelation of God which we have in fact received. At the same time in an experiential construct of the Trinity we cannot self-consistently espouse an Augustinian explanation of the divine unity. Our account of the vital identity of the divine persons must also try to avoid some of the difficulties that attend a theory of substantial identity. More specifically, the divine persons should not be identified with a fourth, essentially simple reality. Nor should the unity of the divine persons be so conceived that it seems to be a fourth person. Our theory should also explain how the Father alone can generate the Son efficaciously and how the Father and Son alone can spirate the Holy Breath even though in Their impact on creation, the divine persons remain perfectly co-active.

Our survey of trinitarian constructs has also yielded two hints of the direction in which an explanation of the divine unity might advance. We must find a way of conceiving the vital identity of the divine persons which nevertheless preserves the personal autonomy that makes them distinct divine selves. We also need to understand better what it means to say that the divine persons exist in one another. And we must determine whether mutual inexistence provides something like an explanation of their vital identity.

The reflections of the preceding chapters have also sanctioned on the whole the legitimacy of attempting to understand the triune God on an analogy with human social experience. For not only does the term "experience" interpret the divine reality disclosed in the historical missions of Son and Breath, but the same historical self-revelation of God also demands that we acknowledge the tripersonal character of the divine experience. The history of trinitarian doctrine offers one important caution. Any social construct of the triune God must avoid the heretical extreme of tritheism.

133

In the present chapter we are trying to understand how a tripersonal divine experience achieves unity. Why do the three divine persons share an identity of life? We confess all three as perfectly and equally divine. All three are one and the same God. Let us begin to probe more deeply the social structure of human experience for whatever light it may shed on this complex theological question.

Human experience certainly needs integration at a biological, affective, intellectual, moral, religious, and socio-political level. And because human experience enjoys a relational and transactional structure, all five forms of integration, when achieved to any extent, advance through interaction with the other selves that constitute one's world. Some of those selves are persons. Inevitably, then, the human search for integration takes on the character of a social process.

No one hands integration to us on a metaphysical platter. We must achieve it from one moment to the next. Because human persons are finite, fallible, and sinful, the perfect integration of human experience remains an ideal that in this life we approach only as a limit. All too often we live at odds not only with other people but even with ourselves.

In the human search for integration, both our bodies and our histories function ambiguously. Both can effect social separation, division, and disintegration. Our bodies need constant maintenance. Competition for food, shelter, and the control of the physical supports of life suffuse society with violence and conflict. Physical separation can breed forgetfulness, indifference, the cooling of friendship, the death of love. Our histories insert us into different environments and contrasting social settings; and diversity of historical experience abides as a perennial source of social misunderstanding and confrontation. How easily class loyalty degenerates into class conflict! And cultural diversity will betray even the well intentioned into mutual misunderstanding.

But the conflicts born of physical separation and historical diversity can be transcended through mutual consent. Instead of squabbling over the physical supports of life, humans can if they choose collaborate to meet their common physical needs. Love, friendship, and mutual commitment can survive the test of physical separation. And patient, mutual commitment breaks down the social, cultural, and historical barriers that divide individuals and groups.

Neither physical separation nor historical diversity explains ultimately the disintegration of experience. Only dissent does, the conflict of adamant and irreconcilable decisions and commitments. Our environments crush, thwart, and oppose us when they ignore or contradict our own will to live. We torment ourselves when through contradictory decisions we build conflicting attitudes, beliefs, and aspirations into our personalities. We oppose, battle, shoot, shell, and bomb those who contradict us and our own vested interests.

134

Dissent fragments experience by denying, avoiding, excluding, or destroying some hated person or thing. Consent affirms, includes, welcomes, nourishes, integrates. Consent gives life, and mutual consent is mutually life-giving.

One of the primordial human instances of nurturing consent is a mother's care for the child in her womb. The mother's body forms the immediate environment from which the foetus draws its existence. Because they are physically bonded, their relationship comes closest to effecting the perfect mutual inexistence of two human persons. But we nurture life in one another in other ways as well: by tending the bodily and psychological needs of others, by the exchange of enthusiasms and insights, by sharing what we have and who we are. Moreover, through consenting acts of nurture we become part of one another. We exist in one another in life-giving ways.

The sharing born of mutual, nurturing consent intensifies the similarity between two human experiences. Children resemble their parents not only physically but also in their habitual responses to the world. Friends and spouses share the same minds and hearts through love. Teachers and students experience common enthusiasms, common view-points, common judgments about the world.

The corporeal character of human experience prevents human persons from ever sharing a perfect identity of life. You will never own my body. As a consequence, my history and the self that I am becoming will never be perfectly identical with the self that you are. But things stand otherwise with the divine persons. They suffer no physical separation, for the divine experience is eternal and all-encompassing. Moreover, as Victorinus saw clearly in the fourth century, the eternity of the Christian God is not static but vital. In God indestructible, interpersonal life wells up eternally.

The divine persons exist in one another. As long as western theology remained dominated by Aristotelian categories and by Augustinian patterns of thought, **perichoresis** lay in our theological attics, a term largely forgotten and unused. For while two substances can be intentionally present to one another, one does not normally speak of two substances interpenetrating one another or existing in one another. In a world of created substances, divine persons who are subsistent, interpenetrating relationships remained an anomaly. In the words of Boethius, Their reality was scarcely comprehensible.

But experiences can and do interpenetrate one another. For what is experienced stands within experience and makes it the kind of experience it is. When reality is understood as experience, **perichoresis** ceases to be the anomaly it once seemed and becomes instead the order of the day, the way in which any two interacting realities come to be what they are. In a world of experiences, the divine persons do not differ from creatures because

135

They alone experience **perichoresis.** Rather through Their mutual inexistence the divine persons enjoy an identity of life, while human persons being separated by their bodies, by their histories, and by their dissents enjoy only vital similarity.

The perfect mutual inexistence of the divine persons constitutes their vital identity. That identity of life we designate as the **"ousia"** that makes all three equally God. Moreover, if the divine experience bears an analagous resemblance to human social experience, one would expect its unification to result from the mutual consent of the divine persons to one another. Does the historical revelation of God we have received support such an hypothesis?

The Son's relationship to the Father was finally and fully revealed in His death and glorification. In death he gave himself freely and lovingly into the hands of the Father (Lk 23:46). His death crowned a lifetime of obedience to the Father's will.

If Jesus' death reveals in the starkest and clearest terms the Son's self-gift to the Father, the revelation of His resurrection can be legitimately interpreted as the disclosure of the Father's perfect gift of Himself to the Son. The risen Christ confronted the apostolic witnesses not only as Son and savior but as Lord, **Adonai,** the bearer of the Father's divine name, authority, and vitality (Ph 2:1-11).

The Son also gave Himself in love to the divine Breath. His self-gift to the Father was revealed in the perfection of His obedience to the Father's will. He was obedient to death, even death on a cross. But the Holy Breath relates to the Son as the divine principle of illumination Who revealed to the Son the will of the Father. In obeying the Father perfectly, He obeyed Her inspirations no less perfectly. In giving Himself to the one He gives Himself to the other.

The self-donation of the Breath to the Son was also revealed in His resurrection. For in His risen glory the Son confronts us as a life-giving **pneuma,** as so totally transformed in the divine Breath that they share an identity of life (2 Co 3:12-18). She also inspires the creative, providential wisdom of the Father; for Father and Son share the same mind (1 Co 2:6-16). She gives Herself to both Father and Son by enlightening Them.

The self-gift of the Father to the Breath is historically revealed in the fact that She is the saving presence of the Father as well as of the Son. He receives from Her sapiential enlightenment; She from Him, divine creative efficacy.

Finally, the perfect, mutual self-donation of the divine persons comes to historical visibility in this fact: that whenever one of Them speaks and acts in history, the others are perfectly co-present and co-active. Their mutual self-donation within the Godhead gives significance

136

to a standard principle of trinitarian theology: namely, that in the triune God everything is common except where a relation of opposition prevents. Relations of opposition within God result from the processions, for the procession of one divine person from another demands their mutual distinction. Self-donation is, however, not a relation of opposition but a unitive relation. It effects the perfect mutual inexistence of the divine persons and creates the identity of life that makes them equally divine. And there can be no relation of opposition between the divine persons and the life by which they live. Far from being only an abstract metaphysical principle, however, this old scholastic trinitarian maxim in fact describes the totality and perfection with which the divine persons give themselves to one another in selfless love.

In giving themselves to one another, the divine persons do not, however, loose Their autonomy, otherwise They would cease to be persons. Without autonomy They could initiate no activity at all, including procession, mission, and self-donation. For autonomy does not separate persons from one another; dissent does. Indeed, the fact that each person remains an autonomous center of activity within the Godhead justifies the appropriation to a specific person of divine activities in fact common to all three. The Father is justly called creator of heaven and earth because, even though all three persons act simultaneously in creation, the Father abides as the eternal source of spontaneous creative efficacy within the Godhead. The Son is correctly called redeemer and savior, because even though all three persons act simultaneously in the redemptive process, the Son alone became incarnate and saved us by His perfect obedience to the mission of the Father and the illumination of the Breath. The Breath is aptly called the source of gracious enlightenment because even though the Father and Son also act in the gracing of human experience, She abides as the eternal source of enlightenment within the Godhead.

Predicates which envisage the relation of the divine persons to one another are traditionally called notions. If the preceding reflections enjoy validity then in speaking of the triune God one must distinguish two kinds of notional predicates, those which envisage relations of opposition and distinction within the Godhead and those which envisage the mutual self-donation of the divine persons. The latter relations unite and give rise to the perfect mutual inexistence of the divine persons and to the identity of life which they enjoy.[9]

For example, the relation which distinguishes the Breath from Father and Son is traditionally called passive spiration. Her unitive relation to the Father, sapiential enlightenment; Her unitive relation to the Son, conception. For as the divine interpretant She is the mind of both: She is the Wisdom who guides the Father creator; She is the meaning of the Word He speaks. Similarly, the Father who efficaciously generates the Son and with Him spirates the Breath is united to both in a creative act of free-self-donation, while the Son is united to both the Father and the Breath in an obediential act of free self-donation that transforms Him into the one through whom They act.

Our theological construct for interpreting the divine unity then advances fairly straightforwardly. It argues that because God stands historically revealed as both tripersonal and triune, the unity of the divine experience cannot be the unity of utter simplicity. Complex realities are unified by their internal relational structure. The unity of the triune God is the identity of life which the divine persons enjoy. That identity of life is achieved by Their perfect mutual inexistence. And Their mutual inexistence results from Their perfect mutual self-donation to one another in the supreme perfection of selfless love. Finally, we have discovered in the analogy of experience a way of making both the mutual inexistence of the divine persons and Their identity of life thinkable.

At this point a critical reader might be inclined to interpose, "Just one moment my friend. Aren't you playing fast and loose with traditional Christian beliefs? Trinitarian theologians have traditionally held that the Father alone generates the Son and that the Son derives His being entirely from the Father. All this talk of the Holy Breath conceiving the Son seems to change all that. And it creates a terrible muddle. Instead of the Holy Breath proceeding from the Son as co-spirator with the Father, **He** now seems to proceed from **Her**. Aren't you putting the cart before the horse? If the Holy Breath proceeds from the Son, then must not the Son exist **before** the Holy Breath can proceed from Him? How then can **She** conceive **Him**? You've got it all backwards. Why don't you just admit that like every other trinitarian theologian you end by talking jabberwocky."

The objection is trenchantly put. And it deserves a reply. Our experiential construct of the Trinity demands that we understand procession as an efficacious process. In generating the Son, the Father gives rise to Him efficaciously. In the order of efficacy, the Son derives all that He is from the Father. But the Holy Breath functions within the divine experience as the divine interpretant. She gives rise to evaluative rather than efficacious responses within the Godhead. For that reason no one proceeds from Her. Her conception of the Word is an act of enlightenment. She does not generate Him efficaciously as the Father does. There can then be no question of His proceeding from Her.

Moreover, in speaking of God in experiential terms, we must exercise continual care not to project into the Godhead traits proper to spatio-temporal experiences as such. The divine experience subsists as an eternal process. We cannot then properly speak of a before or after either in the procession of the divine persons or in the eternal unification of the divine experience. Both the efficacious processions (which create the distinction of persons in God) and their mutual gift of themselves to one another (which creates their perfect mutual inexistence in an identity of life) occur simultaneously. We misconceive the divine experience, therefore, if we imagine the procession of the persons and their unification as a temporal succession. Under such a supposition, the divine experience would have to fragment first into three persons and then somehow come back together into a single divine reality. But the eternity of God excludes such a ludicrous conception. In other words, our experiential construct of the Trinity neither denies traditional Christian belief about the generation of the Son, nor does it offer a contradictory account of the origin of the divine persons and of their unification into a single divine reality. Quite the contrary, an experiential construct of the unity and trinity of God offers a plausible solution to an ancient and perplexing problem: namely, why does no one proceed from the Holy Breath? No one proceeds from Her because the divine interpretant functions as an illuminative rather than as an efficacious principle within the Godhead, while procession results from the autonomous exercise of causal efficacy.

If, moreover, we concede that the procession and mutual self gift of the divine persons occur simultaneously, then an experiential construct of the Trinity allows us to clarify somewhat the way in which the Breath proceeds from the Father and the Son. She functions in the divine experience as the divine interpretant, as the mind of both Father and Son. Human minds consist of complex and interrelated systems of habitual beliefs and attitudes. Habitual beliefs and attitudes are fixed and therefore created through decision. The mutual self-donation of the Father and Son within the Godhead fixes forever the evaluative shape of the divine experience, at the same time that the Breath's illuminating gift of Herself to Them motivates Their mutual self-gift and Their gift of Themselves to Her. In fixing efficaciously the evaluative shape of the divine experience, Father and Son give rise within the Godhead to the divine mind. In other words, they actively spirate the Holy Breath.

The fact that the divine experience is integrated through the perfect, mutual self-donation of the divine persons has three important consequences. First, it prevents Them from being persons in the same identical way that humans are. Second, it defines the evaluative shape of the divine experience. Third, it explains the divine unity. Let us reflect on each of these propositions in turn.

(1) **The divine persons are not persons in the same identical way that humans are.** Human persons think their own thoughts. Their minds advance or recede with independent self-awareness. But in God the Holy Breath is the mind of both Father and Son. The three divine persons enjoy the self-same omniscient consciousness.

Human persons must spend some vital energy on self-development and self-maintenance. Being spatio-temporal, human persons come into being and risk physical annihilation. The divine experience, however, subsists eternally. It had no datable beginning and will have no datable end. Being eternally self-existent, the divine persons need expend no vital energy on their self-constitution and self-maintenance. As a consequence, they are free to give themselves to one another with a totality that is inconceivable for humans.

139

Human persons can act independently to transform their world. Within the Godhead only the Father generates the Son; and the Father and Son together actively spirate the Breath. She, however, inspires Their understanding and insight. But because the divine persons enjoy an identity of life and are perfectly and mutually inexistent, when they act on some reality outside the Godhead they are simultaneously and perfectly co-active.

Humans think with spontaneous egocentrism. We imagine all too easily that because we are persons we define what personal existence ought to be. The same egocentrism causes us to speak of ourselves as persons and of the divinity as transpersonal. But the self-revelation of God as both tripersonal and triune pricks the inflated human bubble of personal self-importance. It challenges us to recognize in God the supreme exemplification of interpersonal experience. The divine persons exhibit a perfection of love and social generosity which we can only approach as a limit. Nevertheless, the social communion into which we humans are called by God reflects imperfectly and sacramentally the supremely perfect communion of the divine persons within the Godhead. By the same token, their mutual love is not utterly alien to the human love we know. In the mutual love of the divine persons we encounter interpersonal communion in its supreme perfection. For no union among persons could be conceivably greater or more intimate than one which effects total mutual inexistence and perfect identity of life.

There are important practical issues at stake here, issues we will attempt to explore in greater detail in subsequent chapters. For we become what we worship, since we worship what we value ultimately and absolutely. The way we understand what we worship will then have consequences for the kind of persons we become. Those who look upon God as a metaphysical monad flee society to dwell alone with the Alone. Those who look upon God as an inexplicable mystery to which one must blindly submit will see little relationship between the reality of God and day-to-day living. Those who believe in a vengeful God will preach holy wars. But those who look upon the reality of God as the perfection of interpersonal communion will discover the divine in community.

We Christians worship a mysterious God but not an alien mystery. The true mystery of God is the mystery of love lived in its supreme perfection. Our human love is blemished by defect. It is marred by egotism, distorted by neurosis, caged by limitation, paralysed by fear. Yet we do love. And when we love a triune God we are drawn individually and collectively into the supremely perfect communion of the divine persons, into the mysterious divine knowing that is loving, into the purifying fire of a divine self-gift so total that it effects the perfect vital identity of the divine persons and the death of every form of selfish human egotism.

(2) **The mutual self-donation of the divine persons defines the evaluative shape of the divine experience.** Within human experience

emotional reactions occur with a certain spontaneity. Joy and sorrow, disappointment and satisfaction, attraction and aversion, love and hate grip my heart unannounced. But my attitudes, my habitual ways of perceiving reality affectively are above all the fruit of decision. I learn to perceive the world with habitually loving eyes by performing the deeds of love. Those who live violently see with eyes that hate.

The divine reality is an experience with an evaluative shape. Its habitual attitudes may then be expected to be shaped by the transactions that structure it. Within the Godhead, however, we have discerned two kinds of activity: the efficacious procession of the persons from one another and their mutual self-donation in perfect love. Divine persons who give themselves to one another eternally in the supreme perfection of self-surrender can only experience one another lovingly. Their relations to one another can never be marred by the slightest trace of the negative feelings that divide human persons from one another. The eternal transactions of the divine persons display no shadow side, no egotistical selfishness, no neurotic defensiveness, no repressed violence, no guilty self-hatred, none of the coercive trauma that scars human social intercourse, no whisper of dissent. Moreover, in dealing with a sinful world the divine persons can never violate the love that defines the supreme perfection of the divine experience. Though we abandon Them, They can never deny Themselves by hating us. Divine love prefers, therefore, to suffer sin and its consequences rather than to stoop to vindictive retaliation. Such is the love Jesus preached. Such is the love with which He died.

Moreover, because God is an experience that perceives every reality lovingly, the Holy Breath functions as the simultaneous source within God of both enlightenment and of love. As we have seen, Augustinian trinitarian theology stumbled on this precise point by ascribing enlightenment to the **Logos** and love to the Holy Breath. The Bible, however, ascribes both to the Breath.

At the root of this theological blunder lies an inadequate psychology of love, one which fails to recognize that loving actions express loving perceptions. For like all decisions the deeds of love are specified by the evaluative processes they terminate. Love then does not reside in the will alone. It is an affection and therefore a way of knowing. As cognitive, love gives evaluative shape to an experience. It is an affective interpretant. In God it is conceived by the divine interpretant and expressed in God's creative and redemptive actions.

(3) **The mutual self-donation of the divine persons explains the divine unity.** We humans would succumb to arrogance were we to claim that we have comprehended God. Our "explanation" of the divine unity makes no such speculative claim. But it does attempt to interpret in human categories the historical revelation of God we Christians have been vouchsafed. As an interpretation of the Trinity it enjoys certain advantages. It is rooted in the analogy of experience. It appeals to the

human experience of mutual inexistence through social consent in nurturing love. And it discovers in God the supreme exemplification of such an experience, the perfection of that loving, interpersonal communion to which we are called as a Christian community.

But it might seem to some finally impossible to give oneself totally and simultaneously to two distinct persons. If we give ourselves to one totally, what remains to be given to the other? The very totality of the gift would seem to exclude a multiplicity of beneficiaries.

Human persons must select the objects of their love. The legitimate claims which family, friendship, and even religious and moral idealism make upon us force choices among the people who will be the recipients of our love. But we should not be too quick to project into the love of the divine persons limitations that are rooted in human finitude. Our selectivity in loving follows inexorably from our finite, corporeal existence. Our lives blend only at their circumferences. As separately embodied centers of life we can also withdraw socially.

But things stand otherwise with God. The divine love is infinite and all encompassing. Its character is revealed to us most clearly in Jesus. His loving obedience to the will of the Father was identical with His loving fidelity to the enlightenment of the Breath. In giving Himself to the one He did not withold Himself from the other.

Moreover, we ourselves experience in some measure this facet of the divine mystery. In giving myself to the Son in loving obedience I do not withold myself from the Father He proclaimed or from the Breath which He breathes into my heart. Nor can I truly give myself to God while witholding myself from those whom God loves. There is, then, a mystery in the self-donation of personal love which transcends the limitations inherent in the gift of some thing, some object, some bauble or prized possession. Our finite loves glimpse the mystery. And because we in some measure experience it, the mystery ceases to be utterly incomprehensible.

Our account of the divine unity raises, however, another difficulty. Jesus gave Himself to the Father and to the Breath by His obedience. That obedience was an act of decision. We have described the Holy Breath as the mind of God and of Christ. As such She functions within God as a principle of illumination rather than of decision. But how can an entity which is not a principle of decision give Herself at all? To give Herself to Father and Son, mustn't She decide to do so?

Once again we must be chary about projecting the limitations of human experience into the social life of the Godhead. The divine persons share an identity of life. Unlike human persons They cannot be complete persons separated from one another. The capacity of the Breath to give Herself to Father and Son is rooted, not in some habit of decision, but in Her power as a self to act. She acts within the Godhead as a source of illumination rather than of decision. As a consequence She gives herself to Father and Son by illumining Them. She gives Herself to them by being Their mind.

But if the divine persons give themselves to one another totally, what remains of the person once the gift is made? In the case of the Father the autonomy remains that constitutes Him the eternal source of divine creative efficacy, generator of the Son and co-spirator of the Breath. In the case of the Son the autonomy remains that makes Him the eternal source of obediential and redemptive efficacy and co-spirator of the Breath. In the case of the Breath the autonomy remains that makes Her the eternal source of divine illumination.

In an experiential approach to the unity and trinity of God one can, moreover, offer some reply to the objections raised by Barth and Rahner in their reluctance to call Father, Son, and Breath "divine persons." We legitimately distinguish three divine persons as facets of the divine experience. But They do not enjoy three distinct personalities because unlike human persons They enjoy not a mere similarity but an identity of divine life. Human personalities differ because human persons are separated by their bodies and by their histories. But the divine persons experience no physical separation and subsist eternally. And the perfection of their mutual inexistence ensures that in all things they act with identically the same mind and will. Nor does the fact that the divine persons possess autonomy necessarily lead to tritheism. For the divine persons use their autonomy to give Themselves to one another so totally that they are perfectly one, equally divine, and enjoy an identity of divine life.

There is, however, a sense in which the significance of the tripersonal life of God remains, as Rahner has suggested, hidden in the transcendent mystery of God. For while the divine and human experiences of interpersonal relationship manifest a certain number of analogies, human persons have no direct experience of what it would be like to share an identity of life with two other persons. The very existence of such an experience had to be revealed historically before it could be known as such. Nevertheless, in the perfection of their mutual love, Father, Son, and Breath exemplify the supreme perfection of interpersonal communion. And we humans become fully personal only to the extent that our finite loves approximate the eternal self-gift of the divine persons. If we speak of Them as "modes" we must call Them modes of interpersonal experience.

1. Elmar Klinger, "Modalism," in Sacramentum Mundi, edited by K. Rahner, et al. (6 vols.; New York: Herder and Herder, 1969), IV, pp. 88-90; J.N.D. Kelly, Early Christian Doctrines (London: A.C. Black, 1965), pp. 119-126.

2.   Juan Ochagavia, S.J., Visibile Patris Filius: A Study of Irenaeus'
Teaching on Revelation and Tradition (Rome: Gregorian, 1964), pp. 22-24;
L.W. Barnard, Justin Martyr (N.Y.: Cambridge, 1967), p. 34; Raoul Mortley,
Conaissance Religieuse et Hermeneutic chez Clement d'Alexandrie (Lieden,
E.J. Brill, 1973), pp. 8-13, 71-85; E.F. Osborn, The Philosophy of Clement
of Alexandria (Cambridge: Cambridge University Press, 1957), pp. 25-31;
Rolf   Goegler,   Zur   Theologie   des   Biblischen   Wortes   bei   Origenes
(Dusseldorf: Patmos Verlag, 1963), pp. 128-130.

3.   Hermann Dorries, De Spiritu Sancto: Der Beitrag des Basilius zum
Abschluss des trinitarischen Dogmas (Gottigen: Vanderhoeck and Ruprecht,
1956), pp. 121-124; Edward R. Hardy and Cyril Richardson, Christology of
the Later Fathers (Philadelphia: Westminster, 1954), pp. 138-159; Roger
Leys, S.J. L'image de Dieu chez S. Gregoire de Nysse (Paris: Desclee,
1957), pp. 3-55, 62-79.

4.   Ancius Manlius Severinus Boethius, The Trinity is One God, Not
Three Gods, I, II, 29-54, IV, 24-34; John Scotus Erigena, De Divisione
Naturae, III, 16; Anselm of Canterbury, Monologium, XVII, XXVII; Hugh of
St. Victor, De Sacramentatis, I, iii, 4; Richard of St. Victor, De Trinitate,
V, iv,V, xvii; Thomas Aquinas, Summa Theologiae, I, i, 3.5.

5.   In the twelfth century Gilbert de la Poirée (1076-1154) wrote a
learned commentary on Boethius's De Trinitate. In Boethius Gilbert found
a distinction made between a reality (id quod est) and that in virtue of
which the reality is what it is (quo est). He was accused of extending the
distinction to the Christian God. In effect Gilbert was accused of holding
that there is a reality in the Godhead called "God" distinct from "divinity,"
or that by which God is God. On such a presupposition, in addition to
Father, Son, and Breath and the divinity common to Them there would be a
fourth reality in the deity called "God." Gilbert denied holding any such
doctrine and seems to have defended himself successfully at the Council of
Rheims in 1148.   And indeed he probably taught that the distinction
between the quo est and the quod est applies only to created things and not
to God. Scholars, however, like Gilbert's own contemporaries have been
divided in their assessment of his position [Cf. M.A. Schmidt, Gottheit und
Trinität nach dem Kommentar des Gilbert Porreta zu Boethius De Trinitate
(Basel: Verlag fur Recht und Gesellschaft, 1956)].

The controversy evoked a guarded response from Rome. The pope
ruled that no reasoning about the trinity is "to divide nature and person and
that God should not be called the divine essence only in the ablative but
also in the nominative" (DS 745). In other words, not only should the three
persons be said to exist in a divine manner; They should all three be said to
be God.

Richard of St. Victor was also concerned to exclude quaternity from
God. But he wanted to deny a quaternity of persons within the Trinity
rather than to deal with the more abtruse issues that had worried Gilbert.
Characteristically, Richard's rejection of quaternity involved an attempt to

show that within the Godhead there are only three ways in which the divine love can be shared. Love, he argued, is either gratuitous or owed. The Father's love for the Son and Breath is utterly gratuitous, for He is Their source but proceeds from no one. The Son's love is owed to the Father from whom he proceeds, but it is gratuitous with respect to the Breath Who proceeds from Him. No divine person proceeds from the Breath. Her love is, therefore, owed to both Father and Son and non-gratuitous. Hence, the Father's love is gratuitous, His Son's is both gratuitous and owed, and the Breath's is simply owed. Since these three kinds of love exhaust the possible modalities of love, there can be only three ways of sharing divine love and therefore only three persons in God (De Trinitate, V, xv-xviii). The reader who finds these pious reflections less than logically coercive will, of course, be understandably pardoned.

Peter Lombard (c. 1100-c.1160) also flourished in the twelfth century and wrote one of the most successful theological textbooks ever penned. In medieval universities his Book of Sentences became a standard companion text to the Bible. Innumerable commentaries were written on it, some as late as the seventeenth century. In the first volume of his Sentences the Lombard had written that "the divine essence did not generate the essence. Since the divine essence is a certain reality that is one and supreme, if the divine essence generated the essence the same reality would generate itself, which is altogether impossible; but the Father alone generated the Son, and from the Father and Son proceeded the Holy Breath" (The Book of Sentences, I, d. 5).

Joachim of Flora (c. 1132-1202) was a Cistercian Abbot active in the latter half of the twelfth century. He was a prophetic figure whose writings influenced the spirituality of the Fratecelli. A visionary with a reputation of great personal holiness, Joachim showed less skill in tight rational argument. On the basis of the passage from the Sentences cited in the last paragraph, he seems to have decided that the Lombard had transformed the divine essence into a fourth reality in the Godhead distinct from the divine persons. He feared that in the process Peter had introduced quaternity into God and denounced him as an "insane heretic."

The Fourth Lateran Council (1215) vindicated the Lombard's orthodoxy. It also excluded quaternity from God on the basis of the fact that each of the divine persons is that "reality," "substance," "essence," or "nature" we call God (DS 803-804). The council also tried to introduce a measure of order into trinitarian speculation by canonizing a certain number of technical theological terms. It restricted the term "generator" to the Father, "generated" to the Son, and "the one who proceeds" to the divine Breath. And it denied that the divine essence generates, is generated, or proceeds. Technical terms are helpful. But the council left theologians largely in the dark as to how the unity of the divine persons is finally to be conceived.

6.   The problem begins to surface in the writing of Thomas Aquinas. In his Summa he argued that the divine intellect and will, both of which are

identical with the divine substance, are the powers within God which explain the generation of Son and Breath. He conceived the Son's generation as an act of the intellect, the Breath's as an act of the divine will. (Summa Theologiae, I, xxvii). But John Duns Scotus (c.1265-c.1308) grasped the implications of Aquinas's suggestion with the greatest clarity. Like Aquinas, Scotus thought in matters trinitarian like a systematizing Augustinian. With Augustine, Scotus discovered a vestige of the Trinity present in every human mind; for the mind is composed of memory, understanding, and will. With Augustine, Scotus used the triadic structure of the mind as a way of conceiving the unity and trinity of God. And with Aquinas he appealed to the powers of the divine substance as a way of explaining the divine processions. But Scotus seems to have sensed more keenly than Aquinas the difficulty of explaining the act of a single divine person or of only two of Them by appealing to a power of activity common to all three. He therefore distinguished an operative and a productive aspect of the divine memory. As an operative principle the divine memory causes the divine intellection common to all three divine persons. As productive, the divine memory gives rise to the **Logos.** Productive memory therefore resides in the Father alone, who is the sole generating principle within the Godhead. The divine will too has both an operative and a productive aspect. As operative it effects the divine love common to the three divine persons. As productive it is proper to the Father and Son, Who are cospirators of the divine Breath (Opus Oxoniense, 1, d. 2, q. 7, n. 18; 1. d. 12, q. 1, n. 2; 2. d. 1, q. 1, n. 9, 13). Scotus failed to explain adequately how in its operation the productive aspect of the divine memory and will could be proper to specific persons while in its operative aspect the very same faculty was common to Father, Son, and Breath.

7.   Gaius Marius Victorinus, Traites théologique sur la trinité, edited by Paul Henry with an introduction by Pierre Hadot (Paris: Editions du Cerf, 1960), pp. 23-27.

8.   Leonard Prestige, "**Perichoreo** and **Perichoresis** in the Fathers," The Journal of Theological Studies (April, 1928), pp. 248-249.

9.   We find a hint of this insight in the writings of Alexander of Hales (d. 1245). He saw that relationship is a potential source not only of distinction within God but of unity as well (Summa Theologiae, I, n. 64, ad. 4, n. 319, ad. 4, n. 330, ad. 4.). Jürgen Moltmann also seems to be groping his way to a similar insight in his distinction between "person" and "form" within the trinity. But he muddles matters terribly by associating the concept "form" with a misguided denial of the **Filioque.** Moltmann holds that the Breath proceeds from the Father of the Son but not from the Father and the Son, and that She receives Her "form" from both the Father and the Son. He defines the "form" of the Breath in the following terms: "When we talk about the **form** of the Holy Spirit, we mean his face as it is manifested in his turning to the Father and to the Son, and in the turning of the Father and the Son to him." (Moltmann, The Trinity and the Kingdom, pp. 178-187).

Moltmann's rejection of the **Filioque** seems to spring from a desire to enter into ecumenical dialogue with orthodox theologians. But it suggests serious theological deficiencies in his own position. With Karl Rahner he wants to coordinate his account of the immanent and the economic trinities (Moltmann, op. cit., p. 154). But had he understood clearly that the missions reveal to us the way the divine persons relate to one another and provide trinitarian theology with its only principle of verification, he would never had denied the **Filioque**. The fact that the Holy Breath is sent by the Son reveals to us that She proceeds eternally from Him. Moltmann's discussion of the **Filioque** ignores as well important aspects of the history of this controversy: that the Photian position rested initially on a serious misreading of Latin theology, that some of the Greek fathers speak of the Breath's procession from the Father through the Son, and that every attempt in the past to discuss this question ecumenically in council has led to the reaffirmation of the Latin position.

Moreoever, in the experiential construct of the Trinity defended in these pages, one may reply systematically to the key Photian objections to the **Filioque**. Let us reflect on those objections in turn.

(1) **If the Son can produce the Holy Breath within the Godhead, why cannot She produce the Son?** The Son functions as an autonomous principle of obediential efficacy within God. The Holy Breath functions as the divine interpretant, as an autonomous source of inefficacious, evaluative response. The Son can function as cospirator of the Breath because Her production within God is an efficacious act and because the Son, being perfectly obedient, does whatever the Father does, being perfectly one in will with Him. But the Breath cannot produce the Son because within God She acts as a source of conscious illumination rather than as an efficacious principle of production.

(2) **If there are two causes in addition to two processions within the Godhead must there not be composition in the deity?** This objection fallaciously presupposes that the Father and Son spirate the Breath as two independent principles. Moreover, one must distinguish the relations which give rise to the divine persons from the relations which unite them. The relations which unite them result from their mutual self-donation, a self-gift so perfect that it grounds the identity of divine life which They enjoy. The identity of life precludes composition in the deity. In addition, because Father and Son share perfectly the same will, in producing the Breath, She proceeds from Them as from a single co-principle.

(3) **What does procession from the Son add to the Breath that is not already contained in procession from the Father?** It adds Her ability to be historically revealed as the Breath of both Father and Son. For mission manifests procession.

(4) **Would not procession from Father and Son as from a single principle lead to modalism?** Modalism discovers that there is only one divine person in God who was historically manifested under the distinct modes we call the Son and the Breath. But the cospiration of the Breath

147

does not entail that Father and Son are one and the same divine person. For in the act of cospiration each functions autonomously and therefore as a distinct divine person. The Father spirates the Breath as Her aboriginal creative source within the Godhead; the Son, as an obediential principle perfectly one in will with the Father.

(5) **If the distinction of Father and Son as causes of the Breath is maintained, might it not lead to polytheism?** A polytheistic interpretation of the Christian deity would maintain that Father, Son and Breath are not three persons in one God but three distinct Gods. In fact, because the Breath is sent to us simultaneously by both Father and Son, She is historically revealed as proceeding from both as from a single co-principle perfectly conjoined. The fact that Father and Son co-spirate the Breath does not, however, negate the identity of life which all three divine persons enjoy, for that identity is grounded not in their procession but in the unitive relationship of mutual self-donation which unites the divine persons in a single divine nature.

(6) **If there are two causal principles within the Godhead instead of one why are there not three?** The procession of a divine person is an efficacious act. Because Father and Son function as efficacious principles within the Godhead, they can simultaneously co-spirate the Breath, one as creative, the other as obediential cause. The Breath, however, stands historically revealed in Her mission as the mind of God. As such She produces the divine evaluative response. Evaluations lure experience but effect nothing efficaciously. Hence, the divine Breath cannot function within God as the efficacious source of another person.

(7) **If the Father as a person causes the Breath, how can the Son who is hypostatically distinct from the Father also be Her cause?** The perfection of the Son's obedience to the Father allows Him to act in perfect concert with the Father without surrendering His autonomy.

(8) **How is it possible to predicate the same hypostatic property of two divine persons?** Predication is a logical act of the mind. It occurs within propositions when a predicate is referred to a subject. But every proposition is linguistic shorthand for an inference. And every inference is properly understood as the evaluative grasp of significant relationships. When we understand the "hypostatic property" we call cospiration, we grasp evaluatively how Father and Son relate to the Breath within the Godhead. That relationship stands historically revealed in Her mission. Since the Son sends the Breath in obedience to the Father, He stands toward her as an obediential source. Since the Father initiates the mission of both Sin and Breath, He stands toward Her as her aboriginal source. The doctrine of co-spiration does not predicate the selfsame "hypostatic property" of Father and Son, but differentiates the way they function in originating the Breath.

(9) **Because the procession of the Breath from the Father is divine, it is perfect. Hence Her procession from the Son can add nothing to it.** The procession of the Breath from the Son adds nothing to the divine perfection of the Father's act in spirating Her. But it does ground the possibility that

She could be sent historically as the Breath of both Father and Son. Since the Father grounds divine creativity within the Godhead while the Son grounds redemptive efficacy, did the Breath proceed from the Father alone, She could confront us as a divine source of creative but not of redemptive efficacy. For Her coming reveals the source from which She proceeds. But in Her historical mission She confronts us not only as the creative Breath of the Father but also as the redemptive Breath of the Son. She therefore proceeds from both.

(10) **Every perfection in the Trinity is either common to all three persons or proper to one alone. If then the production of the Breath is a property of one person, must it not belong to the Father alone?** "Cospiration" does not designate a qualitative perfection but a relationship of origin within the Godhead. How the divine persons relate to one another cannot, however, be deduced **a priori.** The knowledge of their interpersonal relationship within the Trinity we possess we must glean from their historical missions. Because the Breath is sent us simultaneously by both Father and Son, She is historically revealed as proceeding efficaciously from both as from a single principle. But her relationship to each within procession is not identical; for She proceeds from the Father as from an aboriginal, creative source and from the Son as an obediential redemptive source.

CHAPTER VII:

THE HOLY BREATH OF JESUS

We have not yet completed our task. We have elaborated a trinitarian construct that interprets major themes in biblical pneumatology. But a theology of the Holy Breath raises Christological questions as well. Because the Breath is sent us by both Father and Son, She confronts us as the Breath both of God the Father and of His Christ. Moreover, Jesus stands historically revealed as the messiah, as the Christ, precisely in His role as the Breath-baptiser in whom She dwells in eschatological plenitude, precisely as the one divinely sent to pour Her out on all flesh: Jew and Greek, slave and free, male and female.

An adequate pneumatology must then attempt to understand Her relationship to the Word incarnate. It must examine the ways in which the New Testament portrayed that relationship in narrative and image. But it must also deal with the abstract, speculative issues raised by the Christian tradition. Those issues divide into two sorts: Christological and trinitarian. We will not, of course, be able to treat the development of Christology in the same detail as the growth of trinitarian doctrine. But we must address those Christological issues directly related to a trinitarian theology of the divine Breath. We must probe the mystery of the incarnation, the hypostatic union in a single divine person of both divinity and humanity; for Jesus' relation to the Holy Breath flows from that union. We must ensure that our theological construct of the hypostatic union can be reconciled with our account of the Son's place and function within the divine experience. And we must attempt to understand the speculative implications of the major affirmations of the New Testament about the relation of the Son and Breath to one another within the Godhead.

To this complex set of issues we now turn. We shall find the New Testament witness making three interrelated affirmations about the action of the Holy Breath in Jesus: (1) As Son of God and Breath-baptiser, Jesus stood in an utterly unique relationship to the Holy Breath. (2) Because Jesus was a messiah in the image of the suffering servant, the Breath which proceeds from Him prolongs the divine judgment pronounced upon the world in His death and glorification. (3) Because the Holy Breath proceeds from the risen Christ, She enters the experience of the Breath-baptised as a principle of resurrection. Let us examine each of these statements in turn and reflect on their implications for Christian pneumatology.

(1) **As Son of God and Breath-baptiser, Jesus stood in an utterly unique relationship to the Holy Breath.** As we have seen, in the Old Testament the Holy Breath was experienced as an immanent source of divine enlightenment. That enlightenment found expression in both words and deeds. The prophets and wise men gave voice to the Breath. The divinely inspired leaders of Israel incarnated Her enlightenment in action.

151

Isaiah imagined Yahweh orchestrating the entire exodus through the Holy Breath He had imparted to Moses (Is 63:7-14). Though the Breath in question is sometimes interpreted as an angelic presence, the author insists in verse nine that the salvation of which he speaks was not effected by any angel or messenger but by the living presence of Yahweh Himself, a presence effected by His holy **Ruah.**

Moses ranks, of course, as the first and greatest of the inspired leaders of Israel. But the **Ruah** acted too in the judges and in some of Israel's anointed kings. Inevitably, then, as biblical writers reflected on the activity of the Breath, they were forced to wrestle with Her relation to Israel's social and political structures.

The question surfaces in the book of Numbers. Moses, exhausted with the burdens of leadership, asks Yahweh for relief. Accordingly seventy elders are chosen and made to stand around the tent in which the ark of the covenant resides. Some of the **Ruah** in Moses is then transferred by God to the seventy, including two tardy ones who had not made it to the tent. As a proof that the Breath of Moses has descended on them, they begin to prophesy (Nm 11:10-30; cf. Ps 106:33).[1]

The Deuteronomic tradition viewed inspired leadership in more individualistic terms. In the book of Judges, individual leaders arise sporadically. The **Ruah** raises up Othniel, Jephthah, Gideon, and Samson to save the nation in moments of crisis (Jg 3:10, 11:29, 6:34, 7:2, 13:25, 14:16, 15:15).[2] With the establishment of the monarchy, however, the **Ruah** reveals the ritually anointed king, first Saul and then David, as the individual prophetically chosen by Yahweh to wear the mantle of national leadership and authority (1 Sm 9:26-10:16, 16:13).[3]

It also fits the Deuteronomic pattern that the **Ruah** of leadership should pass from one individual to another. Joshua leads the conquest of Canaan enlightened by the breath of practical wisdom imparted to him by Moses (Dt 34:9).[4] More striking still is the story of the transfer of royal authority from Saul to David. The prophet Samuel under divine inspiration anoints Saul to be king of Israel. The prophet's act is confirmed by God when the **ruah** of prophecy descends suddenly upon Saul as Samuel had predicted it would (1 Sm 9:26-10:16).[5] The Breath of God remains with the new king until he disobeys the Lord. When Samuel anoints David to replace Saul, the divine **Ruah** departs from the ill-fated Saul and rests instead on David as an abiding presence (1 Sm 11:15, 16:23).

Although Solomon, David's successor resembled his father by his legendary stature, the manifest wickedness of most of the Hebrew kings disqualified them as plausible bearers of the divine **Ruah,** with the exception of the pious king Josiah. As a consequence, both hope and disillusionment shaped the attitudes of the prophet Isaiah as he contemplated the careers of the successors of David he had known. In the book of Emmanuel he had responded to the faithlessness of the wicked king

Ahaz by predicting the birth of another king whose name would be Emmanuel, God-with-us, so abundant would be the blessings his reign would bring. Hezekiah, who succeeded Ahaz, while an improvement on his father, was no Emmanuel. The prophet therefore spoke a second oracle predicting that at some indefinite future date a king would be born of Davidic stock who would be filled with such a plentitude of the divine Breath that he would effect an eschatological age of peace and blessing.

> There shall come forth a shoot from the stump of Jesse and a branch shall grow out of his roots. And the Breath of the Lord shall rest upon him, the Breath of wisdom and understanding, the Breath of counsel and of might, the Breath of knowledge and of fear of the Lord (Is 11:1-3).[6]

In a later age Trito-Isaiah would renew Jewish hope in the coming of an anointed liberator:

> The Breath of the Lord God is upon me, because the Lord has anointed me to bring good tidings to the afflicted; He has sent me to bind up the brokenhearted, to proclaim liberty to the captives, and the opening of the prison to those who are bound; to proclaim the year of the Lord's favor and the day of vengeance of our God, to comfort all who mourn...(Is 61:1-2).[7]

The Breath does more than enlighten the coming savior; She anoints him to be a royal leader. The anointed one will not merely foretell the coming of an era of peace and prosperity; he will in the power of the Breath effect a season of jubilee (Dt 15:1-18; Lv 25:8-12) in which the desolation and suffering of the past will give way to an era of reconstruction and renewal: "They shall build up the ancient ruins, they shall raise up the former devastations; they shall repair the ruined cities, the devastations of many generations" (Is 61:4).

Finally in the writings of Deutero-Isaiah the action of the **Ruah** is linked to the mysterious figure of the suffering servant. A prophetic figure inspired by the Breath, the servant atones tragically for the sins of God's people by his innocent suffering. As bearer of the divine **Ruah,** the servant will vindicate the cause of Israel and establish God's justice upon earth (Is 42:1-4).[8]

The New Testament proclaims the good news that Jesus fulfills these ancient Hebrew hopes and prophecies. He is the new Moses who brings into existence a new Israel by fulfilling the meaning of the Passover through His death and glorification, the Davidic messiah, the expectation and judge of the nations, the eschatological prophet in whom the plentitude of the divine Breath dwells, the suffering servant of the Lord, Who by His innocent death reconciles a sinful world to God. Jesus establishes His claim to all these titles through His death and glorification. The risen Christ baptises with the Holy Breath all those who believe in Him and thus effects liberation, reconciliation, and judgment.

The synoptic tradition attributes to John the Baptist the prophecy of the coming Breath-baptiser. In their accounts of the Baptist's ministry both Matthew and Luke sample important themes in his preaching. Mark shows less historical concern. In Mark John merely prophesies that one greater than Himself is coming who would exercise a more significant ministry than the Baptist's own:

> After me comes he who is mightier than I, the thong of whose sandals I am not worthy to stoop down and untie. I have baptized you with water; but he will baptise you with a Holy Breath (Mk 1:7-8).

The Baptist's prophecy gives no hint of who the "mightier one" will be or how he will effect Breath-baptism. But Mark's full theological intention in citing the Baptist's prophecy becomes quite apparent as the narrative unfolds.[9]

For Mark's account of Jesus' own baptism follows immediately after the Baptist's prophecy. And it discloses the true meaning of John's prediction.

> In those days, Jesus came from Nazareth of Galilee and was baptised by John in the Jordan. And when He came up out of the water immediately He saw the heavens opened and the Breath descending upon Him like a dove; and a voice came from heaven: "You are My beloved Son; with You I am well pleased" (Mk 1:9-11).

Jesus at the moment of His baptism is proclaimed by the voice from heaven as the "mightier one" John had foretold. And the divine **Pneuma** descends upon Him to inaugurate His public manifestation as the Breath-baptiser whom John expected.

In Mark the violent rending of the heavens at Jesus' baptism recalls the apocalyptic rending of the sky in Is 63:7 and 74:11. The rending of the heavens announces the end time. And from the riven sky the Breath descends to betoken that Her action in Jesus begins the last age of salvation.

The Breath descends under the sign of a dove. The Hebrews kept doves as pets, and the rabbinic tradition often spoke of Israel as God's dove, His pet, the object of His special delight and favor. The voice from heaven now announces that Jesus is the specially beloved of God, the incarnation and beginning of a new Israel.

The dove symbolizes the descending Breath of God. And the Breath hovering over Jesus' baptismal waters reminds us of the action of the divine **Ruah** at the first creation. There She blew over the waters of chaos to render them docile to God's creative word. Now She descends on Jesus that He might hear the voice from heaven and through docile obedience to God and to His Breath become the beginning of a new creation.

In Genesis the return to Noah's ark of a dove bearing an olive branch had signaled the ebbing of the flood waters. The waters had served as Yahweh's righteous instrument for expunging human sinfulness from the face of the earth. And their retreat foreshadowed a new covenant sealed between Yahweh and Noah, the one divinely chosen to found the human race anew. In his death and resurrection Jesus will become the new Adam, after having washed the world clean of sin and sealed the new covenant in His atoning blood.

The descent of the Breath upon Jesus also probably seeks to remind the reader both of Isaiah's prophecy of the coming of a virtuous king who would enjoy the plentitude of the divine **Ruah** and be a compendium of all the great charismatic leaders of Israel (Is 11:1-9) and of the prophecy of Trito-Isaiah that a messianic leader would one day appear to proclaim in the power of the divine Breath a season of liberation and of jubilee (Is 61:1-4).[10]

Finally, the voice from heaven informs Jesus that He is to be messiah in the image of the suffering servant described by Deutero-Isaiah. The voice combines two messianic texts. The first recalls Psalm 2: "You are my son; this day I have begotten you" (Ps 2:7). The psalm is a royal psalm and the verse in question addressed to the royal descendant of David. A promise of worldwide dominion follows. But in Mark the voice from heaven combines this allusion to the Davidic monarchy with the first verse of the first of the servant songs in Deutero-Isaiah: "Here is my servant whom I uphold, my chosen one in whom I am well pleased" (Is 42:1).[11] It comes then as no surprise to find Jesus in Mk 10:38 referring to His impending death as the completion of His baptismal anointing and as the ordeal awaiting any disciple who aspires to sit at His side in glory.

The other synoptics endorse and embellish these Markan images. In the infancy narrative which prefaces Matthew's gospel, the evangelist insists that Jesus was miraculously conceived of a virgin in the power of the Holy Breath (Mt 1:20).[12] Jesus' miraculous conception by the Breath underscores the uniqueness of His relationship to Her and excludes any adoptionist reading of Her descent upon Him at the time of His baptism. From the first moment of His conception Matthew's Jesus confronts the reader as both messiah and Son of God. His conception in the power of the Breath is both mysterious and miraculous. Matthew finds in the event a fulfillment of Isaiah's prophecy of Emmanuel, God-with-us. In consequence of His privileged relationship to the Holy Breath, the messiah will both incarnate and effect a new presence of God in the midst of His people.[13]

155

In both Matthew and Mark the Breath comes to Jesus under the sign of the dove to reveal that He is the object of God's delight and the beginning of a new Israel. But Matthew's Baptist prophesies that She will come to Jesus' disciples under the sign of fire (Mt 3:11). In the Bible fire symbolizes the holiness of God. It purifies those who believe in Him and consumes those who oppose Him in the flames of divine judgment. That the Breath will perform both functions is further suggested in the Baptist's promise that the messiah will act like a winnower. In Hebrew husbandry wind and fire winnowed the grain. Unwinnowed wheat was tossed into the air. The heavier grain was separated out and fell to the ground. But the chaff was blown away to be gathered up later and burned. Such would be the judgment effected by the coming Breath-baptiser.

Matthew does not describe Jesus' baptism by John, although he admits that it occurred (Mt 3:13, 16). Moreover, before the baptism happens the evangelist inserts a dialogue between Jesus and John in which the Baptist protests the impropriety of what he is about to do. "I need to be baptized by you," John objects, "and do you come to me?" (Mt 3:14) But Jesus brushes aside John's scruples with the assurance that their action will "fulfill all righteousness" (Mt 3:15). Jesus seemingly asserts that in submitting to John's baptism He is doing no more than any devout Jew would do.[14] But the evangelist may have intended Jesus' reply to connote a deeper meaning. The theme of "fulfillment" bulks large in Matthew's gospel: Jesus comes to fulfill the law and the prophets. His reply to John suggests therefore that He has also come to fulfill the Baptist's own prophetic ministry as well and to give new meaning to his baptism of repentance. And Jesus accordingly reminds John that what they are about to do is "only for the time being": an action acceptable only as a passing moment in a larger providential design.[15]

In Mark the voice from heaven addresses Jesus personally. Mark's account suggests that Jesus alone heard it. In Matthew, however, the voice speaks to the reader and through the reader to the world. But the message remains the same.

Luke, like Matthew, both endorses and embellishes the main lines of Mark's baptismal narrative. Luke too opposes an adoptionist reading of Jesus' baptism with the assertion that Jesus' very conception was effected by the divine **Pneuma**. At the annunciation the angel promises Mary "A Holy Breath will come upon you and the power of the Most High will overshadow you; therefore the child to be born will be called holy, the Son of God" (Lk 1:35). The angel's imagery has also been read as suggesting that the descent of the Breath will transform Mary into a living temple. Moreover, Jesus' designation as messianic Son of God has an eschatological ring: His miraculous conception (rather than His baptism) inaugurates the end time.[16]

All the other references to the Holy Breath in Luke's infancy narrative also look forward to Jesus' baptism at the Jordan. The Breath inspires Elizabeth to exclaim to Mary: "Blessed are you among women and blessed is the fruit of your womb; and why is it granted to me that the mother of my Lord should come to me?" (Lk 1:42) Later, Zacharias under the enlightenment of "a Holy Breath" prophesies that John's ministry will be conducted in the image of Elijah, whose return was supposed to foreshadow the arrival of the messiah. Both inspired sayings acknowledge the superiority of Jesus' messianic mission to John's prophetic one (Lk 1:67, 76). Finally, Simeon, the old man on whom "a Holy Breath rested" prophesies that Jesus is destined for a life of conflict. He will be "a sign of contradiction" and is destined "for the rise and fall of many" (Lk 2:34). Clearly, the multiple references to the divine Breath in Luke's infancy narrative are linked more or less directly to themes relevant to the meaning of Jesus' own baptism at the Jordan: the exclusion of adoptionism, the inauguration of the last age of salvation, the revelation of Jesus as messiah, the primacy of Jesus' mission over John's, the fact that Jesus was destined from the beginning to be a suffering messiah. Moreover, the abundance of Her inspirations at the time of Jesus' birth also foreshadows the eschatological abundance with which She will come on Pentecost. Her arrival at that time will fulfill the Baptist's prophecy of the coming of a Breath-baptiser (Cf. Ac 1:16, 2:30, 4:25, 28:25).[17]

In his account of Jesus' actual baptism by John, Luke drawing perhaps on the same primitive traditions about the Baptist as Matthew, adds the words "and with fire" to the Baptist's prophecy that one would come who would "baptise you with a Holy Breath" (Lk 3:16). For Luke as for Matthew, then, the Breath comes to Jesus to reveal Him as messiah, beloved of God and the beginning of a new Israel. But She comes to the community He will found in purification and in judgment.

Of the three synoptic evangelists Luke alone asserts that the Breath-dove descended upon the messiah "in bodily form (**somatiko eidei**)" (Lk 3:22). The phrase attenuates somewhat the apocalyptic tone of the narrative and transforms Jesus's vision into a semi-miraculous event. But the words seem to lack any further theological significance.

Moreover, Luke states that Jesus' messianic commissioning in the power of the Breath occurred only after John had finished baptising and while Jesus was at prayer (Lk 3:21). Matthew and Mark both place the vision immediately after Jesus emerged from the water (Mt 3:16, Mk 1:10). Very likely Luke separates Jesus' vision and the descent of the Breath from the event of the baptism itself lest his readers misinterpret John's baptism as the cause of Jesus' messianic anointing. But he may have also desired to parallel the descent of the Breath upon Jesus with Her descent on the disciples at Pentecost (Ac 1:14, 2:11). Both events seem to have occurred during prayer.[18]

In contrast to the synoptics, John the evangelist omits any reference whatever to the fact that John did indeed baptise Jesus. Instead he suggests that Christian baptism was foreshadowed in a baptism of repentance similar to John's which Jesus Himself administered for a time and which His disciples continued to use after Jesus Himself had abandoned it (Jn 3:22-23, 4:1-3). As a consequence John the Baptist enters the pages of the fourth gospel not as Jesus' baptizer but as the one sent by God to bear witness to His Son.

As we have seen, in Luke's account of Jesus' baptism, the dove descends on Jesus in a physically visible manner. In the fourth gospel, the descent of the Breath is witnessed by the Baptist. How the Baptist came to see the Breath descend remains obscure. But the vision leaves the Baptist with no doubt that Jesus, not himself, is God's Chosen One (Jn 1:31-34).[19] As a consequence, the Johannine Baptist shows none of the hesitations about Jesus and His mission displayed by the Baptist of the synoptics. Rather, John's Baptist confesses only that, prior to the descent of the Breath, he himself was ignorant of the fact that Jesus was indeed God's Chosen One.

Moreover, in what may be a theological gloss on the Baptist's final witness to Jesus, the evangelist insists that the **Pneuma** descends on Jesus as an abiding presence in order to empower Him to impart Her to others. For She dwells in Him "without measure."

> He who comes from above is above all; he who is of the earth belongs to the earth, and of the earth he speaks; He who comes from heaven....bears witness to what He has seen and heard, yet no one receives His testimony; he who receives His testimony sets his seal on this, that God is true. For He whom God has sent utters the words of God, for it is not by measure that He gives the **Pneuma**; for the Father loves the Son and has given all things into His hand. He who believes in the Son has eternal life; he who does not obey the Son shall not see life, but the wrath of God rests on him (Jn 3:31-36).

Is it the Father who gives the Son a measureless portion of the divine **Pneuma**? Or does the Son pour forth the Breath in measureless abundance? Both meanings are possible, and perhaps both intended. In either case Jesus alone in virtue of His heavenly origin and unique dignity as Son of God has access to the divine Breath in measureless plentitude either as Her vessel or Her wellspring. Not only, then, does the divine Breath abide with Jesus; She dwells in Him as an inexhaustible source of life.[20] And She abides as the source of His testimony concerning God. Consent to that testimony in faith, to the truth that is God, opens the gateway to eternal life (Jn 3:5-8).

In a private conversation with Nicodemus, John's Jesus subsequently insists:

Truly, truly, I say to you, unless one is born of water and **Pneuma**, he cannot enter the kingdom of God. That which is born of flesh is flesh, and that which is born of the **Pneuma** is **Pneuma**. Do not marvel that I said to you "you must be born anew." The wind (**pneuma**) blows where it wills, and you hear the sound of it, but you do not know whence it comes or where it goes. So it is with everyone who is born of the **Pneuma** (Jn 3:5-8).

"Breath" (**Pneuma** without the article) functions, as we have seen, as a generic term for the life common to Father, Son, and Advocate. "Breath" designates life from above, "flesh" designates life from below. The life from above is divine, abiding, eternal; the life from below is human, fragile, deathbound. "The Breath" (**Pneuma** with an article) gives birth to "Breath." Who is this Breath? Who but the divine **Pneuma** who has descended on Jesus and dwells in Him in immeasurable plentitude.

By conceiving **Pneuma** in those who believe, the **Pneuma** effects rebirth from above and is revealed as a principle of divine regeneration. Moreover, because the **Pneuma**, like the Son in whom She dwells comes from above, those from below cannot comprehend Her origin and dynamic movement. Those born of the **Pneuma** are swept along by Her impulse. But for John as for Paul the precise shape of the salvation which is dawning remains obscure even for believers.

John's account of Jesus' divine commissioning to be Breath-baptiser differs in certain respects from the synoptic tradition. John's failure to include in his gospel an account of Jesus' baptism lends a different flavor to his description of Jesus' relationship to the Breath. The witnessing Baptist in the fourth gospel does call Jesus the Lamb of God (Jn 1:29, 35-36), designating Him at one and the same time as the victorious messiah of apocalyptic literature, as the lamb of paschal sacrifice, and as the suffering servant who goes to his death with the meekness of a lamb. But we do not find in John's gospel the same rich clustering of theological images with which the synoptics surround Jesus' baptism. We find no rent heavens, no descending dove, no voice from the sky. In the fourth gospel as in the synoptics, the Baptist designates Jesus as the Breath-baptiser (Jn 1:33). In addition, however, the fourth gospel also insists that entry into the kingdom is effected by baptism in water and the Holy Breath. Like the synoptics the fourth evangelist recognizes that Jesus' relation to the Breath is charged with eschatological significance. Jesus mediates Her outpouring in eschatological abundance. Moreover, John insists more explicitly than the synoptics that She dwells in the Son as an abiding source. Despite superficial differences we find then a clear convergence between the Johannine and the synoptic traditions in their understanding of Jesus' relationship to the Holy Breath.

Moreover, in the New Testament witness to Jesus as Breath-baptiser we can identify three distinct but interrelated doctrinal strains. The title "Breath-baptiser" tells us something about the scope of Jesus' mission and His relation to His disciples. It also tells us something about His relation to the Father. And it suggests the uniqueness of His relation to the Holy Breath. Let us reflect briefly on each of these doctrinal strains.

The title "Breath-baptiser" points to Christian baptism as an eschatological event: through it the believing Christian enters the last age of salvation, the season of jubilee inaugurated by the incarnation, death and resurrection of Jesus. The risen Christ is the first-born of a new creation. And those baptised in the Holy Breath stand united to Him in His risen glory. The Christian baptismal covenant, therefore, transcends and fulfills the baptism of repentance proclaimed by John. It establishes a saving bond between the Christian community and the risen savior. Through their baptismal experience, Christians enter into the Passover of the Lord: they experience a new exodus, a decisive liberation. They are incorporated into the new Israel. They are twice born of water and Breath. But they can also expect to be drawn into the mystery of the Passion of Jesus. Moreover, they encounter the Breath of Christ both as a source of purification and as a judgment upon human sinfulness.

In confessing Jesus as Breath-baptiser, the Christian community also asserts something about His relation to the Father. Jesus alone has power to baptise in the Holy Breath because He alone is the sinless Son of God. The Holy Breath comes to Him neither in purification nor in judgment but only to reveal Him as the Father's beloved Son. The Son incarnates the living presence of God. He is Emmanuel, God-with-us. Through His virginal conception in the power of the Breath, He transforms Mary into a living temple, the dwelling place of God. His revelation to us as Son is accomplished in His obedient fulfillment of the mission He received from the Father through the illumination of the Breath. He is sent to be messiah in the image of the suffering servant, to proclaim the forgiveness of sins and accomplish it by His atoning and innocent death upon a cross, and to bring into existence a new Israel baptised in His Holy Breath.

The gospel proclamation of Jesus as Breath-baptiser also asserts something fundamental about His relation to the Holy Breath. As Son of God and Breath baptiser, Jesus stands in a very different relationshp to Her from His disciples. They must be born again of water and Breath. Sinners recreated in the image of God's incarnate Son, they must either be purified by Her Pentecostal fire or consumed in the flames of the divine judgment She effects. But Jesus, the innocent servant of God has a very different experience of Her enlightenment. He knows Her instead as the one who reveals to Him the full scope of His relation to the Father. The sinless Lamb of God, He needs no purification. Nor does He stand under the divine judgment. Instead, He pronounces it in obedience to the Father's will. His disciples are twice-born, but the Breath-baptiser is not. His sinlessness demands that His relationshp to Her begin at the moment of His conception. He knows Her therefore as an abiding source of empowering enlightenment. That She dwells in Him in eschatological fullness is revealed in the gracious transformation of all those who confess the risen Christ as their savior and Lord.

Does the foundational pneumatology developed in the preceding pages provide us with a way of interpreting these basic biblical insights and images? We approach the triune God is experientially. We seek to discover the experiences that ought to lie at the basis of Christian doc-trinal assertions. And we understand every reality, including that of the Christian God as an instance of experience.

We should also attempt to understand Jesus' relation to the Holy Breath no less experientially. Can we then understand the incarnation of the divine Word and His relation to the Holy Breath in experiential categories?

In 451 a.d. the Council of Chalcedon defined the doctrine of the hypostatic union. It asserted that the incarnate Son of God is both fully divine and fully human and that in Him the divinity and the humanity do not blend in order to form some third reality. Instead, they are two natures (**physeis**) united in a single entity (**hypostasis**).[21]

When these insights of Chalcedon are reformulated in the language of experience, the results are illuminating. In a world of experiences, everything exists in God naturally, graciously or sinfully. The incarnation effects the gracious transformation of the Son's human experience. But because of the analogy of experience, that transformation need not have been accomplished in exactly the same way as ours. In point of fact, it was not. We Christians are graciously transformed in the Holy Breath of God. But Jesus was graciously transformed in the **Logos.**

The divine Breath functions within the Godhead as a principle of illumination. She is the divine interpretant, the source of God's evaluative responses. Evaluative responses, however, lack all efficacy. They lure experience. They invite decisions. But they do not effect them. Those therefore who are graciously transformed in the Holy Breath of God are wooed by Her rather than ruled by Her. Our response in faith to Her divine invitation remains as a consequence autonomous, free, and interpersonal.

But things stood otherwise with Jesus. He was graciously transformed in the **Logos,** the Son. And the Son stands within the divine experience as a principle of obediential efficacy. By this we do not mean that the Son's human experience did not stand in a graced relationship to the Breath, only that its relationship to the Breath results from its transformation in the Son. As a principle of obediential efficacy the Son rules His human experience decisively in ways that ours are not divinely ruled. Indeed, the biblical witness provides evidence for saying that the

161

Son so ruled His human experience that it ceased to enjoy the individual autonomy that other human experiences enjoy. It remained constituted of the same generic kinds of qualitative, factual, and legal variables that shape other human experiences. But the laws that shaped the human experience of the Son did not function in exactly the same way as the laws that shape other human experiences, because, being ruled by the **Logos**, they lost their capacity to function autonomously. The biblical witness provides warranty for such an inference. In all the gospels, Jesus nowhere acts and speaks as a human person who stands in an autonomous interpersonal relationship with the Son of God but as the Son of God Himself. The Son certainly enjoys an interpersonal relationship with the Father. But Jesus enjoys no interpersonal relationship with the Son. Whenever He speaks and acts, He speaks and acts **as Son.**

Here we should recall that the laws which shape experience can function either autonomously or not. Autonomy consists in the ability to initiate decisive or evaluative response. Only those experienced laws which function autonomously deserve to be called selves. And only those selves which enjoy responsible and responsive social self-awareness qualify as persons. When autonomy vanishes, so too does the ability to say "I" and with it the ability to exist as an independent self, as a person. For autonomy, as we saw in Chapter II, constitutes an indispensable diagnostic trait of personal existence.

One of the most serious objections to the doctrine of the hypostatic union is that it attempts to unite in a single person two incommensurate natures: one finite and created, the other infinite and divine. But as soon as Jesus' divinity and humanity are understood as experiences, that particular problem vanishes. The divine experience enjoys infinity because it contains everything and is contained by none. The infinity of the divine experience follows, in other words, from its supremacy. As supreme, God experiences everything conceivable. As a consequence, everything exists in God, and nothing exists outside of Him.

Panentheism also grounds remotely the possibility of our gracious transformation in God. For one must first exist in God naturally if one is to be graciously transformed in Him as well. But a human experience need not be perfectly commensurate with the divine in order for it to be graced. The gracing of a human experience demands only the ability to consent to God in faith. The gracious transformation of a finite experience in an infinite, divine one implies, then, no incompatibility between them.

Moreover, the analogy of experience allows for the possibility that not every human experience will be graciously transformed in God in exactly the same way. Only those human experiences directly and immediately transformed in the Holy Breath retain their autonomy, for She functions within the Godhead as a source of evaluative rather than of decisive response. The Son, however, functions within the Godhead as an

162

omnipotent source of causal efficacy. Any human experience transformed in Him forfeits its autonomy in being ruled efficaciously by Him. In losing its autonomy it ceases to be a human person without ceasing to be a human experience. Rather its human actions and choices become those of the Son of God Himself. In other words, if one is willing to conceive the triune God as an experience, the hypostatic union becomes less of a metaphysical conundrum than it once seemed to be. It becomes instead an unavoidable, practical consequence of the manner in which the Son functions within the divine experience.

But if the Son's human experience is ruled efficaciously by Him, must it not forfeit its freedom? Here the distinction between autonomy and freedom made in Chapter II begins to assume Christological importance. Freedom is an aspect of the evaluative shape of an experience: it consists in the ability to act or not to act, to do this rather than that. It therefore roots itself in the ability to distinguish action from inaction or this kind of activity from that. Because it is measured by the degree of evaluative differentiation present in any experience, freedom, like consciousness, flickers. It knows more or less.

Autonomy, by contrast, consists in the capacity to initiate evaluative or decisive responses. Unlike freedom autonomy knows only either-or, never more or less, in this sense: that my heartbeat, my gestures, my digestive processes, my words, my thoughts, affections, loves, hates, and deeds are never more or less mine. They are either mine or someone else's. Because autonomy roots itself in habit and because habits develop and decay, one may speak of an apparent development in autonomy in this sense: that with the growth of new habits, I acquire new ways of functioning autonomously. But the development in autonomy is only apparent. When I acquire a new habit, I become more skilled but not more autonomous. In the exercise of my newfound skill, the action initiated remains always either my own or someone else's.

Every autonomous human response is more or less free. But not every free human response need be autonomous. The free human choices of the Son of God constitute the exceptional case that proves this rule. The Son's human experience could be efficaciously transformed in the **Logos** without loss of freedom because freedom and autonomy inhabit different provinces of experience. Freedom inhabits the realm of quality; autonomy, that of law. The suppression of autonomy does not alter the free quality of a choice; it only makes it the free choice of someone else. Had the Son's human experience retained its autonomy, His acts would have been those of a human person. But because His human experience is efficaciously ruled by His divine person, His free human choices become the free human choices of God's incarnate Son. But His human decisions continue to enjoy the same kind of freedom as the choices of human persons in that they proceed from a more or less conscious, differentiated sense of possible alternatives of action.

These insights into the Christological consequences of our experiential construct of the Trinity also illumine the uniqueness of Jesus' relation to the Holy Breath. And they cast light on the character of the experiences that lie at the basis of a Christian confession of the hypostatic union.

Matthew and Luke both teach in their infancy narratives that Jesus from the first moment of His conception stood in a positive relation to the Holy Breath. The New Testament witness also insists at several points that Jesus was sinless. These two affirmations illumine one another. The belief that Jesus was sinless was not the result of a statistical survey of the moral quality of His human acts undertaken in the apostolic church. It followed inexorably from His revelation as Savior and Lord. The one who saves cannnot Himself be a sinner in need of salvation. Nor can the Lord commit sin.

Matthew's and Luke's repudiation of adoptionism can be similarly interpreted. If Jesus had begun to be Son of God only at His Jordan baptism, we may be morally certain that up until that moemnt His human experience would have resembled other human experiences in being more or less sinful, more or less morally compromised, more or less selfishly egotistical. Instead of being our redeemer, He would Himself have needed redemption.

The action of divine grace does not rule us decisively; God woos us persuasively, like a lover. To respond autonomously to divine grace, we must recognize it as such. Grace, therefore, enters our experience as an impulse that we can not only resist but utterly ignore, an impulse that we must also be educated to recognize.

But Jesus did not need to recognize divine grace consciously in order to respond to it. His human experience was transformed decisively in the **Logos,** not persuasively in the Breath. Grace was worked efficaciously in Him in ways that it is not worked in us. More specifically, we cannot claim to stand in a graced, life-giving relationship with God from the first moment of our existence. As foetuses we are simply incapable of conscious religious acts. As a consequence we are born in the state called original sin. For the situation into which we are born is marred by sinful forces that stand within experience and mold our attitudes efficaciously in both conscious and unconscious ways.

In order to stand in a gracious, life-giving relationship with God we therefore need to be justified. We are justified when we pass from a state of nature marred by sin to a state of grace. That passage is effected by faith in the divine forgiveness revealed in Jesus. Even after our justification we remain vulnerable to the sinful forces that shape us as experiences. But after we are graced, we feel such impulses as concupiscence. They are not our own personal sins, but they come from sin and lead to sin.

Our conscious faith floats on a sea of unconscious attitudes. And in that sea glide monsters with sharp, rending teeth. Their names are rage, fear, and guilt. Our path to gracious enlightenment leads therefore through repentance. For we must surface the monstrous things within us and allow the grace of God to dissipate their terror and teach them the playfulness of Leviathan.

But because the gracing of Jesus' human experience proceeded efficaciously rather than persuasively, even His unconscious decisions were ruled from the first by the **Logos** and hence were untainted by sin of any sort. He therefore would never have felt the need to repent. Between His conscious and unconscious decisions loomed no yawning gulf of fear. The human decisions which shaped His human growth were so governed by the Word that they remained impregnable to every impulse of evil whether conscious or unconscious. At no point then did Jesus need justification. And at no point did the sinfulness of His situation shape the character of His choices. Never, therefore, was His religious situation the one we call "original sin." Nor did Jesus know concupiscence. "Concupiscence" designates those forces in the situation of the graced believer that come from sin and lead to sin. Sinful forces enough surrounded Jesus. But because Jesus was efficaciously transformed in the **Logos** from the first moment of His conception, His every human decision was guided by the will of the Father and the illumination of the Holy Breath. At no point therefore did the forces of evil that Jesus encountered lead Him to sin.[22]

The relation of the Father to the Son within God is traditionally called generation; for the Son experiences the Father as the aboriginal, efficacious source of divine life. The unitive relation of the Breath to the Son is, as we have seen, called conception; for She conceives within God the saving wisdom the Son proclaims. All persons, whether divine or human, are relational realities. Hence, the Son's human experience of His own divine person, whether conscious or unconscious, was from the first the experience of being generated by the Father and conceived by the divine Breath. As a consequence, She dwelt in Him in eschatological abundance.

Nevertheless, Jesus' human decisions were, like our own, conditioned. His human consciousness, like ours, flickered. In any given situation His human options remained limited. His human perspective on Himself and His world was finite, though expanding. So too was His ability to conceive and explain to others who He was and what He had been sent to do or to suffer. But He never knew the moral and emotional paralysis born of unrepentance. Angry He could have been and was, but never vindictive. Apprehensive, even fearful, but never neurotically rigid. Nor could He have known gnawing guilt or morbid self-hatred. Loving obedience to the Father and to the Breath must have come as instinctively to Him as egotistical self-serving too often comes to us.

165

Jesus the man would have been realistically aware of His human limitations. He could know surprise or disappointment. Some things He ignored altogether. He would have thrilled to the excitement of learning. Nor would He have comprehended from the first the full implications of His relationship to the Father and to the Breath. His passion to obey Them may even on occasion have left him humanly bewildered. Indeed, the gospel narratives suggest that only after His baptism by John did His personal self-awareness mature into a driving sense of mission.

Jesus' Jordan experience focused and reintegrated the human experiences He had known up to that point: parental and familial relationships, religious upbringing, personal friendships, poverty, labor, the beauty of the Palestinian landscape, the oppression of Roman rule, synagogue worship, Jerusalem pilgrimages, temple cult, the Torah, the prophets, the writings of the Hebrew sages, a growing awareness of the religious and political movements of His day, the preaching of the Baptist. But at the Jordan these experiences were transmuted and refocused by a creative impulse stemming from the Father and illumined by the Breath. Together they led God's obedient Son to a new human clarity concerning both the Father's will and the meaning and purpose of His own life.

The gospels give us solid evidence for affirming that Jesus was a man of prayer. Not only did He attend synagogue worship, but He also seems to have been drawn to personal prayer. He addressed God spontaneously with the familiar term **"Abba** (Papa)." He also sensed, as we have seen, that His personal relationship to **Abba** was distinctive. For although He invited His disciples to become children of God, in speaking of His own relation to the Father He seems to have used only the first person singular. He spoke of My Father and of your Father; but He did not join His disciples in saying "our Father," even though He instructed them so to pray.[23]

The gospels also give us reason to believe that Jesus' sense of being Son of God in a personally distinctive way resulted from His conscious openness to the divine Breath. Moreover, in a subtle and complex way, Her presence to Him endowed His religious self-awareness with an eschatological character. Through Her empowering inspiration He claimed to cast out demons. He seems moreover, to have felt that the eschatological reign of God He proclaimed was already being established on earth though Her action in Him. Accordingly, while the Baptist preached an immanent divine judgment, Jesus announced a joyful end time already in process of realization, even though its final fulfillment still lay in the future.[24]

Needless to say, these germinal Christological insights need further elaboration and more systematic justification. Such an elaboration is in process of preparation. But a detailed examination of the issues raised by the development of Christological doctrine lies beyond the scope of this book. Our focus remains pneumatological. But it certainly lies within the purpose of the present study to note in passing that an experiential construct of the hypostatic union offers a promising approach to a number of Christological problems, as well as an orthodox alternative to the sometimes heterodox Christologies emerging from American process speculation.

(a) An experiential construct of the hypostatic union offers a way of thinking the perfect interpenetration of the human and the divine in Jesus without blending them together into some third kind of reality. God's experience of the world does not cease to be divine because it experiences finite, created realities. Nor does the Son's divine experience of His humanity cease to be divine simply because He experiences something human. By the same token, the Son's human experience does not cease to be human because it is the human experience of being a divine person. Not only, then, does an experiential Christology sanction the attempt of John of Damascus to extend the idea of **perichoresis** to the hypostatic union, but it also offers a contemporary set of philosophical categories which render the mutual interpenetration of the divine and the human in Jesus thinkable.

(b) An experiential construct of the hypostatic union frees Chalcedonian teaching from the abstractness with which it was originally formulated. Instead of speaking of the simultaneous presence of two natures in the same entity, an experiential Christology would attempt to understand the dynamic development of the Son's human experience of Himself and its gracious transformation in the divine experience. The language of the Bible is not only concrete but richly experiential. An experiential Christology would, then, also seem at first blush to give promise of being able to account better than the abstract Christology of Chalcedon for the images and insights that give meaning to the biblical witness to Jesus.

(c) An experiential construct of the hypostatic union also provides a theological context in which to reconstruct Jesus' human psychological development. The success or failure of such a reconstruction must of necessity be conditioned by the limited nature of the evidence we possess. The gospels by and large make no attempt to paint a psychological portrait of Jesus. But the "new quest" for the historical Jesus has yielded some important insights into the shape and scope of His religious exper-ience, insights which an experiential construct of the hypostatic union ought to be able to accomodate.

(d) Finally, an experiential construct of the hypostatic union gives some promise of being theologically comprehensive. In his perceptive dialectical analysis of the development of Christology, John McIntyre has argued persuasively for the existence of three major speculative approaches to the hypostatic union. The first approach is Chalcedonian: it attempts to understand the incarnation as the union of a divine and a

167

human nature in a single divine person. The second approach is psychological: it uses the techniques of historical, critical exegesis to reconstruct Jesus' religious experience. The third approach is revelatory: it speaks of Jesus in symbolic, sacramental terms as God's historical self-revelation. And it tends to portray the self-revelation of God in Christ as a self-authenticating religious event.[25]

As we have already seen, an experiential construct of the hypostatic union gives some initial promise of being able to take account of the insights of both a Chalcedonian and a psychological approach to Christological questions. But an experiential Christology would also defend the symbolic structure of experience in general and of religious experience in particular. It would conceive the gracing of the Son's human experience as a symbolic, sacramental act of divine self-revelation. It should, therefore, be able to take into account the best insights of a self-revelatory Christology. In other words, an experiential construct of the hypostatic union gives initial promise of offering a fairly comprehensive way of conceiving the incarnation, one which can incorporate into itself the best insights of three other major Christological constructs. But we must resist following these inviting theological leads until another day. Our present concern with Christological problems remains subordinate to our primary interest in understanding the reality of the Holy Breath.

The reader may find it helpful at this point to recapitulate the results of this initial exploration into Jesus' relationship to the divine Breath. We have examined the New Testament witness to Jesus as the Breath-baptiser and found there three distinct but interrelated doctrinal strains. The title describes the scope of Jesus' mission and His saving relation to His disciples. It calls attention to His unique relation to the Father. And it underscores the uniqueness of His relationship to the Holy Breath: He stands in a graced relationship with Her from the first moment of His conception. The experiential construct of the Trinity developed in the preceding chapters provides not only a way of conceiving the hypostatic union but also a way of explaining how it was possible for Jesus to live in a graced relationship to the Holy Breath from conception on. Because the Son stands within the divine experience as a principle of obediential efficacy, His divine omnipotence overrules the autonomy present in His human experience. Jesus appreciates, thinks, and acts as the Son of God Himself. In Her function within the Trinity as divine interpretant, the Breath relates to the Son as His mind. She conceives the truth that His acts express. Jesus' graced relation to the Breath from the moment of conception on was then the direct consequence of the way the Son and Breath relate to one another within the divine experience. The Breath conceives the truth the Son incarnates. As a consequence, Jesus and Jesus alone possesses the Breath in eschatological abundance. In confessing Him as Breath-baptiser we enter the last age of salvation when God stands historically revealed as tripersonal and triune and when those who are united to the Father through the Son and in the Breath look forward to risen life with Christ.

168

Jesus' baptism only inaugurated His public revelation as Breath-baptiser. That revelation culminated in His death and glorification. As the Breath of Jesus, the Advocate stands in an important relationship to both events. She prolongs the divine judgment upon human sinfulness they effected. And She enters the religious experience of believers as a principle of risen life. Let us, then, examine in greater detail both of these facets of Her saving action in Jesus.

(2) **Because Jesus was a messiah in the image of the suffering servant, the Holy Breath prolongs the judgment on human sinfulness effected in His death and glorification.**

Already in the preaching of the pre-exilic prophets the illumination of the Holy Breath is associated with three interrelated theological themes: prophetic witness, suffering, and divine judgment. The Breath's illumination authorizes the prophet Micah to stand in judgment over Israel's moral infidelity (Mi 3:8). Isaiah likens the judgment of Yahweh to the wind that blows away the chaff from threshed grain: it purifies the people of their moral filth and prepares them to accept the salvation Yahweh is preparing (Is 4:40).[26] Hosea speaks more pessimistically: the chaff scattered by the wind of divine judgment is Israel herself (Ho 4:19). And in the twilight of the Hebrew monarchy, Jeremiah's prophecies foresee only doom. Repentance comes too late, judgment brings only retribution:

> A hot wind from the bare heights in the desert toward
> the daughter of my people, not to winnow or cleanse, a
> wind too full for this comes. Now it is I who speak in
> judgment upon them (Jr 4:11-12).

In the preaching of the pre-exilic prophets the divine **Ruah** effects judgment because She inspires the moral uprightness and covenant fidelity the prophets proclaimed. As a consequence, stiff-necked resistance to Her sanctifying enlightenment transforms Her into the instrument of divine judgment. For the enlightenment which sanctifies lays bare the vanity of false prophecy and false mysticism. It rebukes moral disobedience which betrays covenant faith. And it demands retribution of those who persecute the prophets Yahweh sends to pronounce judgment in His name.

We find a similar interweaving of the themes of witness, suffering, judgment, and pneumatic inspiration in the synoptic gospels. Mark was the first synoptic evangelist to insist that the Breath-baptised follow a messiah who is also the suffering servant of God. But the other synoptic gospels heartily concur. And like Mark they urge the witnessing disciple to look to the Breath of Jesus for inspiration and courage to testify under persecution (Mk 10:28-30, 13:9-13; Mt 10:17-20, 19:23-26; Lk 18:24-27, 21:11-12). Moreover, as we have seen, Matthew and Luke differentiate more clearly than Mark Jesus' relation to the Breath from Her relation to the Christian community. She comes to Him to reveal that He is the beloved Son of God, the messiah in the image of the suffering servant, and the beginning of a new Israel. She comes to the Christian community in the fire of purification and of judgment.

Of the three synoptics, Luke links Jesus' own death most explicitly to His enlightenment by the Holy Breath. Luke insists more explicitly than either Matthew or Luke that Jesus conducted His own ministry under Her inspiration and guidance. He even portrays Her as the source of Jesus' self-awareness as Son (Lk 4:14-15, 10:21-22).[27] And Luke also suggests that His death resulted in part from His courageous docility to Her inspirations. Luke concludes his narrative of Jesus' early ministry with the story of His preaching in the synagogue at Nazareth. The conflict between Jesus and the Nazarenes begins almost immediately after He lays claim to being the fulfillment of a messianic prophecy:

> The Breath of the Lord is upon me because He has anointed me to preach good news to the poor. He has sent me to proclaim release to the captives and recovering of sight to the blind, to set at liberty those who are oppressed, to proclaim the acceptable year of the Lord (Lk 4:16-19, Is 61:1-2).

The prophecy interprets the meaning and purpose of Jesus' entire ministry. The Holy Breath which descended on Him at the Jordan now impels Him to proclaim a time of jubilee in which misery and oppression will be overthrown and the poor and suffering will be gathered into God's kingdom.[28] The townsfolk of Nazareth respond to this good news with brief wonder and superficial enthusiasm, then almost immediately with scepticism, and finally violently, as Jesus warns them that the unbelief of His own people will cause God to extend His favor to the gentiles. Their attempt to cast the Breath-filled messiah from a precipice clearly foreshadows His eventual crucifixion at the hands of the chief priests in Jerusalem. Both events, however, follow inexorably from His proclamation of the good news in the power of the Holy Breath.

Moreover, Luke describes in greater detail than the other synoptics the judgmental action of the Breath in the Christian community. Pneumatic judgment is pronounced in Acts in three different contexts: the unbelieving are rebuked and summoned to repentance, the sinfulness of believers is unmasked and punished, and official decisions are taken concerning matters of common concern to the Christian community (Ac 2:1-41, 5:1-12a, 27-33, 6:1-7, 15:22-29).

In Acts the apostles' courageous witness to the resurrection plunges them into immediate and abiding conflict with the same religious and political forces as crucified Jesus. The twelve are first harrassed then flogged by the Sanhedrin (Ac 4:1-31, 5:21-42). Peter escapes martyrdom only by a miraculous deliverance (Ac 12:1-19).

170

Paul's ministry in Acts also dramatizes the way in which the judgment effected by the apostle's witness draws him inexorably into the passion of Christ. When the Lord in a vision sends Ananias to baptise Saul, He assures the disciple that this former persecutor is "a chosen instrument of Mine to carry My name before the gentiles and kings and the sons of Israel; for I will show him how much he must suffer for the sake of my name." Ananias obediently summons the temporarily blinded Saul to baptism with the assurance that he will be "filled with the Holy Breath" (Ac 6:41, 9:15-16). Thereafter She presides over the apostle's ministry of proclamation by confirming it with abundant charismatic signs of healing and deliverance (Ac 19:11-12). At Her inspiration Paul and Barnabas are "set apart" for a mission of evangelization to Asia Minor (Ac 3:12). Their practice of baptising uncircumcised gentiles culminates in the council of Jerusalem where a confirming judgment pronounced by the divine Breath (Ac 15:5-29). On Paul's second missionary journey the divine **Pneuma** prevents him from going to Bithynia (Ac 16:7). At Troas he is called by a vision to Macedonia (Ac 16:9). And She descends on the disciples of the Baptist whom he baptises at Ephesus (Ac 19:1-7). But the Breath-filled apostle must also suffer with the Lord he proclaims. He is stoned at Iconium (Ac 14:19-20), flogged in Philippi (Ac 16:22), driven from Thessalonika (Ac 17:1-9), harried at Ephesus (Ac 19:23-20:1). On his final mission as he turns back to Jerusalem, he is prophetically warned by the Breath that imprisonment and persecution await him in the holy city (Ac 20:22-23, 21:11-14). The calm with which the apostle continues his journey recalls the courage with which Luke's Jesus had set His face toward Jerusalem where betrayal, suffering, and death awaited Him (Lk 14:31-35).

In the gospel of John a similar fate awaits every witnessing disciple. In His farewell discourse Jesus promises His disciples that the Paraclete will teach them to bear witness to Him. But in doing so they will experience the same kind of persecution as He did. For "the world" will no more heed their witness than it did His (Jn 15:20-21). They will be expelled from synagogues. Like Jesus they will be murdered by pious hypocrites who will explain their crime as an act of divine homage (Jn 16:1-2). Some of the disciples will fall away; even with the Paraclete to strengthen them they will not be able to bear the things that are to come (Jn 16:1).

But the witness of the suffering disciples prolongs the divine judgment accomplished in the death and glorification of Jesus. In opposing Jesus the dark powers of this world were forced to come out into the light and reveal themselves for what they are: murderous, tyrannical, hypocritical. Exposed by the testimony of Jesus they stood judged before the divine presence within Him. In prolonging Jesus' witness, the disciples also prolong the judgment of this world accomplished in Him (Jn 8:31-59, 10:22-38, 11:45-54, 12:44-50, 18:28-19:22). In convicting the world of sin, the Paraclete will vindicate the innocence of Jesus and testify against the murder of God's Son. In the witness of His disciples She will testify to His victorious ascent on high. That victory manifests His righteousness, His

171

justice, which the world refuses to acknowledge because it refuses to own its murderous injustice in executing Him. Hence, before the testimony of the disciples, the dark powers of this world will stand judged. And the judgment pronounced will be the same that Jesus pronounced over Satan, the prince of this world. For by being lifted up in suffering and in glory, Jesus broke the power of the prince of darkness (Jn 16:7-15). For their part the witnessing disciples will recognize the presence of Satan in the unbelief and injustice of their persecutors. And their witness will render their adversaries liable to the same judgment as Jesus pronounced over the Evil One. With Satan, their persecutors will be cast out from the divine presence (Jn 14:30-31).

Witness, suffering, judgment: these three themes are interwoven in the theology of both the Old and New Testaments. And the thread which binds them together is the Holy Breath. For She inspires the prophetic witness that sets one in opposition to the forces of evil, forces that take satisfaction in the persecution and suffering of God's holy ones. But the witness that leads to suffering stands in divine judgment upon those who ignore it, a judgment sanctioned by the authority of the divine Breath Who inspires it. What insight does the interweaving of thse theological themes yield into Her reality and into Her relationship to the Son of God?

The gospels give us good reason to believe that Jesus' Breath-consciousness shaped His religious experience in significant ways.[29] She taught Him the meaning of the mission He had received from the Father. And She endowed His proclamation of God's reign with a charismatic authority that was further confirmed by the miracles He worked with divine power.

It is, then, altogether plausible that Jesus' own pneumatology would have reflected His personal experience of the Breath. She had revealed to Him that He was **Abba's** Son; His disciples would then come to know through Her inspiration that they are called to be God's children in Jesus' image. If She inspired His prayer, She would teach them the meaning of authentic worship. If She dwelt as a divine life force within Him, Her indwelling would effect rebirth in them. If She drew Jesus into conflict with the powers of darkness, She would draw them into the same conflict and inspire their witness under persecution as She had inspired His. Finally, we blaspheme the Breath, mistake Her action in Jesus for anything but the presence of God, when we refuse the divine forgiveness the Father had sent His only Son to proclaim. We then stand under God's judgment whether one utters the blasphemy in this life or in the next.

Whether or not these propositions describe accurately Jesus' own experience of the Holy Breath, they certainly interpret accurately the way in which the gospels portray Her saving action in His disciples. We are, however, presently concerned with Her judgmental activity and its relationship to Jesus' passion and death. How is that relationship to be understood?

172

In His healing ministry Jesus took upon Himself the sin and broken-ness of humankind in order to cure it. When it would not be healed, in His passion He suffered mockery, lashes, the cross, if that was needed to reveal to sinners the full scope of God's forgiving love. If God responds to our sins as Jesus did, He suffers them with a forgiving atoning love that is simply there.

Only the Son was crucified. He therefore stands historically revealed as the person in the Godhead who first receives into the divine experience the destructive consequences of the world's sinfulness. Our sins once nailed God's Son to the cross. But they continue to make a difference to God even now. They effect, therefore, the Son's enduring passion.

Only the Son was crucified. But His passion is also the compassion of the Father and of the Breath. Human persons experience only human compassion. We suffer in the misery of those we love but without ourselves experiencing the very pain of those whom we compassionate. For being human, our experiences remain only analogous. But things stand differently with the divine persons. For so perfectly do They give Themselves to one another that they share not just a similarity but an identity of life. When, therefore, the Son of God hung from the cross on Calvary, we may be sure that the Father and the Breath did not gaze on His torment with detached indifference. Even less would They have turned from Him or abandoned Him.[30] Instead they compassionated Him with the kind and quality of compassion that is possible only to persons who give themselves to one another so totally they share not a similarity but an identity of life.

These conclusions lend theological support to devotion to the Sacred Heart of Jesus. Jesus' crucifixion was not just an unrepeatable historical event. It reveals to us a perennial truth about God. The incarnate Word even in His glory continues to receive unto Himself the sinfulness of the world and to suffer its rejection with the kind of compassion that He embodied when He walked among us. And the enduring passion of the Son is the compassion of the Father and of the Breath.

The Son functions within the divine experience as a personal principle of obediential efficacy. The Father and the Breath speak to us through the words and deeds He enacts in obedience to Them. The judgment He pronounces expresses God's evaluative response to human sinfulness. It is conceived within God by the divine interpretant. She abides also as the final interpretant, the one whose judgments measure the truth or falsity, the innocence or the guilt of every human act. As the interpretative principle within the Godhead, She functions within the divine experience as the one through whom the judgment which the Father sends the Son to pronounce upon the world is deliberatively reached.

Human judgments as often as not express apprehension, fear, resent-ment, vindictiveness. But God judges the world with a compassionate and

173

atoning love that expresses the evaluative shape of the divine experience. The divine interpretant perceives all things lovingly; and every judgment She inspires is pronounced in love. God's abiding judgment upon human sinfulness can therefore only be a judgment of compassion. The Pentecostal flame which comes to purify human hearts blazes with love. It does not seek our condemnation but our justification in repentant faith. We often fear God's judgment. But even to be convicted of sinfulness before a loving God counts as a supreme act of divine mercy. Conviction invites repentance. And until we repent we remain imprisoned in the fear, rage, and guilt that festers in our hearts. We are justified by accepting the divine forgiveness Jesus proclaimed and incarnated. We are sanctified by learning to deal with one another with His own atoning compassion.

For God judges the world by the simple expedient of telling us lovingly the truth about Himself and us. The more clearly God reveals to us the full extent of His love and forgiveness, the clearer the contrast between His goodness and holiness and our unrepentant sinfulness. The passionate witness of Jesus' disciples seeks to prolong historically the judgment He accomplished in dying, rising, and sending the Holy Breath. Like Jesus we ask that if possible the cup of suffering pass us by. "Do not bring us to the test, but save us from the Evil One." But when confrontation cannot be sidestepped, the true follower of a servant messiah enters with Him into the crucible of pain. But our suffering will prolong the judgment He pronounced on the cross only if it too incarnates the forgiveness with which He died. For that judgment will be Breath-inspired only if it is uttered with divine compassion and love.

(3) **Because the Holy Breath proceeds from the risen Christ, She enters human experience as a principle of resurrection.** Ezechiel the prophet in his vision of the valley of dry bones, had linked the Breath to the idea of resurrection (Ez 37:1-14). But Paul the apostle expanded this cryptic hint into a rich theology of resurrection. In Pauline theology the pneumatic life that flows from the risen Lord seeks to reanimate every aspect of the human person. It stands therefore irreconcilably opposed to the flesh. "Flesh" signifies the whole person as earthbound, deathbound, sinful (Ga 5:13-26).[31] Pneumatic life triumphs over the flesh by enabling the believer to participate even now in the risen Christ's own experience of transformation in God. In baptism we are buried with Him and rise to the life that is eternal (Rm 6:1-11).[32] Our present participation in the Breath of the risen Savior stands, however, only as a divine "down payment." The full purchase will be completed when we too rise in glory to a world recreated in Christ (2 Co 1:21-22).[33] But our very yearning for the fulness of risen glory is conceived in us by the divine Breath who prays within us for final deliverance with sighs too deep for words (Rm 8:18-27).[34]

For Paul, then, the divine Breath functions as an eschatological principle of continuity within salvation history. She functions as a vitalizing link between the risen Christ and the community of believers,

174

between the present moment in salvation history and the resurrection of the just. Her saving activity gives rise to a vectoral thrust within history itself toward the future God has prepared for those who love Him. Indeed through her present action in believers that future is already being realized in the present.[35]

In the Johannine tradition the Holy Breath is described as a font of living water welling up to eternal life. The first mention of living water in the fourth gospel occurs during Jesus' conversation with the Samaritan woman. Jesus tells the woman: "If you knew the gift of God and who it is that is saying to you, 'Give me a drink,' you would have asked Him, and He would have given you living water" (Jn 4:14). Living water flows; and where it flows it brings life: to fish, plants, animals, humans. It contrasts with stagnant water and with the saline waters of the Dead Sea. The living water which Jesus promises will quench the human thirst for life after death. A mysterious gift, it wells up spontaneously within those who receive it. And it flows from Jesus as its source.

Jesus tells the woman that she would have asked Him for living water had she known the "gift of God" and Jesus' own messianic identity. The phrase "gift of God" in rabbinic Judaism referred to the Torah. And as we have seen in another context, the Hebrew wise men extolled the divine wisdom born of meditation on the Law as a gift from on high. Jesus, however, offers as a gift the living water itself. Those who receive it will participate in God's own wisdom and will know Him therefore for who He is, the One who comes from above.

In Jesus' encounter with the Samaritan women, the precise nature of the living water remains obscure. But in his account of Jesus' activities in Jerusalem during the feast of Tabernacles, the evangelist makes it quite clear that the "living water" Jesus has promised is in fact His Holy Breath.

> On the last day of the feast, the great day, Jesus stood up and proclaimed, "If any one thirst, let him come to Me and drink. The one who believes in Me, as the Scripture has said, 'From within him shall flow rivers of living water.'" Now this He said about the Breath (**peri tou Pneumatos**) which those who believed in Him were to receive; for as yet the Breath had not been given, because Jesus was not yet glorified (Jn 7:37-39).

In the passage just cited Jesus does not quote sacred scripture directly but refers only vaguely to a divine outpouring of living water. But His invitation, "If anyone thirst, let him come to Me and drink," echoes the invitations of divine Wisdom in the writings of the Hebrew sages (Pr 9:5, Si 24:21, Is 55:1). The living water Jesus will dispense, the divine wisdom He will freely bestow, is, however, now clearly identified with the Breath that

175

will proceed from Him in His risen glory. But Jesus' promise: "From within him shall flow rivers of living water" is ambiguous. Does the phrase "from within him" refer to the Christ who gives the living water or to the disciple within whom the living water will well up spontaneously? Both meanings are possible, and both are probably intended. For the phrase recalls Jesus' promise to the Samaritan woman: "The water I shall give will turn into a spring inside him welling up to eternal life." But it also looks forward to the resurrection when the Breath will be sent into the world as the Breath of the risen Christ.

Jesus must be lifted up in glory before He can mediate the Breath. He will also be lifted up on the cross. But on Calvary the sign of blood and water anticipates in symbol Jesus' victory over death. "When they came to Jesus and saw that He was already dead, they did not break His legs. One of the soldiers thrust a lance into His side, and immediately blood and water flowed out" (Jn 19:33-34).[36] The thrust of the soldier's lance is meant to prove that Jesus has died. But it is followed by a sign that promises eternal life. For the water flowing from Jesus' side recalls His promise of the living water and looks forward to its fulfillment on Easter day.[37] The water flowing from the side of Christ also recalls the prophecy of Ezechiel that a torrent of water would pour from the temple of God to purify a sinful land and make it bloom with new life. Jesus' pierced body is the temple of God: the cleansing water, the Breath Who will proceed from His lips on Easter day in forgiveness and in judgment (Ez 47:1-12; Jn 20:19-23).

The precise relationship of the first letter of John to the fourth gospel is disputed among exegetes. But there can be no doubt that both documents emerge from the same tradition. Moreover, the sign of water and blood given on Calvary parallels the doctrine of the first letter that the Breath, the water, and the blood all testify as one (1 Jn 5:5-8).[38] At the very least the two texts reflect a similar doctrinal strain within the Johannine tradition. Moreover, when these two passages are compared, they illumine one another. The Breath testifies with the water in inspiring the baptismal faith of Christians. She testifies with the blood by leading the baptised to acknowledge that they are saved through the passion and death of God's Son.

How then are we to interpret the New Testament witness to the fact that the Holy Breath comes to believers as a principle of resurrection? Jesus preached in the power and anointing of God's Breath. But the full implications of the divine purpose behind His invitation to us to live as God's children in His image could not be grasped until He was glorified. Only then could we grasp the full meaning of His invitation. For if we are to be graciously transformed in His image, His resurrection reveals the goal of that transformation. We are graced so that we might rise with Him. And His enlightening Breath graces us. Jesus' glorification reveals to us therefore God's faithful intention to glorify all those who share His Breath.

The Holy Breath of God functions as a principle of resurrection because She conceives within God the saving wisdom revealed in Jesus. She establishes the resurrection of the just as the goal of God's saving interventions in human history. And as the source and inspiration of Christian hope She enters salvation history as a divine vector pointing us toward risen glory.

But there is more. Resurrection completes the process of gracious transformation in God that begins with justifying faith in His Word. Through faith the creative power of the Father begins to transform us into the image of His Son, and the redemptive power of the Son effects our reconciliation with God and with one another. But when we confess that the Holy Breath is a source of risen life, we assert that resurrection involves more than efficacious transformation in God. We rise in the power of the Breath when we experience Her illumination. Insofar as it is the work of the Breath, resurrection consists in the experience of gracious enlightenment. And our present enlightenment only whets our appetite for the glory that lies ahead when we will see God face to face.

As the supreme exemplification of experience, God experiences everything that is and everything that could conceivably be. All things therefore exist in Him. A body is the immediate spatio-temporal environment from which each human self emerges. Through digestive assimilation we organize elements in the physical universe into a personal life-support system. When we die, we begin to exist in God without a physical body. We are promised a risen body. We can only imagine its actual character. Paul the apostle, who saw the risen Christ, assures us that risen bodies differ from physical ones (1 Co 15:35-53). But the fact that both are bodies suggests some analogy between them. As a consequence, the way in which we understand our physical bodies will to a certain extent condition the way in which we imagine our glorified bodies. If we believe that our physical bodies are quantified matter, we will probably imagine our risen bodies as quantified matter mysteriously spiritualized. But is quantified matter the best way to describe a physical body? If a complex, self-coordinated, spatio-temporal process constitutes a somewhat more accurate description, might we not suppose that our risen bodies too will be some kind of self-coordinated process? Our physical bodies result from the successful integration into our biological processes of the life-sustaining forces in our spatio-temporal environments. Isn't it possible, then, that our risen bodies will also be something that we ourselves will have to put together? Might they not be the result of the integration into our experience of the divine and created forces which will impinge on us on the other side of the grave?

We may also anticipate that purgatory will consist of an experience of existence in God after death with unrepented sinful habits still in need of acknowledgment and gracious healing in faith. Those in need of purification will find it in loving communion with the divine persons and with the support of those who draw their life from Them. But they will not yet see the beatific vision, for their sins will prevent them from knowing God as He is, a God of pure love. The pain of purgatory will, therefore, consist in the pain of discovering sinful truths about myself that still separate me from God and which I have for a lifetime been terrified to face. And our purification will be accomplished in confrontation with that loving, transforming holiness that is the fire of divine love. Purgatory will then bring to completion the divine Breath's compassionate judgment of my sinfulness begun in this life.

Heaven will consist of the face-to-face vision of God that results from final purification in Him. In heaven we enter into communion with the divine persons and with the saints with a love unmarred by sin in any form, a love conceived in us by the divine Breath.

Those dead will descend into hell who exist in God after death while rejecting Him and His love, while lacking the physical supports of life, while and existing in a state of unrepentant subjection to those dark powers that are God's enemies. The damned oppose God in such a way that even His loving approaches become a source of pain and terror; for the damned recognize that the fire of His holiness and love contradicts everything to which they cling. In other words, the damned choose to blaspheme God's Breath not only in this life but in the next.

In the present chapter we have examined three important affirmations which the New Testament makes about the divine Breath and Her relationship to the Word made flesh. In the chapter which follows we will begin to explore the experience of Breath baptism for what it reveals to us concerning the third person of the Trinity.

1.   Montague, op. cit., pp. 13-16; JBC, 5:26; von Rad, Old Testament Theology, I, pp. 289-296.

2.   von Rad, Old Testament Theology, I, pp. 237-334.

3.   Ibid., pp. 334-347.

4.   Montague, op. cit., pp. 31-32; JBC, 6:78; von Rad, Old Testament Theology, I, pp. 296-305.

5.   Montague, op. cit., pp. 18-19; JBC, 9:20.

6.   Montague, op. cit., pp. 40-42; JBC, 16:25-29; von Rad, Old Testament Theology, I, pp. 168-175; Moody, Spirit of the Living God, pp. 19-27.

7.   Montague, op. cit., pp. 53-54; JBC 22:59-61.

8.   Montague, op. cit., pp. 51-53; JBC, 22:16; von Rad, Old Testament Theology, II, pp. 250-262.

9.   Montague, op. cit., pp. 238-239; JBC, 42:9.

10.   Catherine Hargrove, R.S.C.J., "Why A Dove?" Worship (May, 1966), pp. 231-237.

11.   Montague, op. cit., pp. 239-242; JBC, 35:20, 42:10; Barrett, op. cit., pp. 25-45; Dunn, Jesus and the Spirit, pp. 62-67.

12.   Barrett, op. cit., pp. 5-24; Raymond E. Brown, The Birth of the Messiah (New York: Doubleday, 1977), pp. 123-144.

13.   Brown, op. cit., pp. 143-153.

14.   JBC, 43:24.

15.   JBC, 43:11.

16.   JBC, 44:31; Montague, op. cit., pp. 264-266; Brown, op. cit., pp. 286-328.

17.   JBC, 44:43; Montague, op. cit., pp. 267-268; Brown, op. cit., pp. 339-355; 367-392, 435-470; John Navone, Themes of St. Luke (Rome: Gregorian, 1970), pp. 151-154.

18.   Navone, op. cit., pp. 158-159, 163.

19.   Montague, op. cit., pp. 340-341; JBC, 63:53; Brown, The Gospel According to John, I, pp. 55-72; Felix Porsche, C.S.Sp., Pneuma und Wort (Frankfurt: Knecht, 1974), pp. 19-51.

20.   Brown, The Gospel According to John, I, pp. 161-162; Montague, op. cit., pp. 343-344; JBC, 63:74.

21.   DS 300-302.

22.   Cf. Gelpi, Charism and Sacrament (New York: Paulist, 1976), pp. 97-153.

23.   James Dunn, Jesus and the Spirit (Philadelphia: Westminster, 1975), pp. 15-40.

24.   Ibid., pp. 44-89.

25.   John McIntyre, The Shape of Christology (Philadelphia: Westminster, 1966).

26. Montague, op. cit., pp. 34-38; von Rad, op. cit., II, pp. 143-146, 165-169, 176-187; JBC, 15:16, 16:13, 17:17.

27. When the seventy-two disciples return from their mission of proclamation, they report joyfully to Jesus that "even the devils submit to us when we use your name." Jesus assures them that their success is indeed a sign that Satan has been cast out from the heavenly court. But he cautions them against self-infatuated preoccupation with their own charismatic power (Lk 10:17-22). Then Luke notes:

> In that same hour, He rejoiced in the Holy Breath and said: "I thank you, Father, Lord of heaven and earth, that you have hidden these things from the wise and understanding and revealed them to babes; yes, Father, for such was your gracious will. All things have been delivered to Me by My Father, and no one knows who the Son is except the Father, or who the Father is except the Son and any one to whom the Son chooses to reveal Him (Lk 10:21-22).

Jesus' hymn of praise recalls a common theme in wisdom literature: true wisdom descends from on high as a gift of God. Jesus, however, offers here a new interpretation of the enlightenment which descends from heaven. True wisdom, true enlightenment, frees the heart to recognize the arrival of the messianic era in the person of Jesus and in His proclamation of the Father. That proclamation emerges from Jesus' awareness that He stands in a unique and special relationship to the Father. Moreover, Luke's Jesus Himself proclaims this double truth under the inspiration of the divine **Pneuma** sent Him by the Father. She, then, inspires His messianic awareness that He is indeed Son of God in a unique and privileged sense (Cf. JBC, 43:77, 44:101; Dunn, Jesus and the Spirit, pp. 26-40; Navone, op. cit., pp. 156-160.

28. G.W.H. Lampe, "The Holy Spirit in the Writings of St. Luke," in Studies in the Gospels, edited by D.E. Nineham (Oxford: Blackwell, 1955), pp. 159-178; JBC, 44:56; Montague, op. cit., pp. 262-264.

29. Dunn, Jesus and the Spirit, pp. 11 ff.; C.K. Barrett, The Holy Spirit and the Gospel Tradition (London: SPCK, 1947); Philip J. Bosato, S.J., "Spirit Christology," Theological Studies XXXVIII (September, 1977), pp. 423-449; Walter Kasper, Jesus the Christ, translated by V. Green (New York: Paulist, 1977).

30. While the position taken in these pages converges in some respects with that of Jürgen Moltmann, it offers a different interpretation of the death of Jesus from his. Moltmann suggests that Jesus on the cross experienced rejection and abandonment by the Father [Jürgen Moltmann, The Crucified God, translated by R.A. Wilson and John Bowden (New York: Harper and Row, 1973)]. Moltmann would, however, seem to contradict the

180

gospel of John on this important point (Jn 17:32). His interpretation of Jesus' death also rests on a questionable reading of the synoptics. It is opposed by a strain in New Testament theology which insists that Jesus' crucifixion expressed his rejection not by God but by the principalities and powers of this world (1 Co 2:8, Eph 3:10, 1 Pt 1:12, Jn 14:30-31, 15:18-27). And it introduces a dividedness into the divine decisions irreconcilable with the co-activity of the divine persons.

Mark and Matthew place on the lips of the crucified savior the words "My God, My God, why have you forsaken me?" The words cite the first verse of Psalm 22. As in the case of other such citations of the Old Testament in the New, the evangelists presupposed a familiarity with the Hebrew scriptures that would supply the context of the cited passage. For the context gives the citation its full theological significance. Psalm 22 is a prayer of the innocent poor man who laments to God for sufferings unjustly borne. But it is also a prayer of hope in God's saving fidelity.

We have no way of knowing whether Jesus actually said these words on the cross. In placing them on the lips of Jesus the evangelists are certainly making a theological statement about His death. They are in effect affirming that Jesus dies the death of the innocent poor man, clinging to God despite the injustice He suffered at the hands of sinful humanity.

New Testament theology did in fact take into account Moltmann's interpretation of Jesus' death. Matthew especially recognized that His crucifixion could be understood as His actual abandonment by the Father. That very idea would seem to be implicit in the mockery of Jesus' enemies as He hangs on the cross. Matthew places Moltmann's interpretation of Jesus' death on their lips. They speak the interpretation of the unbeliever. If Moltmann is correct, then Jesus' cry, "My God, my God, why have you forsaken me?" would have been His acquiescence in His enemies' interpretation of the meaning of His death. Instead of being the prayer of faith uttered by the innocent poor man, Jesus' words would become a confession of unbelief and despair. Such a conclusion is, however, both theologically and exegetically unacceptable. It makes the Son a sinner.

Finally, Moltmann's position is also vulnerable to William Ellery Channings' moral argument against Calvinism. For it seems to exempt the Father from the most basic kind of moral decency. See also: Moltmann, The Trinity and the Kingdom, pp. 20-60.

31. Montague, op. cit., pp. 198-203; JBC, 49:30; Stanislaus Lyonnet and Leopold Sabourin, Sin, Redemption, and Sacrifice (Rome: Biblical Institute, 1970), pp. 48-55, 74-84; Hoyle, op. cit., pp. 62ff.; Cerfaux, op. cit., pp. 446-466.

32. Montague, op. cit., pp. 206-208; JBC, 53:83.

33. Montague, op. cit., pp. 185-187; JBC, 52:10.

34. Montague, op. cit., pp. 209-213; JBC, 53:83.

35. Hamilton, op. cit., pp. 17-25; Hermann, op. cit., p. 98; Cerfaux, op.cit., pp. 157-234, 313-372.

36. Montague, op. cit., p. 349; Brown, The Gospel According to John, II, pp. 932-960; JBC, 63:172.

37. Porsch, op. cit., pp. 327-340.

38. Montague, op. cit., pp. 337-338; JBC, 62:26.

CHAPTER VIII

THE DIVINE ICON

We are examining the implications of confessing that the divine interpretant is also the Holy Breath of Jesus. We saw in the preceding chapter that the Christian proclamation of Jesus as the Breath-baptiser asserts the uniqueness of His relation to both the Father and the Breath. We have examined how an experiential pneumatology might conceive that relationship. But Breath baptism also establishes a relationship between Jesus and His disciples. As we have also seen, it empowers them to prolong the judgment of divine compassion accomplished in His death and glorification. And it inaugurates a process of graced transformation in God that culminates in final resurrection. We experience the Holy Breath as a source of risen life when we allow Her sanctifying enlightenment to conform us to the risen savior. We are conformed to Him when we put on His mind, when we live the religious vision He proclaimed and incarnated. Let us reflect in greater detail on the practical consequences of Breath baptism for what it reveals to us about the third person in the Trinity.

Our argument will advance in four stages. First, we will examine the biblical witness for what it has to teach us concerning the sanctifying consequences of Breath baptism. Second, we shall attempt to understand what the sanctifying enlightenment of the divine Breath tells us about her reality. Third, we will examine a second consequence of Breath baptism: its ability to bind Christians together in a charismatic community of mutual service. Fourth, we will attempt to understand how the enlightenment effected by Breath baptism transforms the Christian community into a social icon of Her divine person.

Of all the New Testament writings the synoptic gospels provide us with the clearest insight into the sanctifying moral consequences of Breath baptism. They do so indirectly in the course of describing the practical results of Jesus' own enlightenment by Her. For Breath-baptism conforms the Christian community to Jesus in faithful obedience to His doctrine. The Breath Herself inspired Him to proclaim that doctrine to His disciples. And it makes specific demands of them.

In **Mark** the Breath that descended on Jesus at His baptism catapulted Him into immediate conflict with the powers of evil.

> The Breath immediately drove Him out into the wilderness. And He was in the wilderness forty days, tempted by Satan, and He was with the wild beasts; and the angels ministered to Him (Mk 1:12-13).

The wilderness into which Jesus is driven for forty days suggests the desert in which Israel wandered for forty years. Those years had been a time of testing. As the beginning of the faithful Israel, Jesus must now undergo a similar ordeal.

But the wilderness into which Jesus is driven also suggests the Yahwist account of creation in the second chapter of Genesis. There God transforms a wilderness into a fruitful garden and creates Adam to tend it. He then leads the beasts of the garden to Adam to see if he can discover in them a proper mate. Jesus, the beginning of the new creation, stands in the wilderness surrounded by brute beasts like the new Adam He is. And like the first Adam Jesus must also confront temptation. He enters into conflict with Satan. The book of Wisdom had long since identified the devil with the ancient serpent, who had, of course, been one of the beasts in the garden (Ws 2:24). And Mark may have conceivably intended this allusion to wisdom literature.[1]

The beasts that surround the messiah are, however, also desert animals. For the Hebrews the absence of life in the desert transformed it into a sinister place, abandoned and cursed by God. It was feared as the haunt of death-dealing, demonic forces, whose symbols were the strange and powerful beasts that lurked in deserted places (Cf. Lv 16:10, Is 13:21, 14:23, 30:6, 34:11-16; Zp 2:13ff). Although Mark does not say explicitly that Jesus did battle with the beasts, there is a hint of demonic conflict in his reference to the ministering angels. Apparently God sends these heavenly hosts to sustain the messiah in His initial struggle with Satan.

Finally, since Mark seems to have written his gospel for Christians persecuted under Nero, the evangelist may have intended the desert beasts surrounding Jesus to suggest to his readers the beasts of the Roman arena.[2] The images that structure Mark's account of Jesus' temptations link the ordeal to His baptism. That same Breath that descended on Him at the Jordan to begin His revelation as messianic Breath-baptiser in the image of the suffering servant now drives Him to confront Satan in the wilderness. This confrontation discloses that Jesus is the new Adam and begins a new Israel. The members of that Israel who are baptised in His Breath may then anticipate that they will be tested as the servant messiah was and be driven by Her into conflict with the ancient tempter.

Matthew's account of Jesus' temptations uses some of the same images as Mark with similar theological intent. In Matthew as in Mark, the Holy Breath which descended on Jesus in His baptism leads Him out to the desert to be tempted as the first Israel was. In Matthew as in Mark the servant messiah's ordeal foreshadows the trials which await His disciples. But in Matthew we find no mention of desert beasts. Instead he transforms Mark's cryptic reference to Satan into a dramatic dialogue between Jesus and the tempter.

Some exegetes would question whether Jesus' desert temptation have any relevance to the lives of His disciples. They argue that in Matthew's narrative Satan prefaces the first two temptations with the same words: "If You are the Son of God." The phrase recalls Jesus' baptism, where the voice from heaven had just proclaimed Him God's beloved Son and messiah in the image of the suffering servant. As a consequence, Jesus' temptations may be legitimately characterized as messianic. And since Jesus alone is messiah, His temptations are sometimes interpreted as only a personal ordeal without relevance to anyone else.

The messianic character of the temptations cannot be contested. But we may not therefore assume that they have meaning for Jesus alone. In point of fact the very opposite is true, for reasons that we have in part already considered. In Matthew as in Mark Jesus begins a new Israel in virtue of His messianic commissioning. He incarnates in His own person the kind of relationship to God that the members of the new Israel will be expected to have. Those who belong to the new Israel will be tested as He was. If they are to live as children of God in His image, they must respond to temptation as He did. Moreover, in virtue of the fact that He is messiah, Matthew's Jesus confronts His disciples as the Breath-filled legislator of new covenant morality. Those baptized in His Breath will be recognized precisely by their willingness to live in obedience to His moral vision. In this context, it is significant that in all His replies to Satan Jesus cites the Torah. For, as we shall see, each citation finds an echo and a fulfillment in His moral preaching. Finally, Jesus' temptations are not so peculiarly messianic that they cannot be experienced by any of His disciples. He is tempted to trust in Himself rather than in God, to set the conditions under which He will relate to God, and to worship the prince of this world rather than the Father. The least member of the new Israel is susceptible to the same temptations and must, as a Breath-baptised follower of Jesus reply to them as She inspired Him to do.

In each of His replies to Satan, Jesus cites Deuteronomy. While the Old Testament context from which the citations are drawn casts some light on the intent of Jesus' replies to Satan, it does not exhaust their meaning. His responses look backward remotely to Israel's desert experience and more immediately to His own baptism. But Matthew's temptation narrative also looks forward to Jesus' ministry, death, and glorification. Matthew, like the other synoptics, intended the witness of the Baptist, Jesus' baptism, and His temptations to introduce the evangelist's entire account of His public ministry. In His temptations Jesus cites the Torah, and in the Sermon on the Mount He will insist that He comes not to abolish the law but to fulfill it (Mt 5:17-19). And each citation of Deuteronomy does in fact, as we shall see, find its fulfillment in Jesus' own doctrine. Moreover, in Mt. 27:32, the crucified messiah is taunted by His enemies with the words, "He trusts in God, let God deliver Him now if He desires Him; for He said, 'I am the Son of God.'" Their taunt recalls both Jesus' baptism and His confrontation with Satan in the desert. On both occasions He had been addressed as "Son of God." For Matthew, then, the messiah's struggle with Satan in the desert foreshadows His final ordeal on the cross. And His citations of the Torah in response to Satan's wiles foreshadow His own proclamation of the new covenant sealed in His blood.

185

We cannot, of course, derive Jesus' entire moral doctrine directly from a reflection on Matthew's account of His desert temptations. But we can legitimately use the temptations as a heuristic device for investigationg Matthew's understanding of Jesus' moral vision. As we shall see, each of Jesus' replies to the tempter foreshadows some facet of His own teaching.

Matthew's Jesus fasts for forty days in the desert. The pious Jew fasted in order to recall that God rather than food or worldly possessions is the ultimate source of life and that those who believe in Him must trust in Him if they expect to live. Fasting reminded the devout of Israel's desert experience when the chosen peple depended from day to day upon the Lord for food to survive. Jesus is first tempted to use His miraculous messianic power to break His fast. The first temptation involves then much more than a crude temptation to gluttony. It seeks to negate the very meaning of Jesus' fast. Were He to yield to it, He would be equivalently asserting that He intends to pursue His messianic career in egotistical reliance on His own miraculous powers rather than in total trust of the Father Who had sent Him. That this is the intent of the temptation is clear from Jesus' reply: "Man does not live by bread alone but by every word that comes from the mouth of God" (Mt 4:4). The citation from Deuteronomy recalls Yahweh's fidelity to His people during their years of desert wandering. Jesus is, then, first tempted to replace trust in the Father with egotistical self-reliance. In repudiating the temptation the Breath-filled messiah establishes trust in God as the first condition for membership in the new Israel.

Jesus' desert fast seems to have been atypical. In contrast to the Baptist He seems to have avoided harsh ascetical practices. While he recommends fasting in secret (Mt 6:16-18), He seems not to have bound His disciples to fasting and penance (Mt 9:14-17; Lk 5:33-39). Moreover, Matthew's Jesus also acknowledges that humans have legitimate physical needs. But He insists that those who live as God's children in His image look first and above all to their Father in heaven to fulfill their physical wants. "Look at the birds of the air; they neither sow nor reap nor gather into barns and yet your heavenly Father feeds them. Are you not of more value than they?" (Mt 6:26) In other words, like Jesus, His disciples must be determined to live from day to day trusting in the Father's providential care, and not by bread alone. "Give us this day our daily bread" (Mt 6:11). Moreover, in Matthew's gospel, this expectant faith in the day-to-day providence of God must also find practical expression in the freedom to share one's bread, one's possessions with others, especially with the dispossessed. The sharing born of faith expresses the determination to look to God rather than to one's worldly goods as the ultimate source of life. It therefore guarantees membership in God's kingdom in the life to come.

> Come, O blessed of my Father, inherit the kingdom
> prepared for you from the foundation of the world; for I
> was hungry and you gave me food, I was thirsty and you

gave me drink, I was a stranger and you welcomed me, I was naked and you clothed me, I was sick and you visited me, I was in prison and you comforted me...I say to you as you did it to one of the least of these my bretheren, you did it to me (Mt 25:31-36,40).

Jesus replies to His first temptation by asserting His determination to pursue His messianic mission in trusting submission to the Father. Satan responds by inviting Him to indulge in a perfect orgy of trust. Let the Breath-filled messiah fling Himself from the pinnacle of the temple and thus force the Father to send angels to rescue Him. But Jesus sees through the deceit. Were He to accede to the tempter's second ruse, He would put the Father to the test. Those test God who set the conditions under which they are willing to trust Him. Jesus refuses to do so: "You shall not put the Lord your God to the test" (Mt 4:7; Dt 6:16). The text from Deuteronomy expresses His determination to live not only by trust in the Father but by a trust that is unconditioned. The Father, not He, sets the terms of Their relationship.

As we have just seen, for Matthew's Jesus the sharing of one's worldly goods with others is a fundamental, practical test of one's trust in the Father's providential care. In His second temptation, Jesus asserts that that faith should be unconditioned. His disciples too must live with such a faith, if they are to claim to be children of God in His image. It comes as no surprise, therefore, to find Matthew's Jesus also demanding that His followers set no conditions in principle upon the scope of the sharing which expresses their faith. Anyone is to be eligible, irrespective of merit.

> You have heard that it was said, "You shall love your neighbor and hate your enemy." But I say to you, Love your enemies and pray for those that persecute you, so that you may be sons of your Father who is in heaven; for He makes His sun to rise on the evil and on the good and sends rain on the just and the unjust. For if you love those who love you, what reward have you? Do not even the tax collectors do the same? And if you salute only your bretheren, what more are you doing than the others? Do not even the Gentiles do the same? You, therefore, must be perfect as your heavenly Father is perfect (Mt 5:43-48).

The Father reveals the perfection of His love by sharing His creation generously with all, whether they deserve His concern or not. Human sharing born of faith in the providential care of the Father seeks to imitate the perfection of His love by also being blind to merit. Even one's persecutors are to be treated with a generosity that exceeds the normal demands of friendship.

> You have heard it was said, "An eye for an eye, a tooth
> for a tooth." But I say to you, do not resist one who is
> evil. But if one strikes you on the right cheek, turn to
> him the other also; and if anyone would sue you and take
> your coat, let him have the cloak as well; and if anyone
> forces you to go one mile, go with him two miles. Give
> to him who begs from you, and do not refuse him who
> would borrow from you (Mt 5:39-42).

Moreover, Jesus Himself sets His disciples the example of such sharing by
His table fellowship with sinners (Mt 9:10-13).

In his third approach to the Breath-filled messiah, Satan offers to
give Him all the kingdoms of this world, if only Jesus will bow down and
worship him. Jesus replies with a third citation from Deuteronomy:
"Begone Satan: For it is written 'You shall worship the Lord your God, and
Him only shall you serve'" (Mt 4:8-11; Dt 6:13). In repudiating the idolatry
of secular messianism, the Breath-filled legislator of new covenant
morality decrees that the kingdom of God must be founded on authentic
worship of the Father. Once again, this two-fold commitment finds an
echo in His moral doctrine. He forbids His disciples the exercise of worldly
power over one another. Instead they must be committed to one another in
an attitude of mutual forgiveness and atoning love.

> You know that the rulers of the Gentiles lord it over
> them, and their great men exercise authority over
> them. It shall not be so among you; but whoever would
> be great among you must be your servant and whoever
> would be first among you must be your slave; even as
> the Son of man came not to be served but to serve, and
> to give His life for the ransom of many (Mt 20:25-28).

Moreover, mutual forgiveness in atoning love shall test the authenticity of
His disciples' worship.

> So, if you are offering your gift at the altar and there
> remember that your brother has something against you,
> leave your gift there before the altar and go; first be
> reconciled to your brother, and then come and offer
> your gift (Mt 5:21-24).

Luke separates his account of Jesus' baptism from the story of His
temptation in the desert by a genealogy which traces His lineage back to
Adam, "son of God." As messianic "Son of God," the new Adam proclaims a
salvation so universal in its scope that it seeks nothing less than the
recreation in grace of the entire human race. The new Israel He founds
reaches out to all, Jew and Gentile alike.

188

Moreover, Luke, like Matthew, expands Mark's cryptic reference to Jesus' confrontation with Satan into the same triple temptation. Jesus replies with fundamentally the same citations from Deuteronomy. But Luke orders the temptations differently. In Luke Jesus' final temptation takes place on the pinnacle of the temple in Jerusalem (Lk 4:9-11). The evangelist seems to have wanted the order of the temptations to parallel the movement of his gospel as a whole, a movement from Galilee to Jerusalem. Moreover, by locating Jesus' final temptation in the Holy City, Luke was able to treat it as a foreshadowing of Jesus' passion. At the close of the desert temptations the vanquished Satan departs from the victorious messiah to return "at an opportune time": at the moment of Jesus' betrayal in the Holy City (Lk 4:13). The parallel is suggestive. Had Jesus faltered under the ordeal of the cross, He would have tested the Father by attempting to fix the terms of Their relationship.

There is, however, another important reason why Luke puts Jesus' temptation to test God last. Luke, like Matthew, takes Jesus' replies to Satan as moral imperatives binding on His disciples. Luke's Jesus is the new Moses who proclaims the tenets of new covenant morality (Lk 6:17-25). Moreover, as in Matthew's gospel the replies Luke's Jesus makes to the tempter find an echo and an elaboration in His own doctrine. As we have seen in reflecting on Matthew's gospel, the disciple of Jesus tests God by placing conditions on personal willingness to share one's worldly possessions with the dispossessed as an expression of faith in God's providential and fatherly care. For Luke to test God is the supreme temptation facing the follower of Jesus.

Like Matthew, Luke regards the renunciation of personal possessions in order to distribute them to the needy and the destitute as the most immediate practical expression of faith in God. But in His concern for the poor Luke's Jesus makes even more radical demands than Matthew's. He promises that the sharing born of faith transforms one into an heir of God's kingdom and that it will be especially rewarded in the life to come (Lk 12:22-34, 16:1-13, 18:28-30). He excoriates the pharisees' love of wealth as "a loathesome thing (**bdelugma**)" in God's eyes (Lk 16:14-15). He warns against trusting in wealth as the source of one's life (Lk 12:15,16:9-12). Because attachment to wealth enslaves one in ways that prevent one's entry into the kingdom, it renders the service of God impossible (Lk 16:13, 18:18-27). And gross avarice plunges one with Dives into the fires of Gehenna (Lk 16:19-31). Moreover, Luke even hints that the cynical love of wealth so contradicts obedient trust in God that it precludes faith in the resurrection (Lk 16:31). On the other hand, willingness to live poorly with a servant messiah marks true discipleship (Lk 14:33, cf. 10:57-58). And hospitality, especially for the poor, finds a special reward in the resurrection of the just (Lk 14:12-14, 21).

In his account of Jesus' desert temptations, Luke, like Matthew, portrays the new Moses demanding not only faith in God but unconditioned faith (Lk 4:9-13). And Luke's Jesus also insists on the unrestricted scope of

189

Christian faith-sharing. None are to be excluded in principle. Moreover, Jesus' disciples must do more than give alms; they must welcome the outcast and dispossessed into their very homes (Lk 14:12-14, 21). For they become the children of God in sharing worldly possessions with a universality and generosity that imitates God's own love (Lk 6:32-36). The sharing born of faith also redefines the purpose of human labor: the true disciple labors not in order to possess but in order to have something to share with others (Lk 12:13-21).

Finally, in both Luke and Matthew, Jesus founds God's kingdom not on power politics but on a worship whose authenticity is measured by personal repentance and by mutual forgiveness (Lk 6:27-38, 11:3).

Luke not only portrays Jesus as a new Moses inculcating the terms of new covenant morality, but he also insists more explicitly than Matthew that obedience to Jesus' moral vision tests one's response in faith to Breath-baptism. He does so in Acts.

In Lukan theology Pentecost fulfills John's prophecy concerning the coming of a Breath-baptiser. Before the risen Christ is taken up into heaven He promises: "And behold I send the promise of my Father upon you; but stay in the city until you are clothed with power from on high" (Lk 24:49). The phrase, "the promise of the Father," refers to the Baptist's prediction of a Breath-baptiser, a prophecy which Jesus now intends to fulfill. The same promise is repeated at the beginning of Acts: "But you shall receive power when the Holy Breath has come upon you, and you shall be my witnesses in Jerusalem and all Judea and Samaria and to the end of the earth." (Ac 1:8) Here the purpose of the promised pneumatic empowering is stated explicitly: Breath-baptism will effect the universal proclamation of Christ.[3]

In Acts, however, the Pentecostal Breath also comes to teach the disciples obedience to the moral vision Jesus had proclaimed. Peter tells the crowds assembled in Jerusalem:

> "Repent, and be baptised every one of you in the name of Jesus Christ; and you shall receive the gift of the Holy Breath. For the promise is to you and to your children and to all that are far off, every one whom the Lord our God calls to Him"....So those who received his word were baptised, and there were added that day about three thousand souls. And they devoted themselves to the apostles' teaching and fellowship, to the breaking of the bread and prayers....And all who believed were together and had all things in common; and they sold their possessions and goods and distributed them to all (Ac 2:37-39, 41, 44-45).

190

Luke's subsequent description of the lifestyle of the Jerusalem community is meant to re-enforce this important point (Ac 4:32).

The repentant faith-sharing practiced in Jerusalem stands, moreover, in sharp contrast to the cupidity of Ananias and Sapphira. Their sin is condemned as "testing God" (Ac 5:9). The phrase recalls Luke's account of Jesus' third and culminating temptation in the desert. So, too, does Peter's question to Ananias: "Ananias, why did Satan fill your heart to lie to the Holy Breath and keep back part of the proceeds of the land?" (Ac 5:3) Like Jesus in the desert, the couple is being tested by Satan; but unlike Jesus they have succumbed to His third and greatest temptation.

But how precisely did Ananias and Sapphira "test God"? As we have seen, for Luke as for Matthew, one tests God by setting conditions on one's willingness to trust in His fatherly, providential care. And trust in the Father is tested practically by personal willingness to share one's possessions, the physical supports of one's life, with others. Unconditioned trust in God demands a willingness to share that is correspondingly unconditioned: no one is excluded in principle, and sharing proceeds on the basis of need rather than merit. In their lying failure to share all their possessions with the community, Ananias and Sapphira stand convicted of setting conditions on their willingness to share their wealth and therefore to trust God. In their stinginess they have tested Him. Moreover, their cupidity stands in stark contrast to the generosity of Barnabas, the "son of encouragement" (Ac 4:32-5:11).[4]

Let us pause and recapitulate our argument up to this point. In Mark's gospel Jesus is driven by the Holy Breath who descended on Him at his baptism out into the desert to be tested as the first Israel was tested and to confront Satan the ancient tempter as the first Adam had. For Mark Jesus' desert experience foreshadows the disciple's own experience of Breath-baptism: like the servant messiah the members of the new Israel will be assaulted by Satan and put to the test. Matthew's temptation narrative expands Mark's cryptic reference to Satan into a prolonged dialogue in which the Breath-filled messiah vanquishes the tempter with three citations from the Torah. When these citations are read in the light of Jesus' own moral doctrine, they take on connotations that go beyond their original meaning in the text of Deuteronomy. The tempted messiah proclaims unconditioned trust in God and worship of the Father rather than of the prince of this world as basic conditions for membership in the new Israel. In Jesus' own teachings trust in the Father's providential care finds its most practical expression in the willingness to share one's bread, one's worldly possessions with others. The unconditioned character of one's trust comes to expression in the gratuity and unconditioned character of one's sharing: like God's own providence it reaches out to anyone, irrespective of the individual's merits. It looks to need rather than to deserts. And it expresses the mutual forgiveness in atoning love which proves the authenticity of Christian worship of the Father. Luke not only endorses the new covenant morality proclaimed by Matthew; he makes even more

191

radical demands in the area of practical concern for the poor. For Luke the supreme temptation of the Christian is to test God: to set conditions on one's willingness to trust in God's providence by also setting limits on one's willingness to share one's possessions with others.

Mark's gospel inculcates a similar moral vision, though less explicitly. Mark's Jesus demands of His disciples a purity of intention (Mk 7:14-23) irreconcilable with religious hypocrisy, formalism, and legalism (Mk 2:23-3:6, 7:1-13, 12:38-40). He summons His followers to a faith in Himself touched by moral ultimacy: they must, in imitation of their Master be willing, if necessary, to die for His sake and for the good news He proclaims (Mk 4:40-41, 5:34, 8:34-9:1, 10:38, 11:20-24, 13:3-13, 14:36). The religious faith to which Mark's Jesus summons His disciples finds expression in practice. It binds one to God in petitionary prayer. It demands obedience to God's will and to the moral demands of His covenant (Mk 3:34-35, 10:19-20). Moreover, God commands us most basically to love Him above all things and our neighbor as ourselves (Mk 12:29-30).

The practical faith which Mark's Jesus demands of His close followers goes beyond the moral exigencies of the Torah. Those who would follow Him must be willing to sell their possessions and distribute them as alms to the needy (Mk 10:21-22). They must recognize that hoarded wealth poses one of the greatest obstacles to obedient submission to the reign of God (Mk 10:21-22). And they must stand prophetically opposed to rich, pious hypocrites who pray long prayers while oppressing the poor and the defenceless (Mk 12:38-40). Instead, the disciples of Jesus must practice an open hospitality toward the dispossessed and the needy that imitates the Lord's own table fellowship with sinners (Mk 2:15-17, 9:37, 10:15-16).

But the faith sharing of worldly possessions in hospitality or in almsgiving must itself spring from a pure intention. It must express belief in the divine forgiveness of sins proclaimed by Jesus (Mk 2:5-12, 15-17). It must therefore incarnate mutual love and mutual forgiveness (Mk 9:41). Indeed, mutual forgiveness must be cherished as the test of the authenticity of prayer (Mk 11:25).

Finally, those who submit in obedient faith to the reign of God must serve one another in the image of Jesus, the suffering servant of God. His disciples must renounce the pride and power of the princes of this world and serve one another instead with the simplicity of children. Among the followers of Jesus the least must be treated as the greatest (Mk 9:34-35, 10:35, 41-45). They must scrupulously avoid giving scandal to one another (Mk 9:42-50). And they must pattern their lives on Jesus Himself Who goes to His death forgiving in advance the betrayal of His followers (Mk 8:3-9:1, 14:36).

For Mark, therefore, as for Matthew and Luke, discipleship demands a faith and trust in God which reaches out to others, especially the needy, to share with them in the Father's name the blessings of this life. That sharing knows no restrictions in principle: it proceeds on the basis of need rather than of merit. And it expresses a mutual forgiveness that tests the authenticity of Christian prayer. Moreover, Jesus proclaims this moral vision in all three gospels in the power of the divine Breath imparted to Him in His baptism.

We have no serious reason for doubting that this value system which the evangelists place on the lips of the Breath-filled messiah is "authentic Jesus". It distinguishes His moral vision from every other. Does then the new covenant morality which He proclaimed in the power and enlightenment of God's Holy Breath tell us anything about the reality of the triune God? More to the present point, does it reveal to us specifically anything about the reality of the divine Breath Herself?

Jesus inculcated a filial morality. That is to say, He taught His disciples how to live as children of God in His own image. His moral vision expressed, therefore, His human understanding of the character of His personal relationship to the Father and to the Breath.

Jesus' human mind remained human even though it was the human understanding of a divine person. It developed, presumably, in much the same way that other human minds grow, even though the hypostatic union certainly introduced important variables into Jesus' human growth absent from ours. But if Jesus' experience was a human one, then we may legitimately suppose that the vision of religious conduct He proclaimed would have ripened within Him over the years.

Human minds develop through dialogue with the world which surrounds them. Living organisms display two ways of interacting with their environments: assimilation and accommodation. Biological assimilation transforms the environment in ways that sustain the organism. Food is eaten, digested, and then incorporated into the organism's physical structure. Assimilation stabilizes life: it strives to repair and restore existing organic structures. Accomodation takes more chances. It adjusts the organism to the environment. It bears fruit in organic change and growth. Similar patterns occur in human cognitive development. Human minds must organize themselves through interaction with their world. Sometimes the world is assimilated to the cognitive structures the mind already possesses. We recognize things that we have already learned. But the mind also accomodates itself to its world by scrapping old beliefs to acquire new ones. Unanswered questions are raised and resolved. In the process the mind acquires new habits of thought and understanding.

Personal decision legislates the habitual structure of each human mind. In order to acquire a belief I must assent to it. Assent is a form of decision. Through decision, too, beliefs become structured into habitual patterns of cognitive response. I may contemplate the possibility that two previously unrelated ideas may in fact stand in a positive relationsip to one another but I must decide that they are in fact related before they will coalesce into a unified belief system.

The beliefs that structured Jesus' human mind were also the fruit of decision. So, too, was the vision of human conduct which He proclaimed and imposed on His disciples. Elements of that vision are found in the Old Testament. In depicting Jesus' moral vision as the fulfillment of old covenant morality, Matthew tacitly conceded that Jesus did not create the moral demands of new covenant living out of whole cloth. Luke's gospel also suggests that Jesus derived His doctrine of faith-sharing in part from the preaching of the Baptist (Lk 3:11). But whatever the sources of Jesus' moral vision, He transformed all of them by reinterpreting them in the light of His own sense of mission and of standing in a unique, interpersonal relationship with the Father. He offered His disciples the vision of a certain kind of faith community, a community which attempts to imitate Jesus' own filial relationship to the Father by living in His image.

But if the shape of Jesus' human mind gradually matured through an alternation of reflection and decision, Jesus' religious maturation differed in one important respect from our own. We grow religiously through the persuasive illumination of the Holy Breath. Jesus' human experience was ruled efficaciously by the **Logos.** Jesus' every human decision was the human decision of a divine person, of the Son who functions within the Godhead as a principle of obediential efficacy. That fact has immense consequences for the manner in which Jesus' human mind developed. Let us begin to explore its implications.

In Chapter II we saw that in the development of experience evaluation, factual transactions, and the development of habits mutually condition one another. The evaluations which precede any decision specify its character. And any alternative I choose either creates or reenforces an habitual inclination to respond in a similar fashion in the future.

Moreover, we saw in the last chapter that the hypostatic union demands that the Son's human experience be ruled by Him in such a way that it loses its human autonomy and is tranformed thereby into the human experience of a divine person. The habits that structured the Son's human mind function within His human experience. Those habits were created and reenforced by the Son's human choices. But the Son's decisions express His obedient submission to the will of the Father and the inspiration of the Holy Breath. In other words, the Son's habitual human beliefs were shaped by decisions that express the evaluations conceived by the divine interpretant. As a consequence, His human mind is Her created icon. We use the term "icon" here in a way that blends its logical and theological meanings.

As a logical term, "icon" designates a representation whose meaning derives from its qualitative resemblance to its referent. A photograph is, for example, an icon of the person or thing photographed. Logical icons are contrasted with indices and with symbols. An index points to a referent. An arrow, a pointing finger, a weathervane all function as indices which direct attention to some reality. A symbol, however, represents its referent by interpreting its significance.

The term, "icon," however, also has a theological meaning. In its theological sense, an icon also signifies in virtue of its resemblance to some transcendent reality. But religious icons in addition negate themselves. In announcing the reality they resemble they make it simultaneously plain that they also differ from the reality in question. In other words, religious icons function as analogous, sacramental symbols of a reality that encompasses and transcends them. They both reveal and conceal the reality they signify.

The icons of the eastern church illustrate the self-negating character of the religious icon. In their beauty and opulence they symbolize the irruption of divine grace and glory into human history. But Christian iconographers as a group eschewed realistic portrayal of religious persons and events. They thus sought to remind those who contemplate the icon that it reflects only dimly the glory of the divine reality it seeks to portray.

The divine mind of the **Logos** is the Holy Breath. The decisions of the **Logos** express His obedient submission both to Her inspirations and to the will of the Father. The habitual shape of the Son's human mind was determined by the decisions that fixed His human beliefs and attitudes. The Son's habitual human beliefs and attitudes were therefore determined by decisions that express evaluations conceived by the divine interpretant. Inevitably, then, they resemble the Breath's own evaluative response to reality. In its historical evolution, Jesus' human mind confronts us as a created icon of Her reality. It truly resembles Her.

But the Son's divine mind is infinite and eternal. His human mind is finite and datable. In its finitude and datability the Son's human mind differs significantly from His divine. It therefore both resembles and differs from the divine interpretant. The human mind of the Son stands therefore as a self-negating religious icon of Her reality.

The Son's human will is also a finite reality. But because the Father and His obedient Son are of one will, we can say with John the evangelist that whoever sees the Son sees the Father (Jn 14:5-10). If then the Son and Breath are also of one mind, we can say just as truly that whoever has understood the mind of Jesus has in that very act penetrated to the evaluative shape of the divine experience and perceived in faith the reality of the divine interpretant who conceives the divine evaluations. Jesus' human mind confronts us therefore as a normative, individual, sacramental revelation of Her reality.

These Christological conclusions follow from the experiential pneumatology developed in the preceding pages. They also lend support to the explanation of the divine unity proposed in Chapter VI. There we suggested that the divine experience being both complex and relational could be unified only by its internal relational structure. We further suggested that the perfection of the Son's obedience to the will of the Father and the illumination of the Breath offers a paradigm for understanding the unitive relation of the divine persons to one another. By His obedience the Son gives Himself freely to both. We hypothesized therefore that the divine experience is unified through the free and mutual self-gift of the divine persons to one another in living love. Because They give Themselves to one another totally, the divine persons exist in one another perfectly and share not a similarity but an identity of life. This insight suggested a further corrolary: namely, that the mutual self-donation of the divine persons defines the evaluative shape of the divine experience.

If Jesus' human mind is a created icon of the divine interpretant, one would expect that the way that the divine persons interrelate within the Godhead would be reflected in some significant way in His vision of the way in which the children of God ought to relate to one another and to God in faith. And in point of fact, Jesus' moral vision does precisely that. It summons His disciples to the free and loving gift of themselves to God and to one another in faith, in hope, and in love. Moreover, the quality of love He demands of His followers reproduces the quality of love that He Himself incarnated. To the extent therefore that Christian communities incarnate the mind of Christ and actually live the moral vision He proclaimed, to that extent they are transformed into social icons of the Divine Breath.

Of all the writers of the New Testament, **Paul** the apostle seems to have grasped this truth most explicitly. The moral vision which the synoptics place on the lips of Jesus functions in significant and suggestive ways in Paul's exhortations to his churches. Most of Paul's letters were, of course, written with a view to specific pastoral problems in the Christian communities he had founded. And their exhortatory sections usually dealt with tensions and questions peculiar to a specific community. An important exception to this pattern was, however, the letter to the Romans. Unlike the other epistles of Paul, it was addressed to a community which the apostle had not personally founded. To introduce himself he attempted to summarize the salient points of his version of the gospel. The moral exhortation which closes the letter is not, therefore, in all probability focused on specific problems peculiar to the Roman community. It expresses rather a general summary of the apostle's vision of Christian living, but with special attention to issues especially bothersome in the early church.

Paul's moral message in Romans alternates between the enunciation of general principles and specific practical applications. Having exhorted the Romans to universal love, even of their persecutors, Paul addresses himself to the relationship which ought to obtain between believers and pagans who wield authority (Rm 13:1-7). Similarly, having exhorted the Romans to mutual love in community, he closes the entire exhortation with an extended reflection on how to deal lovingly with the consciences of scrupulous Christians (Rm 14:1-15). But if these two practical applications are bracketed, the rest of the exhortation describes the general ideals which ought to govern Christian behavior.

Paul makes it quite clear at the beginning of his exhortation that he regards the ideals in question as distinctively Christian. He urges the Romans to live as a community whose worship and lifestyle expresses their transformation in the "newness of the mind **(tei anakainosei tou noos)**" (Rm 12:1-2). In Romans the mind of the believer is transformed and renovated by the illumination of the Breath of the risen Christ (Rm 8:1-39).

That newness of mind finds practical expression in a spontaneous willingness to share in community both the charismatic inspirations of the Breath and the physical supports of human life (Rm 12:3-8). Christian sharing of personal possessions must proceed on the basis of human need. An important form of faith-sharing is hospitality (Rm 12:13). Such sharing should express mutual forgiveness and reconciliation in Christ's name. The same practical love should be shown to one's enemies, since faith sharing in the newness of the mind seeks to unite those whom malice has divided. There must be special concern for the poor; but it must be free from condescension. For Christian faith sharing must express real friendship and mutual service rather than class privilege (Rm 12:9-21; cf. Eph 4:27, Col 3:4-15). Finally, Christian faith sharing must incarnate mutual love. Mutual love in Christ's name and image carries the believer beyond the requirements of the law, for it teaches Christians to act only for the benefit of others, never for their harm, while the law only forbids what is harmful (Rm 13:8-10; cf. 1 Co 13:1-14:1). In other words, the kind of conduct which Paul holds up to the Roman community as expressive of distinctively Christian ideals is thoroughly convergent with the moral vision which Jesus proclaims in the synoptics. Moreover, the same values which Paul affirmed in Romans as distinctively Christian he invoked repeatedly and spontaneously in the resolution of the pastoral problems that arose within the churches he himself had founded (1 Co 11:17-34, 12:1ff; 2 Co 8:1-15; Col 3:5-4:1, Ep 5:21-6:9).

These reflections bring into focus yet another aspect of Pauline moral teaching: the prohibition of forms of conduct incompatible with the mind of God and of Christ. These prohibitions occur in what seem on first reading miscellaneous lists of sins. But when we reflect on these lists in the light of those values which Paul regarded as distinctively Christian, each prohibition violates some aspect of Paul's understanding of Christian moral conduct. An individual committed to the sharing of personal possessions freely and gratuitously with others has, for example by that fact renounced greed, theft, usury, swindle, extortion, economic exploitation, and a spirit of competition. If Christian sharing must express a love as unconditioned as divine love, then it certainly excludes murder, violence,

197

revenge, wrangling, feuding, quarreling, and bad temper. Also excluded are slander, lying, deceit, dishonesty, and boastfulness. Equally reprehensible are sexual expressions of love informed by selfish egotism: like lust, depravity, incest, gross indecency, and pederasty. Finally, the mutual forgiveness demanded by Christian love excludes cliquishness, contentiousness, jealousy, and hypersensitivity (1 Co 1:10-16, 5:1-13, 13:4-6; Rm 1:28-32; Ga 5:19-26).

But Paul's conception of the ideals that govern new covenant morality advances beyond the teachings of Jesus on one important point. Jesus had required of His disciples the willingness to share their worldly possessions with one another and with the poor. Paul extends the notion of faith sharing not only to physical possessions but also to the charisms imparted by the Breath. In order to understand the foundational implications of this basic Pauline insight we must reflect upon four interrelated propositions: (1) A charism of the Breath corresponds to each moment in the growth of human experience. (2) The sharing of all the charisms in community creates the matrix in which Christians learn individually and collectively to put on the mind of Christ. (3) To the extent that the Christian community incarnates the mind of Christ, to that extent it is a social icon of the Holy Breath. (4) The trinitarian structure of the divine experience provides the ultimate ground for Christian sacramentalism.

(1) **A charism of the Breath corresponds to each moment in the growth of human experience.** The first letter to the Corinthians contains two lists of charisms (1 Co 12:8-10, 28-31). Romans and Ephesians each contain one (Rm 12:6-8; Eph 4:9). The lists do not match. In the first of the lists in Corinthians we find the following charisms: teaching wisdom, teaching instruction, faith, healing, miracles, prophecy, discernment, tongues, and the interpretation of tongues. The second list attempts a hierarchical ordering of gifts: apostles, prophets, teachers, miracles, healing, helpers, leaders, and tongues. Elsewhere in the same letter, Paul speaks of marriage and celibacy as charisms of the Holy Breath (1 Co 7:5-7). Romans and Ephesians mention fewer charisms. Romans lists prophecy, administration, teaching, preaching, almsgiving, officials and works of mercy. Ephesians names apostles, prophets, evangelists, pastors, and teachers.

A charism, as we have already seen, manifests in a particular way the grace (**charis**) revealed to us in Jesus and the Breath. The Pauline lists, therefore, name activities and services that were commonly accepted by the members of his churches as concrete manifestations of the graced enlightenment of the Breath. In the course of his letters Paul discourses at some length about the scope and purpose of his own apostolic ministry (Rm 1:3-7, 15:14-16; 1 Co 1:10-4:21; 2 Co 1:8-7:16, 10:1-13:13; Ga 1:11-2:21). In first Corinthians he discusses the relative merits of marriage and of celibacy (1 Co 7:1-40). And he has a fair amount to say about tongues, the interpretation of tongues, and prophecy (1 Co 12:1-11, 14:1-40). But for the most part he assumes his audience knows from experience the way in which the various gifts are to be exercised. But in the absence of extensive exegetical evidence, we in the twentieth century can only make a more or less educated guess at the concrete activities that corresponded originally to each of the Pauline gifts.

An examination of the four lists reveals that they overlap. All four mention prophecy and teaching. And in three of the lists two different kinds of teaching are distinguished. The first list in Corinthians distinguishes teaching wisdom and teaching instruction. The list in Romans distinguishes teaching and preaching. The list in Ephesians links teaching with pastoral leadership and distinguishes it from evangelization. The gifts of healing, of miracles, of tongues, and of apostolate appear only twice. Moreover, tongues, healing and miracles are listed only in first Corinthians. The following gifts are listed only once: faith, discernment, the interpretation of tongues, helpers, leaders, administrators, officials, almsgiving, works of mercy.

We have no reason to suppose that the Pauline lists exhaust the charisms or that they were ever intended to do so. But even if we confine our attention exclusively to the gifts that the apostle names, we can, if we are also willing to consult contemporary religious expeirence, discover gifts that correspond to each moment in the growth of human experience. Let us reflect on how this occurs.

As we saw in Chapter II, experience advances through predictable stages. Sensation provides us with our most basic cognitive contact with the world around us. Our sensations are already affectively charged; and as our affective response grows in complexity, it is transformed into an interpretative perception of the kinds of forces which impinge upon us. We perceive them affectively as either benevolent or threatening. Images endow affective perceptions with greater differentiation. And images universally applicable in intent form an interpretative bridge between concrete, intuitive perceptions on the one hand and abstract generalizations and rational inference on the other. Our evaluative responses can be terminated at any point through decision. Our sensations and decisions insert us into the transactional realm of fact, of dynamic action and reaction. Our affective and inferential perceptions disclose to us the laws, the vectors, the selves that shape experience. Our evaluative responses endow experience with presentational immediacy: that is to say, in responding evaluatively to the facts and forces around us we become present to our world and our world to us.

Within the spectrum of experiences that occur in Christian prayer, some resemble analogously the experience of sensation. We even describe such experiences spontaneously in sensory terms. We speak of being touched by God and of savoring His presence. At such times we know greater receptivity to the divine presence, even though our conscious response is unaccompanied by any clear image or concept. Our sense of God's touch is, however, colored by affectivity.

199

The contemporary experience of the gift of tongues manifests all of these fundamental traits. The charism of tongues is in the first instance a gift of prayer. The tongue speaker comes into the presence of God in an attitude of receptivity, adoration, and praise. Prayer in tongues yields a primitive sense of being moved by God and of responding consciously to Him; but the response is unaccompanied by any clear image or concept. Prayer in tongues is affectively tinged, sometimes with powerful feelings but more often with a deepened awareness of the divine presence. Tongues, therefore, and other gifts of prayer that yield a felt, preconceptual sense of being touched by God, grace the first moment in the growth of experience.

In the second moment in the growth of experience, sensations expand into an imageless, affective perception of oneself and one's surrounding world. In Chapter II we saw that imageless, affective perceptions perform a double function within human knowing. They yield vague perceptions of reality which images and abstract conceptions seek to focus and clarify. But in addition within the realms of affective perception, imageless feelings like fear, anger, complacency exercise a judgmental function analogous to the verification and falsification of abstract inferences. Moreover, judgments of feeling being closer to sensation occur at a more primitive level than inferential judgments and are probably more common as well.

The gift of discernment engages human affective judgments. The discerner must assess prayerfully the kinds of forces that motivate individual and group behavior. The prudent discerner uses more than feeling in reaching a judgment concerning the impulses present in individuals and communities. A wise discernment invokes sound psychological, moral, doctrinal, and ascetical norms. But the judgment of discernment differs from a logical induction or a scientific proof. Abstract criteria function within discernment largely as negative checks upon the felt judgment that the discerner eventually pronounces. That judgment is reached on the basis of feeling. It expresses the discerner's felt sense in prayer of the kinds of impulses that motivate overt human acts. Those forces may be natural, gracious, or sinful. They may breathe of the divine presence. They may express legitimate human needs and desires. Or they may betray violent influences that give evidence of being demonic, diabolical, or Satanic. By engaging judgments of feeling, however, the gift of discernment effects the gracious transformation of the second moment in the growth of experience.

In the third moment in the growth of experience imageless feelings are focused and clarified through imaginative association. Imaginative thinking grasps reality intuitively. The clarifying images may, as we have seen, be remembered, created, or archetypal.

Prophetic discourse addresses the heart. It summons to repentance, to hope, to renewed commitment. Because it demands a change of attitude, prophetic discourse gravitates toward the poetic. The writing prophets were also master poets of the Hebrew tongue. Their visions expressed intuitive perceptions in faith of the saving action of God. By engaging the intuitive imagination, prophecy effects the graced transformation of the third moment in the growth of experience.

In the fourth stage in the growth of experience, the human mind advances beyond lyric and dramatic intuitions to abstract forms of inference. There are three interrelated kinds of inference. Abductive (or hypothetical) inference classifies data on the basis of principles assumed to be true. Deductive inference clarifies the meaning of an hypothesis by predicting its factual consequences. Inductive inference verifies or falsifies deductive predictions and reaches a judgment about the truth of the principle that originally grounded one's abductive explanation.

The prophetic word rends the heart, but it also proclaims a truth. One may then discern within prophecy an inferential as well as an intuitive component. Prophecy characterizes religious events. But its tone is oracular rather than argumentative and carefully didactic.

In other words, in proclaiming divine truth prophecy engages abductive forms of thinking. It offers an initial interpretation of the religious meaning of some situation or occurrence, an interpretation that needs to be illumined by sound teaching and validated through discernment. As a consequence, prophecy straddles two moments in the growth of experience. As a word addressed to the heart it expresses an intuitive perception of the real. As a profession of faith, it addresses belief. Beliefs are formulated in propositions; and propositions are linguistic shorthand for inferences. But because prophecy eschews argument, the propositions it enunciates remain from a logical standpoint hypothetical, or abductive. An interpreted message in tongues has the same experiential impact as a prophecy.

Religious teachers attempt to understand the causes and consequences of those historical events that reveal to us the reality of God. And they must assess the authenticity or inauthenticity of human behavior in the light of those events. As a consequence, charisms of teaching engage all three forms of inference. Teachers must characterize events abductively as religiously significant or not. They must forecast deductively the practical consequences of specific religious beliefs. And they must assess inductively the truth or falsity of the assumptions and generalizations that lie at the basis of spontaneous professions of religious faith.

In the Christian community teaching occurs in two contexts: the evangelical proclamation of the word (teaching wisdom) and ongoing catechesis (teaching instruction). Evangelical proclamation summons the unbeliever or the half-hearted believer to repentance and to faith. Ongoing catechesis seeks to lead the converted to a deeper appreciation and understanding of religious truths already affirmed. All authentic Christian teaching should be accompanied by signs of healing. Minimally, it should effect or deepen conversion. But the proclamation of the good news can also be accompanied occasionally by psychic and physical healings which may or may not be miraculous. Because teaching engages all three forms of inference, it effects the gracious transformation of the fourth stage in the growth of experience.

In its fifth stage experience advances beyond evaluative response to reactive decision. Decisions translate evaluations into action and may interrupt the evaluative process at any of its stages. A number of the Pauline gifts address decision: community leaders (whether official or unofficial), administrators, almsgivers, those engaged in different works of mercy, helpers--all provide important practical services to others. They therefore effect the gracious transformation of the fifth and last stage in the growth of experience.

We may name other Pauline gifts than those we have just considered. Faith is a generic gift exercised by anyone whose witness to Christ achieves a personal intensity and public visibility that goes beyond the faith common to all believers. Marriage, celibacy, and apostolic ministry are vocational gifts. They summon individuals to embrace a specific life style within the community that brings with it specific public responsibilities. But tongues, discernment, prophecy, interpretation, teaching, healing, and the action gifts each address different moments in the growth of human experience and collectively grace experience as a whole.

(2) **The sharing of the charisms in community creates the matrix in which Christians learn individually and collectively to put on the mind of Christ.** The charisms of the Breath seek to heighten shared faith consciousness. Human consciousness develops naturally through discrimination and correlation. We discriminate things that differ in kind: hues, tones, tastes, textures. And we make quantitative discriminations as well: we count, weigh, measure. Both forms of discrimination engage human evaluative responses. We also experience a heightening of consciousness when we grasp the relationship between realities we have already discriminated. We call such correlations insights.

Personal human consciousness begins with the ability to discriminate between one's own body and its impinging environment. It grows as our perceptions of both ourselves and our world acquire affective imaginative, and inferential complexity.

Every conscious act of discrimination and correlation interprets a transaction between a self and its world. Some environments stimulate the growth of consciousness. When a variety of individuals share experiences, viewpoints, attitudes, and ideas, they challenge one another to an ever expanding insight into the significant structure of experience. Some

202

environments, however, stifle consciousness through sameness, routine, and the suppression of diversity and dissent.

The enhancement of personal consciousness through social dialogue differs from the shared consciousness that bonds communities. Often enough it takes the insights of great geniuses generations to be assimilated by the communities in which they lived. Indeed the further individual minds advance in their grasp of problems and solutions of any complexity, the more difficulty they experience in communicating their insights to others.

Communal assimilation lags behind personal insight because **shared** awareness becomes possible only when a community of individuals is committed as a community to a complex process of social dialogue. A community comes to shared awareness of itself as a community only when a certain number of fundamental conditions are met.

(a) Shared consciousness results most directly from shared experiences. Friends who have lived and worked together for years are bound to one another by the things that they have done and suffered in one another's presence. But in communities of any size the direct sharing of experience ceases to be a practical possibility. Geographically large communities and communities with long histories come to initial consciousness as communities when they identify with some past event from which the community dates its origin. Americans remember the War for Independence and its aftermath as the birth of our nation. Christians look back to Jesus and to Pentecost to find their ecclesial origins.

(b) Once a community has identified its founding event, it must then reach a consensus concerning its significance. In interpreting the significance of its founding event a community comes to an initial sense of its specific historical identity. Hence, as long as contradictory interpretations of that event prevail in any given community, its self-awareness as a community will be divided and to that extent dimmed. The Reformation illustrates dramatically how conflicting interpretations of a community's founding event can shatter its unity and diminish its shared sense of identity.

(c) A community is linked to its founding event by its intervening history. The interpretation of that history will then also shape the community's present sense of its identity. To achieve the greatest degree of shared consciousness, a community must therefore also reach a consensus concerning the significance of the history that links it to its founding event.

(d) But human communities have futures as well as historical pasts. If a community is to achieve shared consciousness as a community, not only must it achieve an integrated sense of its present identity through a sound interpretation of its historical origins; but it must also come to a common agreement about the shape of its future. Its members must share common hopes and a practical commitment to organized programs of activity that seek to realize those hopes.

(e)   Communities, however, like individuals advance toward the future through activity. The shared hopes and common projects that bond the members of a community to one another must then be brought to actual realization in shared activity if the community as such is to achieve full self-awareness.

(f)   Moreover, a community's shared self-awareness will be heightened in direct proportion to its ability to engage all its members in the task of interpreting their common origin, planning their common future, and bringing those plans to fruition.   A fully self-conscious community will then treasure the diverse gifts of its members and seek as far as possible to engage them all in advancing its shared life.

(g)   The practical coordination of the personal contribution of the individual members of a community for the advancement of their common cause will demand a variety of leaders with talents proportionate to the diversity of the projects that shape the community's life.

(h)   Freedom waxes and wanes with consciousness. For both grow with the ability to distinguish and correlate the realities that shape experience. The more nuanced my conscious sense of possible alternatives of action and their consequences, the more freely will I choose in any given circumstance.   As a consequence, those communities will achieve the greatest degree of shared consciousness which not only encourage the growth of freedom but also engage the free dedication of their members to a common cause.

(i)   Since freedom, which is a condition for achieving community consciousness, is enhanced by conversion, the shared self-awareness of a community will either develop or decline in direct proportion to the degree of conversion present among its members.

(j)   Finally, since human egotism makes it morally certain that some of the members of any community will at some point selfishly betray the others, no community will be able to maintain the solidarity which is a precondition for achieving shared self-awareness unless it forgives in advance its betrayal by selfish individuals.

The Christian community spans the globe and counts its age in centuries. It faces therefore an enormous challenge if it is to come to shared self-awareness as a community.   Moreover, the awareness that unites Christians must develop in faith; for the event which founds the Christian community and endows it with its present sense of identity is the historical self-revelation of God in Jesus and the Holy Breath. If then the Christian community is to achieve a shared awareness of itself as a

204

community, that awareness must express its gracious illumination by the divine Breath. In other words, the Christian community will achieve full consciousness of itself as a religious community united in a common faith, hope, and love only to the extent that its members share freely with one another Her charismatic inspirations.

Each of the charisms contributes something to the shared faith consciousness of the Christian community. Jesus begins the new Israel. But the disciples He gathered around Him became an eschatological community of faith united in a common creed and a common hope on Pentecost day. The Breath announced Her arrival in Pentecost by pouring out the gift of tongues on those gathered in the upper room. The gift of tongues serves therefore as a living reminder of the ongoing event that founds the Church.

The gifts of prophecy and of evangelization summon the Christian community to repentance and conversion. They therefore demand of Christians freedom of heart to respond to the inspirations of the Breath nd to share them with one another in community.

The different charisms of teaching ensure that the systematic reappropriation of the heritage of the Church advances prayerfully and in faith. That reappropriaton should bear fruit in an enhanced sense of shared communal identity. Moreover, Christian teachers and prophets should nurture Christian hope in the future God has prepared and heighten group awareness of the possible courses of action available to the community and to its leaders. When teaching is confirmed by conversion and other forms of healing, it also yields an enhanced sense of the saving presence of God.

The gift of discernment mediates between the activity of prophets, teachers, and community movements on the one hand and practical community leadership, administration, and decision making on the other. The discerner discriminates between true and false prophecy, between sound and unsound teaching, between authentic and inauthentic religious impulses. The judgment of discernment provides therefore the basis on which sound administrative decisions can be taken in faith.

Finally, action gifts of practical leadership within the Church ensure that the common aspirations engendered by prophecy, evangelization, and day-to-day instruction are translated into shared activity. The chief responsibility of Christian leaders remains, therefore, the evocation, cultivation, and coordination of the charisms of each member of the community for the collaborative achievement of its shared goals and ideals.

As we have just seen in the preceding section of this chapter, each of the Breath's gifts addresses a different moment in the growth of experience. At the same time, individual faith consciousness develops in dialogue with others in community. One may therefore anticipate that in a community in which only some of the charisms operate but not others

205

individual faith consciousness will probably suffer a corresponding diminishment in those realms of experience that should be addressed by the absent gifts. When tongues and other gifts of prayer are absent, individuals will find it more difficult to sustain a sense of the presence of God. When the prophetic voice subsides, hearts harden. In the absence of sound teaching individual faith wavers. Without discernment individual decision falters. And without inspired leadership, activity is scattered and disorganized.

Moreover, unless all the charisms remain operative in the Christian community its shared faith consciousness will falter as well. When tongues fail, Breath consciousness and a shared awareness of Pentecost as the Church's founding event languish. When prophets hold their peace, complacency and despair replace conversion and heartfelt response to God in faith. Without sound teaching Christian communities are tossed to and fro by every wind of doctrine and eventually fragment in their inability to absorb the conflicting forces that trouble them. Without healing, neurosis mars discernment and the sense of God's efficacious presence to His people dissolves. In the absence of effective, practical leadership in faith, living hopes evaporate into empty dreams, and teaching becomes effete and academic.

The sharing of the charisms seeks to enhance the shared faith consciousness of Christians, their awareness of themselves as members of a living faith community. Christians believe that Jesus is the Son of God and the Breath-baptiser. The Breath of Jesus comes to teach us how to live as children of God in His image. We live in His image when our lives incarnate the same values as He lived and proclaimed. In other words, the sharing of the charisms will achieve its purpose when it encourages Christian communities to a living faith in God's providential care which frees each member of the community to share with others both personal worldly possessions and the inspirations of the divine Breath. That sharing will be authentically Jesus-like when it proceeds on the basis of need rather than of merit and when it expresses a mutual forgiveness in His name and image that is acknowledged as the test of the authenticity of the community's own worship. In the community of the Breath-baptised all the charisms of the Holy Breath of Jesus are freely shared in such a way that its members learn both individually and collectively to understand and to live the mind of Christ.

(3) **To the extent that the Christian community incarnates the mind of Christ, to that extent it is transformed into a social icon of the Holy Breath of Jesus.** The hypostatic union transformed Jesus' human mind into an individual, created icon of the Holy Breath. His human mind was ruled in its development by the Son, Whose every decision is taken in obedient submission to the will of the Father and the illumination of the Breath. Because His human mind developed in perfect submission to Her inspirations, it confronts us, as we have seen, as a perfect created icon of the mind of God, of the divine interpretant Who is the Holy Breath.

Breath-baptism seeks to teach the Christian community obedience to the mind of Christ. But our obedience to the will of the Father and the inspirations of the Breath falls far short of His. Even when the Christian community submits to the charismatic inspirations of the Hoy Breath, it perceives both the historical mission of Jesus and the transcendent reality of God through a glass darkly. Jesus no longer walks the earth, nor can we converse with Him directly in order to understand His mind. We perceive the mind of Christ only through a complex and sometimes painful process of social dialogue. For we must grope our way to religious understanding through the ordeal of ongoing repentance and conversion. We must weigh the pros and cons of theological evidence, discern the unconscious motives of prophets, teachers, and charismatic leaders. Jesus' obedience to the Breath's inspiration was worked in Him efficaciously. Our own proceeds by fits and starts. Our personal insight into His mind flickers because we live in communities in which Her charisms are too often little valued or suppressed. As a result, instead of living in the everlasting newness of Christ's mind, we substitute merely humanistic, secular, or sinful values for the true gospel message. We languish in bourgeois complacency or yield to the blandishments of bellicose nationalism.

But in spite of our faltering obedience and frequent failures we do experience moments of enlightenment when saintly individuals and Breath-filled communities challenge us by their fidelity to acknowledge the full scope of our calling as Christians. And in moments of generosoity when we reach out to one another in atoning love, in moments when we share our bread or our faith unstintingly with others without thought of merit or of recompense, in moments when we find the courage to shatter the social barriers that isolate and oppress and to forgive one another in the name and image of Jesus--in these moments even we sinful Christians can still glimpse the rays of divine beauty that glowed in Jesus' eyes and drew to Him throngs of the helpless, the hopeless, and the dispossessed.

When individuals successfully incarnate the mind of Christ to an outstanding degree we venerate them as saints. But we recognize them long before their feasts are incorporated canonically into the liturgical calendar. The Martin Luther Kings, the Dorothy Days, the Mother Teresas bulk large in the Christian community as Gibraltars of heroism.

But communities too can incarnate the mind of the Lord collectively. Christian families, religious communities, and parishes where the charisms of the Breath are cultivated can live a life of faith sharing that excludes no one in principle from charitable concern. Their worship can be rooted in a practical mutual forgiveness that imitates Jesus' own. Moreover, the members of such a community can legitimately claim in consequence of their shared faith experience to perceive the Breath of Jesus in their midst.

We perceive Her presence in Jesus in acknowledging His human mind to be a perfect, created icon of the divine mind. And from our reconstructed perception of His human mind we derive the normative criteria we need to perceive Her presence in ourselves and in others. Among those criteria fidelity to the new covenant morality which Jesus incarnated and proclaimed provides the most fundamental, practical test we have of Breath-filled human behavior. Whenever, therefore, humans are moved by faith in God to share gratuitously the blessings of this life with others, especially with the needy, they dwell in the Holy Breath and She in them. Whenever faith frees human hearts to reach out to the alienated and the dispossessed, they are moved by the Breath of Christ; and we perceive Her inspirations in that act of reconciliation. Whenever people find strength in faith to forgive one another with the atoning love of Jesus and to do so from the heart, in that act the divine interpretant breathes an enlightenment perceivable by those with eyes to see and ears to hear. Finally, when we see people with the strength of faith to proclaim the Lordship of Jesus with the same courage that led Him to lay down His life so that God's reign be established upon this earth, we perceive in their atonement the illumination and vitality of the divine Breath.

To the extent that the life style of Christian communities incarnates the mind of Jesus, to that extent they are transformed into social icons of the Holy Breath, for His human mind was a perfect, individual iconic symbol of Her reality. Then the mutual self-gift of believers to one another in faith, forgiveness, and atoning love mirrors the mutual self-gift of the divine persons and transforms the disciples of Jesus collectively into a created icon of the divine society.

(4) **The trinitarian structure of the divine experience provides the ultimate ground of Christian sacramentalism.** Symbols structure every experience. Facts function as the expressive symbols of the laws in which they are grounded. Facts together with the laws they express endow experience with significance. Evaluations function as interpretative symbols composed of immediate and dynamic interpretants. They endow experience with meaning. Meaning presents significant relationships evaluatively to some self. Communications express meaningful intent. They render experience dialogic.

Expressive and interpretative symbols lend dynamic structure to the divine experience. The Father stands within the Godhead as the source of creative efficacy; the Son, as the source of obediential efficacy. Together they ground the capacity of the divine experience to express itself symbolically. Within the Godhead the Father expresses Himself in generating the Son. The Son expresses His love of the Father by obedient submission to the Father's will. In conforming Himself to the Father's will the Son becomes an expressive symbol of the Father's person and reality.

Within the Godhead the Father and Son express themselves in generating the Holy Breath. She however stands within the divine experience as an interpretative symbol: She is the mind of the Father and the Son. In Her unitive relationship to the Father and Son, She conceives

208

the Word the Father speaks by sending Him into the world. The Son, then, through His obedience to Her inspirations also functions as an expressive symbol of Her reality.

The Son's human experience was ruled efficaciously by Him. His human words and deeds are, therefore, created expressive symbols of His divine person. They communicate to us who He is and how He relates to the Father and to the Breath. The Son's human words and deeds reveal His person because He initiates them with divine autonomy. But in consequence of His obedience, they also express the will of the Father and the saving intentions of the divine interpretant. Since only the Son could by taking flesh function as an expressive symbol of both the Father and the Breath, only He could reveal the inner life of the triune God by becoming incarnate. Only He therefore can inaugurate the last age of salvation in which God stands finally and fully revealed.

The incarnate Word also confronts believers as a uniquely normative, expressive symbol of what they are called by grace to become: namely, children of God in Jesus' image. Our salvation lies in imitating His obedient submission to the will of the Father and to the illumination of the Breath. Since the Son incarnates the Father's will, we obey the Father in obeying Him. And since His human mind stands as a perfect human icon of the divine interpretant, it measures the authenticity of our every religious inspiration. Moreover, through the obedience of faith we ourselves are graciously transformed into expressive symbols of the God who dwells within us. Our words and deeds express who we are and communicate the intentions of our minds. When our minds are conformed to the mind of Jesus, our actions express the saving intentions of the divine interpretant. And when we obey the Son who obeyed the Father perfectly, our lives reveal both their persons and their reality. Faith acts therefore function as expressive symbols of all three divine persons. Individuals of outstanding holiness express the reality of God in personal acts of heroic faith. Ordinary believers reveal the same reality less dramatically. And Christian communities give collective symbolic expression to the Godhead.

Events that express the saving presence of God are sacramental. The term "sacrament" has had a long history. In its broadest sense it signifies any reality that both reveals and conceals God's gracious activity. In its narrow sense "sacrament" designates the rituals of the Church, for they celebrate the paschal mystery by which we are saved. A ritual sacrament may be defined as an act of public worship which challenges individuals and communities either to seal or to renew the new covenant of grace revealed in the death and glorification of Jesus. In proclaiming the new covenant, sacramental rituals engage the faith common to all Christians. Because they are public official acts of the Church they must be performed by an individual who is officially empowered to speak in the name of the Christian community and of the God who commissions it to proclaim the gospel.

209

But sacramentality cannot be confined to the ritual sacraments alone. For they point to events beyond themselves which manifest the reality of God and His gracious presence within human experience. The Word made flesh stands as the supreme sacrament and the norm of sacramental authenticity. For in Him we encounter the person of God Himself. But every event that both reveals and conceals the saving presence of God enjoys genuine sacramentality.

Every human experience takes on a sacramental character when it is graciously transformed in faith. Christian hope, faith, and love are the children of commitment, born of consent to God's saving self-revelation. Each graces a different moment in the growth of human experience. Christian hope graciously transforms human affectivity by freeing the heart to expand to a vision of the salvation we are all promised in the death and glorification of Jesus. Christian faith graces the human mind by leading it to an expanding inferential insight into God's saving intentions. Christian love graces human decision by teaching us to deal with one another in obedience to Jesus' moral vision. The gifts of sanctification mediate the ongoing gracing of human experience by rendering it receptive to the Holy Breath as She teaches us to put on the mind of Christ. The charisms of service effect the gracious transformation of different personalities as they incarnate the mind of Christ in different ways: as prophets, teachers, healers, administrators, helpers, officials, pastors, interpreters, tongue speakers, faith-filled individuals, worshippers.

The ritual sacraments seek to effect the gracious transformation of human experience. Baptism summons us to faith, hope, and love and to lifelong openness to the gifts of sanctification. Confirmation summons us to lifelong openness to whatever service gift the Holy Breath desires to impart. Marriage and orders give institutional sanction to specific charismatic vocations. Reconciliation and the anointing of the sick open us to the healing action of the divine Breath. And we celebrate eucharistically the paschal mystery that is historically revealed in the gracious, charismatic transformation of the community of believers.

The trinitarian structure of the divine experience provides the ultimate ground of Christian sacramentalism by endowing the divine reality with a significant and meaningful relational structure capable of historical revelation. In His incarnation the Son speaks to us in His own person, but by His faithful obedience He also reveals to us the will of the Father and the intentions of the Breath. And by summoning us to the obedience of faith, He invites us to reincarnate in our own lives the vision He proclaimed and lived. We reveal Him to the world by living as children of God in His image and by celebrating our salvation in worship. And since He by His obedience revealed to us both the Father and the Breath, we in obeying Him reveal Them to the world as well. Because the triune God is the supreme experience, we exist in it. And when we consent in faith to the incarnate Word we exist graciously in the divine persons and they in us. And in consequence of that mutual inexistence, we are transformed individually and collecitvely into sacramental symbols of their transcendent reality.[5]

In the heyday of the Enlightenment Immanuel Kant dismissed trinitarian speculation for its irrelevance to religious practice.[6] Anyone who has ploughed through a sterile scholastic textbook in trinitarian theology will readily understand some of the motives for Kant's jibe. But a foundational pneumatology unmasks the theological obtuseness of His remark. The construct for experience which that pneumatology invokes demands that we clarify any conception of the Christian God by projecting deductively its lived consequences. Foundational pneumatology transforms the sterile belief that there is a Holy Breath into a living faith and trust In Her by explicitating the moral consequences of Breath-baptism. Jesus summons the Breath-baptised Christian to live as a child of God in His own image. Breath-baptism draws the Christian inevitably into a community of faith sharing commissioned by God to break down the social barriers separating people from one another. It sets the believer in prophetic opposition to the principalities and powers of this world: to calloused politicians and the complacent rich who oppress God's little ones and walk upon the faces of the poor. Breath-baptism demands active participation in the atonement of Jesus by worshipping God in mutual forgiveness. The value system Jesus lived and proclaimed transvalues every human ethic or code of law. For it demands that they be ruled by the mind of God revealed in Christ. Moreover, once we concede that Jesus' human mind stands as a created icon of the Holy Breath, we can also grasp the practical implications of submitting to the judgment She inspires. For His moral vision reveals to us the terms under which divine judgment is pronounced. Moreover, only when we have reached an insight into the practical consequences of Breath-baptism can we begin to comprehend the meaning of death and resurrection with Christ. We die with Him to the extent that our lives incarnate the vision He proclaimed; for then we also die to this world and the powers that rule it in order to be reborn in the enlightening wisdom of His Breath. Finally, Christian worship will breathe with an experienced sense of the presence of God, only if Christian worshippers submit their lives to the terms of the new covenant of grace by teaching one another to understand and live the mind of Jesus in a charismatic community of faith. In the chapter which follows we will attempt to explicitate even further the ways in which Breath-baptism demands the radical transformation of human social relationships.

1. Montague, op. cit., pp. 242-244.

2. Ibid.; cf. JBC, 42:11.

3. Montague, op. cit., p. 269; Haenchen, The Acts of the Apostles, pp. 135-147; Navone, op. cit., pp. 63-165; Lampe, op. cit., pp. 194-200.

4. Montague, op. cit., pp. 291-292; Haenchen, op. cit., pp. 230-241.

5. In an experiential approach to the Trinity, we can, then, legitimately speak of a sacramental perception of the divine persons. Like every human perception it involve an act of interpretation; for we can perceive things affectively and inferentially. Our perception of Christ's eucharistic presence illustrates the process.

In its traditional formulation, the doctrine of the real presence of Christ in the eucharist slurs over three senses of reality and appearance. "To appear" means in the first instance to become immediately obvious: leaves appear on trees, the actor appears on stage. Here the reality itself appears. It functions within experience as an expressive symbol, for it signifies something capable of interpretation. In the second sense of the term "to appear" reality and appearance begin to be contrasted without being totally separated. Something is said to "appear" in this second sense when something not immediately apparent is grasped interpretatively through things that are immediately apparent. For example, the guilt or innocence of the accused becomes apparent through the testimony of witnesses. Similarly, the instructed mind perceives the working of the solar system in the rising and setting of the sun. In this second sense of appearance, some reality, like a sunrise or a sunset, appears immediately. But what appears immediately stands in a significant relationship with another reality less immediately apparent. The latter appears only when that relationship is grasped. As a result, the second sense of appearance engages both expressive and interpretative symbols. For the less obvious reality must be inferred or intuited in order to be perceived. In its third sense, "to appear" means a "mere appearance." This phrase refers to an interpretative moment in the process of inquiry which is subsequently recognized as fallacious and misleading. For example, a stick thrust into water "only appears" to be bent because anyone would be in error who believed the stick itself bent rather than the light rays emanating from the stick and refracted by the water. We might have said we made a mistake when we said the stick was bent rather than the light it reflected. Instead, we blame the stick.

All three senses of "appearance" are invoked in the doctrine of Christ's eucharistic presence, though they are not always differentiated. The consecrated species "appear" to be bread and wine. Here the doctrine invokes the first sense of "appearance." The species look and taste like bread and wine. But they "only appear" to be bread and wine. Now the doctrine invokes the third sense of "appearance." For the total reality that appears in the use of bread and wine within eucharistic worship is not simply the consecrated elements but the glorified Christ Who in sending the Breath to inspire the Christian community and its sacred symbolic acts is actively transforming both by His saving presence. Here we invoke the second sense of appearance.

The reader will find these and other related issues discussed at more leisure in Charism and Sacrament. Here we rest content to note that in such an understanding of Christ's eucharistic presence one lays claim to the ability to perceive the gracious presence of God in His sacramental manifestations. We perceive the divine presence affectively and inferentially in faith. That claim has implications that extend beyond eucharistic worship. For if we can perceive the divine presence in the eucharist, we can also perceive it in every other sacramental manifestation of the divine. Those manifestations will not reveal Christ's eucharistic presence because they occur outside a eucharistic context.

6. Cf. Fortman, op. cit., p. 249.

THE DIVINE MOTHER

We have been searching in all the preceding chapters for an integrated perception of God's Holy Breath. Our method has demanded that we coordinate as carefully as we can our abstract, inferential perception of Her reality with Biblical pneumatology. We have suggested that the Holy Breath can be legitimately conceived as a facet of the divine experience. And we have concluded that an experiential construct of the triune God can interpret Her person, Her union with the Father and the Son, and Her saving activity within the Christian community.

One final task of coordination remains. In the course of our reflections we have been led to conclude that the divine Breath not only enjoys personal existence but also that She functions as the ultimate personalizing principle in both divine and personal experience. But if we consult Christian iconography we discover there a startling dearth of personal images of the Holy Breath. We have no difficulty of course imagining the Son as a person. He has the face and figure of Jesus. We often picture the Father as an old man riding the clouds or seated on a throne. But we imagine the Breath most commonly as either a bird or a descending tongue of flame. We even lack a personal name for her. These facts should give us pause. For they suggest that our affective perception of the Holy Breath has not in fact kept pace with our theological understanding of Her. As long as we relate to Her differently with our heads and with our hearts, our perception of Her will lack complete integration.

The present chapter focuses then primarily but not exclusively on irrational, intuitive perceptions of the Holy Breath. But it attempts to argue in a systematic fasion a specific thesis: namely, that the archetype of the feminine in its positive, transforming aspects can when properly transvalued in faith organize all those images traditionally associated with the third person of the trinity, thus providing Christian iconography with a needed personal image of Her reality.

Our argument advances in five stages. First, we survey biblical images of the divine Breath and conclude that with the exception of the feminine personification of Wisdom in the Old Testament the Bible provides no other clearly personal image of the Breath. Second, with hints from Gaius Marius Victorinus and other fathers of the church we enunciate the thesis stated in the preceding paragraph and explore some of its implications. Third, we examine two objections to the thesis. The first objection states that given the opportunity, New Testament writers tend to prefer masculine to feminine images of the Breath of God. A close examination of the texts of the New Testament, however, unmasks this first objection as groundless. The second objection states that Jungian archetypal imagery labors under sexist connotations and for that reason should be regarded as theologically unsuitable to interpret the reality of the Christian God. We explore the implications of this second objection in some detail. We examine the transformation of archetypal images into stereotypes and some of the affective motives of that transformation. We do so out of the conviction that most conscious, pseudo-rational objections to imagining the Christian God as feminine root themselves in unconscious attitudes nurtured by the sexist, patriarchal caste of the culture in which we live. The fourth part of our argument begins to examine the ways in which the dark night of sense demands the transvaluation in faith and hope of sexist images and attitudes. We attempt to show that when transvalued by Christian revelation masculine heroic imagery loses its sexist, patriarchal connotations and demands the renunciation of **machismo** with all its works and pomps. We also argue that the transvalued archetype of the feminine provides an appropriate personal image for the Holy Breath. Finally, the fifth part of our argument attempts to show the legitimacy not only of imagining the Holy Breath as the Divine Mother but also of imagining the second person of the trinity as androgynous rather than as purely masculine. The chapter closes with a few observations on the consequences of its conclusions for a socially conscious Christian spirituality.

The discrepancy between the way we imagine the Breath and the way we understand Her rationally may seem to some a small matter. But it assumes greater importance once one decides to take the adorability of the divine Breath seriously.[1] For adoration engages the heart especially. And until Christians have an image of the Breath that represents Her person adequately, their felt affective relationship to Her in prayer will continue to languish in ambiguity.

At first glance biblical pneumatology seems to offer us no help out of this impasse. Its authors seem to have imagined the divine Breath for the most part in feral or impersonal terms. In the Old Testament She is described as wind and associated with fire (2 Kgs 2:9-15; Is 4:4; Ez 37:1-14; Gn 1:2; Qo 11:4). Fire, of course, connotes holiness, purification, judgment, and light; and on one occasion the Breath is compared to a lamp (Pr 20:27). Isaiah speaks of an outpouring of the Breath; and in his preaching Breath images and water images blend in a curious way (Is 32:14, 44:3, 59:21). The descent of the Breath on both Saul and David at the time of their royal anointing by the prophet Samuel justifies imagining Her illumination as a kind of anointing; and this fusion of images eventually fed Jewish messianic hopes (1 Sm 10:2, 16:13; Is 61: 1-3).

The New Testament echoes these impersonal images of the Breath and offers others as well. In all four gospels, the Breath descends upon Jesus under the sign of a dove (Mk 1:10; Mt 3:13-17; Lk 3:21-22; Jn 1:32). But images of wind and of fire dominate Luke's account of Pentecost (Ac. 2:2-3). Throughout the New Testament the association of Breath and water takes on important baptismal connotations (1 Co 6:11, 12:13; Rm 5:5; Mk 1:8; Mt 3:11; Lk 3:21-22; Ac 2:38; Jn 3:5-8). And in the fourth gospel, as we have seen, the Holy Breath is described as living water (Jn 4:10-14, 7:37-39, 19:33-34). In Pauline theology the baptised are imagined as having been sealed by the Breath (1 Co 1:20-21; Eph 1:13, 4:30); but in both John's gospel and the letter to Titus they are described as reborn (Tit 3:5; Jn 3:5-8). Jesus, of course, is conceived by Her power (Mt 1:20; Lk 1:35). She is also commonly associated in the New Testament with temple imagery (1 Co 3:16-17, 6:19; Lk 1:35; Jn 4:23-24). The letter to the Ephesians calls the word of God the Breath's sword; but the sword symbolizes the word rather than the Breath (Eph 5:17). The title "the Paraclete" offers perhaps the closest New Testament approach to a personal image of the Breath (Jn 14:15-17, 26, 15:26, 16:7, 13). The title suggests a dynamic personal function of the Breath; but it conceives that function abstractly and leaves the reader at a loss in imagining the Paraclete.

In the Old Testament the Breath is not conceived as a distinct divine person within the Godhead. Nevertheless the book of Proverbs offers us the only clearly personal image of Her in the entire Bible. There wisdom is personified as a feminine figure who preaches in the streets and public places seeking disciples; and She is identified as the Holy Breath of the Lord (Pr 1:20-13). The book of Wisdom also identifies the Breath and divine Wisdom (Ws 1:6), while Ecclesiastes portrays the Wisdom of God as a kind of goddess who dwells eternally in the Presence of God (Qo 24:1-30).

The fathers of the church failed as a whole to exploit theologically this personal image of the divine Breath, perhaps because many conceived of the **Logos**, the Son, as the mind and wisdom of God rather than the Breath. But we find an interesting exception to this patristic pattern. As we have seen, not all the fathers acquiesced in the **Logos** Christology introduced by Justin and popularized by Alexandrian theologians. Irenaeus, Basil, and Victorinus all identify the Holy Breath with divine wisdom. But of the three Victorinus faced most directly the implications of such an association. He taught that when the New Testament tells us that Jesus was conceived by the Holy Breath, it asserts that She is mother of the Son in heaven and on earth. He writes:

> But because we have said that the **Logos** and the Holy Breath are one and the same motion--the **Logos** insofar as He is life, and the Holy Breath insofar as She is knowledge and intelligence (for that natural order is also divine: since there is power, it was necessary that intelligence be moved to the knowledge of itself)--the Son was born, Who is **Logos,** that is, life, through the generating power of the paternal intelligence, like an eternal source. One would not then be deceived, were one to represent the Holy Breath as the mother of Jesus on high and below: on high for the reason just explained; below for the reason that follows. For it was necessary for our liberation that everything divine, that is, the seedbed of all spirits that subsist universally,

217

that which is the First Being, I mean the universal **Logos**, should take on flesh from lower matter and corruption for the mortification of all corruption and sin....The angel replied therefore to Mary and said to her: "The Holy Breath will come upon you and the power of the Most High will overshadow you." These two, the **Logos** and the Holy Breath, that are movement "came" so that Mary might be with child, that flesh might be built from flesh, the temple and dwelling place of God. The Holy Breath was indeed the power in the movement. But the **Logos** Himself was the source of the movement, "the power of the Most High." For Jesus, the **Logos** is the "power and wisdom of God" (Against Arius, II.i. 58. 11-36).

Victorinus was led to this insight in the course of responding to an Arian jibe. The Arians, it will be recalled, had taunted the orthodox that if the Breath is a divine **hypostasis** She must, like the **Logos**, be generated; as a consequence, She must either be the brother of the **Logos** or the grandson of the Father. Most of the Greek fathers had taken refuge from this rhetorical thrust by citing its lack of biblical proof and by describing the procession of the Breath in vague, abstract terms. But Victorinus, like St. Paul, had no difficulty in applying familial imagery to the Christian Godhead. Moreover, his suggestion that the Holy Breath functions as a maternal principle within the Godhead does not lack for subtlety. The Breath, he argued, is mother to the Son in heaven because, being the divine intelligence, She is the power in the Godhead by which the eternal, lifegiving Word that expresses the Father's mind is conceived. She is His mother on earth because Jesus was miraculously conceived of the virgin by Her power. By punning on the word "conception" Victorinus has transformed Jesus' miraculous conception by the Breath narrated in the infancy gospels into an historical icon of an eternal event within the Godhead.

But does not Victorinus thereby assert that the Breath generates the Son? And does not that assertion contradict traditional Christian doctrine that the Father alone generates the Son? Victorinus will have to answer such an objection himself. But the experiential construct of the Trinity proposed in these pages avoids such a conclusion by insisting on three important points. First, it understands the Father and the Son as the source of divine efficacy. The generation of the Son and the spiration of the Breath transpire efficaciously within the Godhead. The Father alone generates the Son efficaciously. Second, our experiential construct of the Trinity distinguishes between relationships within the Godhead which establish the distinction of the divine persons and those which ground their unity. The former are rooted in the divine processions; the latter, in the self-donation of the divine persons. The Breath unites herself to the Father in an act of sapiential enlightenment. She unites Herself to the Son by conceiving the Word which the Father generates efficaciously and sends into the world. Third, our experiential construct of the Trinity insists that the conception of the Word within the Godhead cannot occur efficaciously act because as the divine interpretant the Holy Breath functions within the divine experience as a source of evaluation rather than of decision. For that reason no divine person proceeds efficaciously from Her. At the same time our experiential construct of the Trinity does sanction conceiving the unitive relationship of the Breath to the Son as one of conception. Mothers conceive children. An experiential approach to the Trinity provides therefore a theoretical frame of reference in which the Holy Breath can be imagined as Mother to the second person of the Trinity.

These foundational insights and images become even more suggestive when they are interpreted in the light of Jungian archetypal theory. As we saw in Chapter II, archetypal images perform an important synthetic function in organizing human affective perceptions. They not only clarify vague imageless feelings, but they also attract other images to themselves in predictable patterns. The archetype of the feminine illustrates how this occurs.

The most elemental archetype of woman is the vessel. Within her womb life is created, contained. From it life emerges. Egg-laying is also a feminine function. As the archetypal vessel of life, the feminine is often identified with the cosmogonic egg from whose shell the cosmos and all the life it contains emerge as from a vessel.[2]

But the womb must first be penetrated by the male sexual organ if it is to engender life. This biological fact links the feminine symbolically to affectively significant enclosures capable of penetration; to caves, houses, churches, temples, cathedrals, gardens, sacred diagrams.[3]

Once conceived, the infant lies in the womb. The archetype of the feminine is, then, also associated with cradles, beds, nests, urns, ships, coffins. Indeed some primitive people return the dead to Mother Earth in a foetal position.[4]

The womb that is both cave and grave links the elemental image of the feminine to the earth. Woman is symbolized by the breast-shaped mountain in which the cave is found, by the chasm, the gulf, the maw that leads to the underworld.[5]

Both menstruation and the amniotic fluid that emerges from the womb in birth link that feminine to water that flows from the earth and therefore to wells, springs, ponds, lakes, oceans, tides.[6]

Mothers not only conceive and bear life but with their breasts they nurture it once born. Accordingly, we imagine the earth as a mother who blesses us with trees, plants, fruit. The Lady of the plants fills life's cornucopia. She is the fruitful field sown with seed and made fertile by the rain.[7]

219

But such elemental images do not exhaust the archetype of the feminine. For women are experienced not only as a biological source of life but also as a transforming presence. Transforming images of the feminine, however, build on the elemental as the latter come to be associated with transcendent forms of life.[8] Then woman's capacity to give birth becomes linked with spiritual or religious rebirth or with birth unto immortality. The lady of the plants functions as a transforming principle when it is recognized that she produces not only nourishing plants but intoxicants and hallucinogens as well. She then inspires ecstasy, flights of the spirit, visions. With the breath of her mouth she utters a transcendent, mysterious wisdom.[9]

As a transforming presence the feminine loses earthly ties and assumes a celestial shape. Ordinarily she is imaged as a moon goddess, for the menstrual cycle links the feminine both to the moon and to the tides it creates.[10] Sometimes the celestial feminine is pictured as a virgin rather than as a mother. This need not necessarily happen. But the image of the virgin who is also a mother is an archetype of special power. For it presents woman as simultaneously engendering and illuminating.

Clearly, the archetype of the feminine viewed as a principle of transformation gives promise of organizing all of the images that biblical writers associate with the Holy Breath. Her Pentecostal fire symbolizes the sanctifying transformation She effects. In the blowing wind the Hebrews heard God breathing. That divine Breath speaks the wisdom that burns like a light, a lamp to the mind and heart. The curious association of the divine Breath with water in the Old and New Testaments becomes intelligible once one is willing to imagine Her as feminine. For the archetype of the feminine connotes both the Breath of wisdom and the water of purification and regeneration. And water imagery links the Divine Mother to all the images that cluster around Christian baptism. The archetype of the feminine connotes sacred enclosures: it therefore links the personal image of the Breath to the temple and to temple and church imagery. Birds lay eggs: the image of the dove viewed archetypally has, therefore, feminine connotations. Those connotations find theological reinforcement in the New Testament, where the dove symbolizes the New Israel, the faithful bride of Christ.

Moreover, the archetype of the feminine also connotes many of the theological concepts that structure Christian pneumatology. First of all, it is a personal image, the only adequate kind of affective interpretant for a divine person who is the ultimate personalizing principle within both divine and human experience. As a personal image for the divine source of transforming enlightenment, the archetype of the feminine connotes not only wisdom but every other kind of prophetic, visionary, or charismatic inspiration. The cosmogonic egg functions as a common archetypal symbol for feminine creative power; and the Divine Mother co-creates the world with both the Father and the Son. The Christian community is graciously transformed in the Holy Breath: in Her relationship to Jesus' disciples She functions therefore as an abiding matrix of divine life. She builds the living temple of God that we call the Church; and She conceives the Word of God Himself in heaven and on earth.

We are not suggesting that the third person of the Trinity is in fact a woman. Rather, we are concerned to understand the dynamic structure of the human imagination and the way archetypes produce intuitive insights into reality. The human mind can grasp truth through logical implication and through abstract inference. But it also grasps truth imaginatively. An imaginative grasp of truth does not obey the rules of logic but of free association and synchronicity. A true image of the third person of the Trinity will spontaneously connote the important images and concepts that interpret Her reality. The image of the Divine Mother does precisely that.

There may be some who would raise biblical objections to such a suggestion. Is it not true, for example, that the gospels portray the Holy Breath as the spouse of Mary and therefore implicitly as masculine? And what about the fourth gospel? John calls the Holy Breath the Advocate. Are not advocates lawyers; and were not lawyers always men at the time the gospel was written? Even more, in designating the Holy Breath as the **pneuma** of truth, does not the fourth evangelist invoke the apocalytic image of an angelic male warrior? In other words, given the opportunity to use a personal image of the Holy Breath, did not the authors of the New Testament clearly gravitate toward masculine rather than feminine imagery? Let us reflect on each of these objections in turn. For if they enjoy validity they call our position into exegetical question.

First of all, nowhere does the New Testament describe Mary as the bride of the Holy Breath or the Breath as her husband. Neither infancy gospel even hints that in Jesus' conception the Breath functioned as an impregnating male principle. Male Greek deities impregnated women with considerable regularity in ancient mythic tales. But both the Hebrew and the Christian scriptures eschew such crudities. Matthew states baldly that Jesus was conceived in the power of the divine Breath. He uses no embellishing images to explain the miracle. Mary by conceiving Jesus is transformed, at least in some readings in Luke, into the temple of God through the sanctifying descent of the Breath. In both infancy narratives Jesus' conception is portrayed as holy and mysterious. But the gospels provide no textual basis whatsoever for imagining the Breath's action as male impregnation. And temple imagery has feminine rather than masculine connotations.

Second, one must concede that at the time of John the evangelist only men practiced law. The image of the Advocate has forensic connotations. But for John the Paraclete functions not primarily as a prosecuting attorney but as a witness and as a witness specifically to Jesus. Moreover, in the fourth gospel some of the greatest witnesses to Jesus are women. The woman at the well first proclaims Him as messiah to the Samaritans, and her act foreshadows His proclamation to the gentiles

221

(Jn 4:25-30). Among Jesus' disciples Martha, not Peter, first acknowledges His messianic mission (Jn 11:17). And Mary of Magdala appears in John's resurrection narrative as the first of the apostles (Jn 20:18). In the mind of the fourth evangelist, then, to function as an advocate for Jesus connotes anything but an exclusive male prerogative. Nor has the image of the advocate decisively male connotations.

Third, the title the "**pneuma** of truth" which John applies to the Holy Breath lacks any clear sexual connotations. The title occurs in the literature of Qumran, where its connotations are angelic. But the **pneuma** of which John speaks is no angel. She is the presence of Jesus and of God. Nor does John ever refer to the "Breath of truth" with a masculine pronoun. Whenever in John's text the masculine pronoun **autos** is used of the Breath, refers to the masculine noun **Parakletos** (Jn 14:26, 15:26, 16:7-8, 13).

But a much more serious objction can be raised to invoking Jungian archetypal imagery to interpret affectively the reality of the Holy Breath: namely, the sexist character of the Jungian archetypes. Were we to invoke a sexist image of an icon of the third person of the Trinity, we would run the risk of re-enforcing the already sexist attitudes of many contemporary Christians. Let us explore the implications of this objection. For if it has validity, we would indeed be better advised to rest content with impersonal or feral images of the Advocate.

The human imagination grasps relationships dramatically. The dramatic role of women in most archetypal thinking follows predictable patterns. Most women are imagined either as mother or as consort to heroic male figures. Typically the male hero must win his freedom from domination by parental figures. His struggle often focuses especially upon the mother. He must slay her either symbolically or literally. If symbolically, he destroys either her servants or one of her feral counterparts, most often a serpent or dragon.[11] Not only must the mythic hero slay the dragon, but he must also rescue the maiden whom the dragon holds captive. And he must return from his adventures bearing her back, often with some treasure that motivated his heroic quest. When his story has a happy ending, he and the maiden are united in wedlock.[12]

Jungian psychology has attempted to discover in the adventures of the mythic male hero an archetypal rendering of the origins of human ego consciousness. In the earliest stages of its development (so the story goes), the human child experiences a powerful empathetic identification with the mother who nurtures it. From the standpoint of the child's affectivity, mother and child fuse into one. In the early stages of conscious growth, the mother functions as a symbol of the larger self which fosters the child's first halting steps toward conscious self-individuation.[13]

As the male child grows in personal consciousness, he must learn to assert his independence from maternal nurture and control and to identify with the person and world of the father. His struggle to do so introduces an ambivalence into his relationship to his mother, an ambivalence that is symbolized by the serpent, the archetypal dragon he must slay.[14]

The serpent has multiple ties to the feminine. It crawls upon the ground and is, as a consequence, especially close to the Earth Mother. It lays eggs. It devours its prey alive and become distended thereafter, like a woman in pregnancy. It symbolizes, therefore, the Terrible Mother, who devours the living offspring of her womb. Finally, the serpent's shape also resembles the umbilicus, which links the child to its mother.

At the same time, the serpent has phallic connotations. But in its closeness to the earth, it suggests a phallus owned and dominated by the Great Mother. As phallic, the serpent also connotes penetration into the mysteries of the feminine. The serpent also functions therefore as a common feral symbol of esoteric feminine wisdom. Finally, as sexually ambivalent, the serpent can take on androgynous connotations, becoming a symbol of wholeness and of the reconciliation of opposites.

The image of the serpent functions therefore as a remarkably apt interpretant for the conflict and ambiguity the male child feels as he attempts to establish his independence from maternal control. Need we wonder, therefore, that in male-dominated cultures, the serpent reappears again and again in heroic deeds of derring-do as the feral counterpart of the Terrible Mother?

Jungian archetypal theory, then, presents the Great Mother as a facet of the developing male psyche. She symbolizes the young male's immature relationship with the feminine. The maiden whom the hero rescues from the dragon performs a similar psychic function. Her marriage to the successful hero symbolizes the young man's re-acceptance of the feminine aspects of his own personality after his adolescent repudiation of them in the dragon fight. She is the Great Mother transformed into the marrying maiden, the faithful wife. Her symbolic purpose boils down to supporting her husband as he enjoys the fruits of his victory over the Terrible Mother and her male consort.

Males dominate the human societies we know directly. In patriarchal cultures, the social roles assigned to women tend to conform to the archetypal patterns which Jung describes. In patriarchal myths men always play the lead role. Men risk, act, achieve. Accordingly, in patriarchal cultures, women stand toward men in a subordinate, passive role. They are expected to live content with engendering, nurturing, marrying, and supporting the males who shape the destiny of the race. But women themselves are systematically excluded from the satisfaction of similar achievements. As a consequence, in patriarchal societies the spontaneous fantasies of the natural male ego ordinarily define the limits of hope for both men and women.

As patriarchal society develops, it also becomes more rational and technocratic. Unfortunately, however, the rational ego remains vulnerable to what Jung has called "ego inflation." The inflated ego confides in its ability to control its own rational destiny and the destinies of others. As ego inflation intensifies, the gulf between the conscious and the unconscious psyche widens. Not that the unconscious ceases to shape behavior. Instead it shapes decisions in ways that the conscious ego cannot or will not acknowledge. As a consequence, a situation is created in which the bizarre and destructive forces which lurk unacknowledged within the darker recesses of the unconscious can work with greater and greater impunity.

In such an impasse the human mind shifts with sad predictability from archetypal to stereotypical thinking. Those who have studied archetypal human responses resist the attempt to characterize them as illusion, and correctly so. Archetypes are not nothing. They grip the mind with either creative or destructive power. But in archetypal thinking the knower and the forces which shape the knower's impinging environment lack differentiation. For that reason archetypes can function at a pre-conscious level. For human consciousness emerges with the ability to differentiate between one's own body and the surrounding world.

When archetypal images cease to be used as images and are transformed into abstract, rational concepts they begin to function as stereotypes. Stereotypical thinking emerges in social situations in which distinct social classes are forced into a process of mutual adjustment while preserving their separate social identities. Then the social fabric divides into in-groups and out-groups. I experience the group to which I belong as my in-group and all others as out-groups. As the members of an in-group seek to understand the actions and motives of members of an out-group, they tend to make facile generalizations about the latter. When contact with the out-group as a group remains superficial, its characterization within the in-group tends to become standardized. And the in-group projects it spontaneously on any member of the out-group.

Viewed logically such projection should be classified as abduction. On the assumption that all members of the out-group possess a specific set of characteristics, the member of the in-group reduces individuals in the out-group to a specific class or category of persons. Like all abductions the judgment of prejudice expresses half-acknowledged affections and attitudes. Abductive thinking follows hunches.[15]

When an out-group becomes threatening, fear and resentment harden stereotypical thinking into bigotry. Moreover, the acting out of prejudicial and bigoted attitudes follows a predictable spiral of violence. Initial aggression expresses itself in **antilocution:** members of the out-group are derided in their absence. They are made the butt of crude and aggressive humor. Their essential inferiority to the members of the in-group is blusteringly asserted. If antipathy increases, antilocution leads to **physical**

avoidance, sometimes at the cost of considerable personal inconvenience. At this point the budding bigot prefers to suffer in minor ways rather than to enter into social contact with the despised out-group. But if social antipathy waxes, it eventually gives rise to **discriminatory behavior.** Organized campaigns exclude the members of the hated out-group from social privileges available to those acceptable to the in-group. Laws of segregation are passed which increase the social visibility of the out-group and invite physical attack. And in moments of heightened fear or aggression the members of the segregated out-group may become the object of **violent or semi-violent activity:** the desecration of the out-group's homes, monuments, or places of assembly, their forceable ejection from neighborhoods or places of work, or their subjection to physical assault. Finally, the members of the hated out-group are **exterminated.** They are lynched or massacred.[16]

The stereotypical traits attributed to the members of an out-group commonly result from superficial social contact. Racial bigotry exemplifies the process. Blacks have in the past been stereotyped as mentally inferior, morally unstable and untrustworthy, overassertive, lazy and boisterous, religiously fanatic, fond of gambling, gaudy and tasteless in dress, ape-like, given to crimes with razors and knives, sexually promiscuous, politically venal.[17] Irish immigrants in the nineteenth century often found themselves similarly characterized by their waspish neighbors. None of these traits display overtly archetypal connotations. But racial prejudice also illustrates the capacity of an archetype to organize bigotry and to suffuse it with affective power.

True bigots often manifest repressed personalities characterized by ambivalence toward parental figures, rigid moralistic tendencies, stereotypical thinking, blind support for strong authority figures, sado-masochism, and the tendency to project onto others their own turmoil and conflict.[18] In other words the authentic bigot lives in terror of the shadow. The shadow, it will be recalled, interprets archetypally the dark, violent, or shameful forces lurking in one's unconscious psyche. The shadow is always a dark figure of the same sex as oneself. When an archetype is feared it tends to be repressed. But repression of the shadow leads to shadow possession. For when repressed any archetype begins to exercise controlling power over behavior in unconscious and potentially destructive ways. Moreover, when an archetype is repressed it also tends spontaneously to be projected onto others. The shadow is a dark figure; blacks have dark skins. Accordingly, the white racial bigot will tend rigidly and stereotypically to project onto blacks the same violence, fear, and guilt that seethes unacknowledged deep within the bigot's own psyche and that threatens any minute to overwhelm the fragile, bigoted, conscious ego.[19]

The archetype of the feminine can perform a similar destructive function when prejudice and bigotry assume a sexist rather than a racist character.[20] Male bigots, for example, tend spontaneously to misogyny. And indeed the social status of women in male-dominated societies

225

parallels in many ways that of blacks in racist societies, despite the fact that the feminist movement is largely a white, middle-class revolt. Like racial traits, sexual characteristics are externally visible and cannot be sloughed. Even more than blacks women can be recognized because of distinctive physique and ways of dressing. Like blacks they constitute an easily identifiable out-group. Like the racist, the sexist imagines women as intellectually inferior to men, as irresponsible, inconsistent, weak, and unstable. Women are regarded as fascinating but morally promiscuous temptresses: **"cherchez la femme."** The racist believes that blacks should be tolerated provided they "keep their place"; and the racist believes complacently that blacks really prefer their inferior social status. The sexist believes that women belong in the home and that women long to be dominated by strong and decisive males. The racist stereotypes blacks as whining and deferential, as prone to lie to white superiors. Sexists imagine that women find their greatest satisfaction in surrendering to men and in ministering to male wants and needs. And sexists remain perennially suspicious of "feminine wiles." Both racist and sexist assume an adversary stance toward those whom they oppress and suspect the tendency of the latter to feign ignorance and weakness as a way of manipulating their oppressors. In patriarchal cultures women provide the butt of sexist humor and ridicule. They are socially segregated in a variety of ways. Limitations are placed on their educational opportunities. Special care is taken to prevent them from acquiring skills that would put them in social, economic, or political competition with men or that would allow them social independence from male providers. When women's education approximates men's they are still prevented from pursuing a career with the same freedom as males. Often such segregation is justified in the name of motherhood and of the family.[21] In other words, in male-dominated cultures women commonly function as an oppressed class. Even within classes that suffer oppression for other reasons, women experience besides the oppression of sexism. And like other oppressed people they are educated to accept and to sanction their own submission to oppression.

Moreover, as in the case of racial prejudice, archetypal images organize and motivate the oppression born of sexism. For women in male dominated cultures are expected to discover in patriarchal myths their own authentic self-image. In the myths of the patriarchy, however, heroes outshine, outnumber and outdo the heroines. Hence, in a patriarchy women are traditionally expected to live content with childbearing, with domesticity, and with buttressing their husbands' aggressive competitive egos.

Constant or exclusive association of women with purely physical or biological functions like childbearing or physical nurture can easily begin to take on pejorative, stereotypical connotations. It begins to be assumed that women cannot transcend the physical, biological functions they are expected to perform. It begins to be felt that men are not merely the only achievers in the race but the only thinkers as well. Women begin to be imagined as lumpish and earthbound; men, as enlightened, rational,

226

insightful.   And prejudice becomes once again a tragic, self-fulfilling prophecy.

Oppressors spontaneously fear the oppressed. For to face the fact of oppression, the oppressor must first face the shadows of violence and of guilt that lurks within his own heart.   In patriarchal cultures, however, misogynism may grow from even deeper psychological roots.   For when child nurture is conducted exclusively or primarily by the female parent, she tends to become either the exclusive or the primary focus of infantile fear and resentment.   When repressed, such feelings lose none of their power, however irrational or unrealistic they might be.   And they can subtly and unjustly transform the beleaguered, nurturing mother into a terrifying, devouring, castrating noumenal presence. Indeed, the irrational, male idealization of femininity and motherhood can all too easily mask fear and resentment of women, especially when they are idealized out of social, educational, economic, or political competition with men.

We have invoked the archetype of the feminine as an apt affective interpretant for the third person of the Trinity. But if, in the process, we only re-enforce the bigoted and stereotypical use of archetypal imagery, our attempt to imagine the Holy Breath as a person would probably do more harm than good.   There is, moreover, another reason to question the advisability of introducing Jungian archetypes into Christian iconography. Every archetype labors under affective ambivalence. Because it interprets both sympathetic and negative feelings, in addition to its benign, lifegiving power, it has a dark, destructive side.

The archetype of the feminine labors under the same ambivalence. The womb which engenders life can become the terrifying maw which devours its own children, as the earth does when corpses are lowered into it.   The cave where worshippers gather in ecstasy to find religious rebirth can also lead into darkness and night. Then it becomes the threshold of the underworld, the vestibule of hell.[22]   The female sexual organs which receive the penetrating male organ to engender life can be hideously transformed into the face of the Medusa which strikes terror into men and turns them into cold stone.   The earth mother who engenders the plants that nourish life can withold them and starve her children.   She who provides the intoxicants that inspire ecstasy can drive her devotees to drunken stupor and madness. [23]   The Terrible Mother can maim her children, castrate them, poison them, dismember them, afflict them with insanity, plague, sickness, death.[24] When the transformation effected by the feminine principle deals death, the virgin-mother wears the face of a witch.   Her consort then becomes a warlock, a sorcerer, or some other male figure of dark and sinister character.[25]   Can any image so emotionally ambivalent truly symbolize any facet of the Christian God?

Some have felt that the widespread recurrence of archetypal symbolism points to the fact that the archetypes are deeply rooted in human nature and express some innate natural law of the psyche. But such a suggestion lacks solid proof. Moreover, it points theologically to a doctrine of natural depravity. For sexism is a form of bigotry; and bigotry is sinful. If then humans are naturally predetermined to espouse sexist attitudes, they are predetermined by nature to be sinners.

But a more benign interpretation of the sexist character of archetypal thinking suggests itself. The kinds of attitudes we build into our psyches reflect our social conditioning. The patriarchal character of human society as we know it offers then a possible explanation of why the images that shape our imaginations possess a sexist bias. But if sexist attitudes are learned through social intercourse, they can also be unlearned.

Christian conversion plunges the convert into the dark night of sense. For it demands the healing of any affective attitude irreconcilable with an authentic commitment to Christ. Since human affectivity encompasses imagistic, archetypal thinking, the dark night of sense also involves the gracious transvaluation of any images that disorient human aspirations in sinful directions.

Christian faith does not abolish human nature. But it does demand the abandonment of sinful attitudes and the gracious transvaluation of natural ones. An image or concept undergoes transvaluation when three conditions are fulfilled. First, the presuppositions which ground the frame of reference in which the image or concept functions interpretatively must be reversed. Second, the reversal must create a novel frame of reference. And, third, the very same image or concept must be used interpretatively in the new frame of reference. Because the image or concept remains the same, some of the denotative and connotative significance it formerly enjoyed will be carried over into the novel frame of reference. But through its use in a novel context, it will also acquire a wholly new capacity to interpret the structure of experience. The gracious transvaluation of an image or concept occurs when the novel frame of reference in which either is employed results from conversion from a natural or sinful interpretation of the world to one that is inspired by authentic faith in God's historical self-revelation.

The archetype of the hero certainly calls out for gracious transvaluation. Not that we need fault heroic imagery as such; we need not decry fairy tales. But the sinful transformation of heroic imagery into a sexual stereotype demands prophetic confrontation.

Heroic imagery interprets the natural maturation of the male ego. Left to itself, the natural male ego develops in predictable ways. It aspires to the rational, self-reliant conquest of its own destiny. It seeks to set and control the conditions of its growth. And it aspires to a social order that follows the dictates of natural reason. The more the male ego succeeds in this enterprise, the more surely will it succumb to ego inflation. And the inflated male ego thrives on sexism. It imagines that women exist primarily in order to give birth to men and to bolster male initiative and enterprise.

Archetypal heroic imagery begins to undergo gracious transvaluation when it is used in faith to interpret the meaning of God's self-revelation to us in Jesus. The first Christians acknowledged Jesus as the messianic Son of David. David strides across the pages of the Bible in one heroic, swashbuckling exploit after another. Predictably, the first Christians imagined the new messianic David as a divine hero. All the standard images that recur in hero myths are applied in the new Testament to Jesus. Like the heroes of old He is miraculously born. He is called by God from obscurity to enter into combat with Satan, the ancient serpentine tempter of Adam and Eve. His response to that call sets Him in conflict with demonic powers. Still, He must submit to the final ordeal of symbolic dismemberment through crucifixion. On the threshold of the grave He is confronted by Judas, a shadow figure and tool of Satan whom He persists in calling friend. But His descent into the underworld results in only seeming defeat. For it effects the atonement that reconciles us to the divine Father. Moreover, after a brief sojourn in the underworld, He returns in royal triumph, bearing a divine elixir, the food and drink of eternal life. This he freely bestows on His virgin bride, the Church, whom He has rescued from the ancient serpent.[26]

One may find similar imagery used in countless mythic tales of heroic derring-do. But for the believing Christian, their application to Jesus transforms the very meaning of heroism. For Jesus incarnates values and ideals irreconcilably opposed to natural heroism and all that it connotes. The natural hero professes rational self-reliance, autonomous control of his own life and destiny, concern to found human society on the rule of natural reason. He struts with **macho** arrogance. But, as we saw in the preceding chapter, Jesus incarnated and inculcated a very different value system. He preached not rational self-reliance but the unconditioned primacy of faith in God. He repudiated any rational attempt to control one's personal destiny by sinfully attempting to set the conditions of one's relationship to God. He demanded instead a faith in God both absolute and unconditioned. God alone, He insisted, dictates the terms of our covenant relationship with Him and He alone controls our destinies even though the path He assigns leads to Calvary. Moreover, Jesus also taught that human society must be founded ultimately, not on rational human contrivances, but in humble submission to the reign of God. He demanded that His disciples renounce political power over one another in order to worship God in the service of atoning love. Mutual forgiveness in Jesus' name and image tests the authenticity of that worship. While the **macho** hero exults in his own personal and sexual prowess, Jesus walks the path of humble self-effacement. He seeks only the glory of the Father and the establishment of the divine reign. And His body is finally penetrated by the soldier's lance, broken, and passed out to share as food.

229

Let me make myself quite clear. I am not arguing, as has been erroneously suggested, that the figure of Jesus functions symbolically in the New Testament witness as an anti-hero. The anti-hero confronts us as a pathetic figure who elicits our sympathy despite the fact that he lacks genuine heroic traits. Instead of being an anti-hero, Jesus transforms and transvalues the very meaning of heroism itself. Authentic faith in Him demands, therefore, the repudiation of **machismo** with all its works and pomps. It demands the repudiation of stereotypical and bigoted use of patriarchal concepts and myths, the abdication of the patriarchal pursuit of power and rational autonomy, and the reformation of patriarchal social structures until they incarnate the mind of Christ rather than male sexual arrogance. Is it any wonder that in **macho** cultures males find Christianity dull?

These insights take on added meaning when they are read in the light of the preceding foundational reflections on Biblical pneumatology. Nowhere in the New Testament is it asserted that Jesus' likeness to God results from His masculinity. On the contrary, His likeness to God is portrayed in terms that excluded any such belief. Jesus resembles God not in His masculinity but in His perfect obedience to the will of the Father and the inspirations of the Breath. Such resemblance to God is universally available to women and to men alike.

Moreover, if the preceding reflections enjoy validity, they yield an important insight into why God became incarnate as a male. He did so not because men enjoy special likeness to God as they sometimes in egotistical arrogance imagine themselves to do, but because in the patriarchal world in which we live males spontaneously tend to align themselves with anti-Christ. God, therefore, became incarnate in a male body in order to die in the flesh to patriarchal prejudice and bigotry and to teach His disciples, both men and women, to do the same. Anyone, therefore, who endorses or acquiesces in sexism stands thereby aligned with the forces of anti-Christ. And those who claim divine sanction for sexist social structures blaspheme.

If then Christians are summoned by God to effect the transformation of human culture until the reign of God proclaimed by Jesus is established on this earth, opposition to sexism within the Church or outside binds every believer with divine authority. For Jesus' incarnation redefines the normative meaning of maleness and reveals that both women and men are intended to live equally as God's children in His kingdom on this earth. In the process the incarnate Word unmasks natural male egotism as farcical, destructive, and one of the major Satanic obstacles to faith in a triune God.

The archetype of the feminine must also be transvalued before it can function as a Christian icon of the third person of the Trinity. The Christian God has no shadow side, no vindictive anger, no fear, no guilt. Images which connote such attitudes cannot then interpret any of the divine persons, including the Holy Breath. If we invoke the archetype of

230

the feminine as Her personal image, then we must eliminate from its imaginative structure both the witch and the Terrible Mother. The Divine Mother neither castrates nor devours Her children. The cup She proffers them contains no deadly or maddening potion. Her intoxication brings enlightenment, not besotted stupor. She lures through love; She does not manipulate through bewitchment.

If, moreover, one accepts the mind of Christ as the normative human embodiment of the wisdom the Divine Mother conceives in Her children, then one must also exclude from Her image any hint of coercive violence. The enlightenment She gives from on high breathes of the gentle wisdom of Christ. It eschews the abrasive clichés of power politics. Any struggle for women's rights must, of course, seek to deal effectively with political, economic, and social oppression. But Christian motivation for that struggle must transcend sexual sloganism. For only they enter the kingdom who renounce Satan and with him the patriarchal principalities and powers of this world. The Divine Mother suffers with the Son and with humankind in their enduring passion, but She yearns in all things to heal the brokenness which ruthless violence wreaks and to transform society according to the vision She inspired in Jesus. For She knows that in the struggle against violence and oppression humans all too easily become what they hate.

But once these qualifications have been made, the archetype of the feminine viewed solely as a positive, life-giving, inspirational presence can and does connote most of those images Christians normally associate with the Divine Breath. She is the womb in which risen life is conceived. Through Her and the laving of baptismal waters, we are born anew. She provides the divine locus, the matrix in which the Church experiences gracious transformation. Every assembled Christian community, every place of Christian worship functions then as Her created icon. So too does the tree of life. We speak, however, not of the phallic tree of the cross but of the sheltering, feminine tree which Jesus described, the tree which gathers into itself all the birds of the air. The image of the Divine Mother connotes the baptismal font, the holy vessel filled with the water of life. Moreover, if the Divine Hero gives us His body and blood as the food of eternal life, the chalice symbolizes the breast from which we drink the holy wisdom which the Divine Mother conceived in Him and breathes into us. Her enlightenment anoints us. The archetype of the feminine is linked through menstruation and amniotic fluid to water. And the Bible tells us that the Holy Breath is poured out upon us. She is the living water that wells up unto eternal life. In myth the lady of the plants supplies hallucinogens and intoxicants. She inspires visions. And Paul the apostle speaks of pneumatic inspiration as a divine intoxication. In archetypal thinking the breath of the Great Mother speaks wisdom from on high. In Christian iconography the Divine Mother is the divine Breath through whom God's word of wisdom is uttered. She conceives within God the wisdom the Son incarnates. The archetype of the feminine connotes not only the birth but the transformation of life; fire in the bible symbolizes the transforming enlightenment the Divine Mother inspires. Finally, women turn to men in love; and wherever the Divine Mother is present Her children speak with Christ the loving name **Abba.** In other words, when transmuted in faith, the archetype of the Divine Mother, viewed exclusively as a positive principle of life and transformation, organizes all of the important images traditionally associated with the third person of the trinity. Persons must be imagined as either male or female. Christian hope needs a personal image of the Holy Breath. The transvalued archetype of the feminine fulfills that need.

Before we close these reflections on pneumatic imagery, however, we need to explore another insight in the theology of Victorinus. Not only did he imagine the Holy Breath as the Divine Mother; but he also suggested that the second person of the Trinity could be legitimately imagined as androgynous. He did so in the course of reflecting on the way grace conforms us to God and makes us like the incarnate Word. The Son, he argued, took flesh in order to become a channel of divine grace and light. As we are assimilated to God through grace, we too become mediators of divine life and light, channels of God's saving activity in this world. In this context, Victorinus observed:

> In testimony thereof the prophet speaks in the following terms: **and God made humankind according to the image of God.** But if God made humankind according to His image, then the Father made it according to the image of the Son. But it then says: **He made them male and female,** and it had said: **He made them according to the image of God.** Hence, it is clear in a highly mystical sense that He created them according to the body and the flesh with the **Logos** existing as male and female and that He was son to Himself in His first and second birth, spiritually and carnally (On the Trinity, I, 58, 11-36).

The two births of which Victorinus speaks are the Son's incarnation and resurrection. Needless to say, from the standpoint of trinitarian theology, to speak of the Son, however mystically, as Son to Himself is confusing, misleading, and finally indefensible. But one need not therefore conclude to the illegitimacy of imagining the second person of the Trinity as androgynous.

Here several points should be noted. First, the man Jesus was certainly male. But His obedience to the Father and to the Breath rather than His maleness revealed Him as Son of God. When both men and women obey Him, they both live as children of God in His image. Second, Jesus' repudiation of **machismo** and His capacity to reconcile great strength and great gentleness in His dealings with others suggest personality traits that can legitimately be characterized as androgynous. Third, no sacramental revelation of a divine person ever fully reveals that person. Hence it would

232

be fallacious to conclude that masculinity alone interprets the person of the Word adequately to human affectivity. Fourth, the Son is historically revealed not only in the humanity to which He is hypostatically united, but also in His mystical body, which is composed of both men and women. Fifth, Jesus by His obedience reveals perfectly not only the Father but the Holy Breath Who is His mind. If She may be imagined as the Divine Mother, the Word may be legitimately and consistently imagined as androgynous. Sixth, as an archetype the androgyne connotes the reconciliation of opposites. The Word whose mystical body we are reconciles Jew and Greek, slave and free, male and female to one another in mutual respect and love. Hence, the divine Father and the divine Mother may be legitimately imagined as acting through their androgynous Son to effect the **coincidentia oppositorum.** Finally, if the Word can be legitimately imagined as androgynous, then women can visibly sacramentalize the presence and action of the divine Word to Christian hope as effectively as men.[27]

We began these reflections by observing that contemporary pneumatology should offer more than instruction for the mind. It should challenge contemporary Christians to rend their hearts as well. We have good reason to believe that despite an initial realization that Jesus' death and glorification had shattered sexist stereotypes, the Christian Church very quickly moved to organize itself according to the patriarchal patterns socially prevalent in the first century. But God is no sexist; and those blaspheme who invoke the blessing of Father, Mother, or Son on bigoted social structures. As a consequence, until we Christians stand united in our opposition to sexist bigotry whether within the church or in human society at large, we live not in the illumination of the Divine Mother but under Her compassionate judgment.

Some readers may question the appropriateness of discussing archetypal theory in a book of theology. But those who understand what it means to approach God experientially will confess not only its legitimacy but its inevitability. Foundational method demands that we probe beneath traditional doctrines and beliefs for a normative insight into the experiences which ground them; and archetypes give shape to the experience of Christian hope. Our construct of experience demands it; for it distinguishes an affective from an inferential perception of the reality of God and demands that we bring both to integration in faith. Our experiential construct of the Trinity demands it by showing us that the Holy Breath functions within the Godhead as the mind of God and of Christ. That insight demands that we also conceive Her as a divine person, for She confronts us in Christian revelation as distinct from Father and Son and as the source of Their interpersonal awareness of one another. A distinct source of interpersonal consciousness within God cannot be less than a divine person. We humans can, however, imagine persons only as male or femals. And the archetypal image of the feminine interprets to human hope not only Her saving illumination but the unitive relation of conception She bears toward the Son. Finally, Jesus' proclamation of new covenant morality in the power and illumination of the Holy Breath provides us with the normative frame of reference we need to transvalue the archetype of the feminine, purify it of all sexist connotations, and transform it into a sacramental icon of Her reality. In other words, the preceding discussion of Christian iconography occupies so important a place in a foundational pneumatology that our reflections on Her reality could never be complete without them.

Our foundational insights into trinitarian iconography impose upon us a burden of conscience. They demand first of all that we look upon every human family as a created, natural icon of the divine society. In the preceding chapters we have concerned ourselves especially with sacramental icons of God. But natural ones exist as well. Things subsist in God naturally when they develop without faith consciousnss or (most often) without any awareness of God whatever. Stones, plants, animals display no overt religious behavior. And many human beings choose to live thoroughly secular lives in ways that are naturally responsible but obtuse to faith and the realities it grasps. The divine experience comprehends all the processes that transpire within it, including natural ones. And some natural processes reveal to us facets of the divine experience, provided we see them with the eyes of faith. The vastness of nature reveals, for example, the divine immensity. However far we advance into space or probe into the meaning of the universe the Divine Experiencer has already been there before us. To those with ears to hear, the majesty of nature speaks of the divine majesty, its power of the divine omnipotence; for God encompasses and transcends them both.

We find initial warranty for imagining human families as natural icons of the divine in Jesus' own proclamation of the Father:

> Or what man of you, if his son asks him for bread will give him a stone? Or if he asks for a fish will give him a serpent? If you then, who are evil know how to give good gifts to your children, how much more will your Father in heaven give good gifts to those who ask him? (Mt 7:9-11)

In Jesus' eyes not even human sinfulness had so blunted the human heart to pity that the love of a father for his son has lost all resemblance to the heavenly Father's love of His own. Jesus' homely comparison invites us to discover the face of God revealed in the most elemental of human experiences: that of belonging to a family. But if the foundational reflections on Christian iconography contained in this chapter can claim normative validity, then we can legitimately discover in a mother's love of her child an image of the Divine Mother's tender care for each of Her little ones. And we can find in the loving relation of brothers and sisters a finite, natural reflection of our relation to the incarnate Son of God.

But if faith can discover in human families a natural icon of the divine society, Christian families are summoned by God in hope, faith, and love to transform those natural relationships into a sacramental icon of the divine persons by giving themselves to one another and to those in need in selfless Christlike love. By the same token every Christian community will fully sacramentalize the reality of the triune God only to the extent that its members are bound to one another in a single family of graced sharing.

In the twelfth century Joachim of Flora looked back to the Old Testament and named it the age of the Father. In his intuitive perception of salvation history, the incarnation marked a second age: that of the Son. And he believed a third age was about to dawn: the age of the Holy Breath.[28] While one cannot subscribe to Joachim's vision of the historical revelation of the Trinity in the same terms in which he formulated it, the prophetic abbot may have been groping his way toward an important truth. If one confesses that the God of Abraham, Isaac, and Jacob has been revealed in the New Testament as the Father of Jesus, then it makes good sense to regard the Old Testament as in some special sense the age of the Father, even though His **Ruah** breathed even then in the great charismatic leaders of the Jewish nation. The New Testament begins the last age of salvation, in which both Son and Breath stand historically revealed as divine persons co-equal with the Father. But for a variety of reasons that we have already considered, the Holy Breath, the Divine Mother, has been eclipsed in popular Christian piety by devotion to the Father and Son. And over the centuries neglect transformed Her into "the forgotten God." If the foundational insights contained in the preceding chapters can claim normative validity, the Christian churches will continue to pass over the third divine person in silence as long as they continue to misprize Her charisms and to invoke divine sanction on sexist social and ecclesiastical structures. The age of the Holy Breath is prepared by every gracious illumination She inspires. It dawned in eschatological force on Pentecost day. But the third person of the Trinity will remain the forgotten God until Her healing inspirations free us to see in women's faces a finite, created revelation of Her own. She comes to teach prophecy not only to God's sons but to God's daughters as well. We will enter upon the age of the Divine Mother in its eschatological fullness when Christians finally die as Jesus did to sexist patriarchal values, cherish women as persons co-equal with men, and give their gifts full scope to flourish within the church and human society. May She Who is faithful accomplish this good work in us soon.

1. Perhaps the most original contribution Basil of Caesarea made to the development of Christian pneumatology came with his insistence on the Breath's adorability. He altered the traditional form of the Christian doxology. Instead of giving glory to the Father, through the Son, and in the Breath, Basil offered glory to the Father, and to the Son and to the Holy **Pneuma.** For this liturgical innovation he was criticized. He responded

that his new doxology had ample justification. It echoed the traditional baptismal formula recorded at the end of Matthew's gospel (Cf. Hermann Dorries, De Spiritu Sancto: Der Beitrag des Basilius zum Abschluss des trinitarischen Dogmas (Göttigen: Vanderhoeck und Ruprecht, 1956), pp. 61-62; Basil, Letter 159:2). He conceded that the older formula had called attention to the relationships which obtain among the divine **hypostaseis.** For all things do indeed proceed from the Father, through the Son, and in the Breath. His new formula, however, insisted on another equally important truth: namely, that the same divine glory is revealed in all three members of the Trinity and that equal glory is therefore due all three (Dorries, op. cit., pp. 46-52). Basil's vindication of the adorability of the divine Breath was warmly supported by the other Cappadocians. And eventually the belief found its way into the Niceno-Constantinopolitan creed recited in the churches every Sunday. The creed ascribes to the Holy Breath the divine titles of Lord and Life-giver. Both Her procession within the Godhead and Her adorability are affirmed (Fortman, op. cit., pp. 83-86).

2.   Erich Neumann, The Great Mother, translated by Ralph Manheim (Princeton: Bollingen, 1955), pp. 39-40, 42.

3.   Ibid., pp. 44-45.

4.   Ibid., p. 45.

5.   Ibid.

6.   Ibid., p. 48.

7.   Ibid., pp. 240ff.

8.   Ibid., pp. 55-65.

9.   Ibid., pp. 281 ff., 325 ff.

10.   Ibid., pp. 315-317; Mircea Eliade, Patterns in Comparative Religion, translated by Rosemary Sheed (New York: World, 1968), pp. 154-187.

11.   Erich Neumann, The Origins and History of Consciousness, translated by R.F.C. Hull (Princeton: Bollingen, 1954), pp. 102-127, 152-191.

12.   Ibid., pp. 195-219.

13.   Erich Neumann, The Child, translated by Ralph Manheim (New York: Harper and Row, 1973), pp. 7-57.

14.   Philip Slater, The Glory of Hera (Boston: Beacon, 1968), pp. 75-122.

15. Gordon W. Allport, The Nature of Prejudice (New York: Doubleday, 1958), pp. 19ff.

16. Ibid., pp. 14-15.

17. Ibid., pp. 192-193.

18. Ibid., pp. 371-397; T.W. Adorno, Else Frenkel-Brunswick, Daniel J. Levinson, R. Nevitt Sanford, et. al. The Authoritarian Personality (New York: Harper, 1950).

19. Allport, op. cit., pp. 349-355.

20. Adorno, et. al., op. cit., pp. 387-477.

21. Helen Mayer Hacker, "Women as an Oppressed Class," Social Forces, XXX (October, 1951), pp. 60-69.

22. Neumann, The Great Mother, pp. 45, 147ff; The Origins and History of Consciousness, pp. 39-102.

23. Slater, op. cit., pp. 20, 318, 320.

24. Neumann, The Great Mother, pp. 72-74, 240-267, 281-305.

25. Ibid., pp. 162-208.

26. Joseph Campbell, The Hero With a Thousand Faces (New York: Meridian, 1934).

27. We note in passing that these foundational insights validate an otherwise baffling strain in the Christian mystical tradition. Both Julian of Norwich and medieval Cistercian mysticism apply maternal imagery to the person of the Son. The image of Jesus the mother has never appealed to popular piety in the way that other mystical images have. Think, for example, of the Sacred Heart. But if we may imagine the Son in androgynous terms, the image has its use and importance. For the image of Jesus the mother invokes not the archetype of the feminine but the archetype of the androgyne by blending in a single individual the masculinity of Jesus with the femininity of the mother.

28. In Joachim's vision, the first age of salvation began with Adam and extended to the coming of Christ. It was a carnal age, the age of the laity, the age of marrying and giving in marriage, the age of Mosaic law and of slavery to the law. During it God was served primarily through courageous deeds. Humankind had not yet advanced beyond spiritual infancy. This was the age of the Father. The second age extended from the incarnation to the mid-thirteenth century. It was the age of the clerics. During this second era the church experienced partial liberation from the trammels of

the flesh. Grace replaced the law; and filial service to God replaced bondage to the law. Teachers supplanted laborers. During this second age the Church advanced beyond infancy to spiritual youth. Such was the age of the Son. The third age began with St. Benedict and extended to the time of Joachim and beyond. This would be the age of the monks, the vanguard of a spiritualized Church purified of the corruptions born of clericalism. It would be an age of love, freedom, spiritual maturity. During it praise and contemplation would receive the honors formerly accorded to teachers. It would be the age of the Holy Breath. Clearly, Joachim's vision of salvation history was marred by a monkish elitism and a dualistic suspicion of the flesh (Henry Bett, Joachim of Flora (London: Methuen and Co., 1930); Ernst Benz, Ecclesia Spiritualis: Kirchenidee und Geschichtstheologie der Franziskanischen Reformation (Stuttgart: Kohlhammer, 1964), pp. 12-27).

Abba: Hebrew word for the familiar address of a father by his child; Jesus' name for God.

Analogy: similarity despite difference.

Androgyne: an image which combines male and female elements.

Archetype: a spontaneous image that recurs in a variety of individuals, epochs and cultures, that is heavy with affective significance and therefore connotatively rich, for it is endowed with a central core of meaning that is linked by free association with images and attitudes of varying degrees of conscious or unconscious evaluative differentiation.

Arianism: the subordinationist, trinitarian doctrine taught by Arius of Alexandria.

Autonomy: the bare capacity to initiate either reaction or response prescinded from the kind of reaction or response initiated.

Charisma (Charism): A Pauline term for a particular, visible, manifestation of the grace (**charis**) of Christ; an enabling call of the Divine Breath.

Classical Theism: a term used by process philosophers and theologians for a more traditional philosophical conception of God as utterly immutable and unrelated to any reality beyond Himself.

Conception: in an experiential approach to trinitarian theology, a notional predicate for the unitive relation of the Holy Breath to the Son.

Coincidentia oppositorum: the reconciliation of contrasting or conflicting realities, usually in God.

Conversion: the decision to assume responsibility for one's subsequent personal development in an identifiable realm of human experience. A conversion may be affective, speculative, moral, religious, or socio-political.

Ditheism: the doctrine that the Father and the Son are not only distinct realities within the Christian God but are two distinct Gods.

Dynamic Interpretant: the habit which evokes the values that disclose the meaning of a sign or significant event.

Ekporeusis: the Greek word for procession, used by the Greek fathers to designate the origin of the Holy Breath within the Christian Godhead.

Emotional (Affective) Interpretant: an affective response evoked by a sign.

Energetic Interpretant: the interpretation of a command.

Eschatological: pertaining to the last age in the history of salvation.

Eschatology: an organized account of the last age of the history of salvation.

Eschaton: the last age of the history of salvation; the period of salvation history inaugurated by Jesus' death and resurrection and by the Pentecostal sending of the Holy Breath,

Essence: what a thing is; as a facet of experience, a quality prescinded from the facts and laws it presents and understood for what it is and nothing else.

Essence Fallacy: the illegitimate reification of an experienced essence or quality.

Experience: a process which integrates relational elements called feelings.

Expressive Symbol: a fact which manifests the law in which it is grounded.

Fact: a decisive action and its corresponding reaction prescinded from the habit in which it is grounded and from the values which present both within experience. The decisive action is an initial fact; the reaction is a final fact.

Feeling: a relational element within experience.

Filiation: the passive relation of the Son to the Father within the Christian Godhead which is the necessary correlate to His active generation by the Father.

Filioque: a Latin word meaning, "and from the Son"; it was added to the article of the Latin creed which attributed the procession of the Holy Breath to the Father in order to affirm that She proceeds simultaneously from the Father and Son. The legitimacy of the addition has been a theological issue between eastern and western Christians since the time of the Great Schism.

Final Interpretant: A response to a sign which grasps exhaustively its meaning and the significance of the reality it interprets.

Final Fact: a decision which terminates evaluative response.

Foundational Theology: a functional specialty within theology which attempts to formulate a normative account of the conversion experience which ought to lie at the basis of a religious tradition.

Freedom: the capacity to act or not to act, to do one thing rather than another.

Generation: the engendering of life; as a technical trinitarian term, the eternal procession of the Son from the Father seen as active causation.

Gnosis: the Greek word for knowledge. It is used in Gnostic religion to designate saving enlightenment.

Gnosticism: a syncretistic religion which developed during the first centuries of the Christian era and which promised an enlightenment that freed one from entrapment in the material, sensible universe.

Grace: beauty; as a technical foundational term, the beautifying transformation of experience effected by faith in God's historical self-revelation.

Heuristic: pertaining to inquiry.

Holy Breath: a term derived from Biblical sources and used here to designate the third person of the Trinity.

Homoiousios: a Greek word meaning similar in being; a term suggested by some opponents of the Nicene Creed as an alternative to **homoousios.**

Homoousios: a Greek word meaning one in being; the term used at Nicea to vindicate the divinity of the Son and His co-equality with the Father. It was eventually applied to the Divine Breath as well to vindicate Her divinity and co-equality with the Father and Son.

Hypostasis: a Greek word for entity, reality; as a trinitarian term, the particular reality of the Father, Son, and Breath as opposed to the divinity common to all three. **Hypostasis** was translated into Latin by the term **persona.**

Hypostatic Union: the union of a divine nature and a human nature in the one divine person of the Son without the two natures blending to form a third reality that is neither divine nor human.

Icon: as a logical term a sign which denotes in virtue of its qualitative likeness to the reality signified; as a theological term a sign which not only resembles what it signifies but which is also self-negating in the sense that it also proclaims itself to be other than the reality signified in some recognizable way.

Immediate Interpretant: the evaluative response to a sign prescinded from the habit which evokes it.

Initial Fact: a decision which evokes evaluative response.

Interpretant: the proper significant outcome of a sign or significant event; the evaluative response the sign or significant event seeks to evoke.

Interpretative Symbol: an evaluative response which seeks to present within experience the significant relational structure of the real.

Ktisma: the Greek word for creature.

Law: a generalized, habitual tendency to react or respond evaluatively or decisively prescinded from the values or decisions it grounds.

Logical Interpretant: an abstract, inferential response to a sign.

Logos: the Greek term for "word." It was a title given Jesus in the Christological hymn which opens the fourth gospel and has been variously interpreted by Christian theologians. Some regard the **Logos** as the mind, or conception, of God; others, as the "spoken" or revealed expression of God.

Meaning: the evaluative disclosure of relationship.

Mission: the sending of one person by another; in trinitarian theology the historical sending of one divine person by another; as a technical foundational term, a gracious transformation of human experience in God which reveals sacramentally the reality of the divine person who is sent, the character of the relation of that person to the other divine person(s) who function in the sending, and the conditions which must be met if the historical mission of the divine person is to be experienced as such.

Modalism (Sabellianism): the doctrine that the Son and Breath are not distinct divine persons but only two ways in which the single person of the Father was historically revealed.

Monarchy: single sway; a theological term used by the fathers of the Church in their defense of the oneness of God: the one God holds single sway over all created reality and is the only source of salvation.

Montanism: a Christian sect of the second and third centuries which regarded its prophetic leader Montanus as a privileged spokesman for the Holy Breath.

Nature: what a thing is, viewed as the reason why it acts in the way that it does; viewed experientially, nature embraces that realm of experience which develops in abstraction from faith in God's historical self-revelation.

Notion: as a technical trinitarian term, a relational predicate applied to one of the divine persons.

Nous: the Greek word for intelligence.

Ousia: a Greek word for reality, being; as a technical trinitarian term, the divine being common to Father, Son, and Breath.

Panentheism: the doctrine that everything exists in God but that God and creation are distinct realities.

Pantheism: the doctrine that everything is God.

Patripassionism: the doctrine that God the Father was crucified for the salvation of the world.

Perichoresis: mutual interpenetration; in trinitarian theology, the mutual inexistence of the divine persons.

Person: as a technical foundational term, a dynamic relational reality, not only subsistent in its own right (that is to say, as a relationally autonomous center of responsive evaluation and decision) but also imbued with vital continuity and with the capacity for responsible self-understanding, for decisions that flow from that same self-understanding, and for entering into responsible social relationships with entities like itself.

Persona: the Latin word for mask. It was used to designate the masks worn by actors in order to identify their dramatic role in a play. It was used also by Tertullian as a designation for the Father, Son, and Breath. Its Greek equivalent was **prosopon.** But Latin trinitarian theologians used it to translate the Greek word **hypostasis.**

Personal Causality: an interaction between persons which establishes or modifies a knowing, loving, interpersonal relationship between them.

Pneuma: a Greek word for breath, or spirit, used to translate the Hebrew word **ruah.**

Pneumatic: related to or caused by God's Holy Breath.

Pneumatology: a theology of the Holy Breath.

Polytheism: the doctrine that there are many gods.

Presentational Immediacy: the quality of the evaluative shape of an experience which causes it to be both an experience of the present moment and the way an experiencer is present to what is actual and real.

Procession: as a technical, trinitarian term, the eternal origin of a divine person within the Christian Godhead. At first it designated the Breath's origin but was extended to the Son's also.

Quality: an instance of particular suchness; a value within experience prescinded from the habit in which it is grounded and from the facts and realities it presents.

Quaternity: the character of a reality composed of four parts; as a technical, trinitarian term, the doctrine that there is a fourth reality in God in addition to the three divine persons and distinct from them.

Reaction: in the broad sense, any decisive retaliation; in the narrow sense, a decisive retaliation that is devoid of the deliberation and reflection that characterizes personal responses.

Relation: the order of one reality to another.

Religious: the character of an experience whose evaluative form is touched by a concern for ultimacy.

Response: a reaction which is motivated by personal deliberation and reflection.

Resurrection: the gracious transformation of a human experience in God begun in this life and completed after death.

Ruah: a Hebrew word for breathing, for air in motion; its English equivalent in this text is Breath.

Sabellianism: see **Modalism.**

Sacramental: the character of an event which both reveals and conceals the reality of God.

Salvation: as a technical term, the process by which creatures enter into a graced, lifegiving relationship with God.

Seminal Logos (Logos Spermatikos): a term from Stoic and Neo-Platonic philosophy designating impulses ingredient in material things which cause them to develop in specific ways.

Sexism: social prejudice or bigotry based on sex.

Sin: evil chosen in violation of God's will.

Soteriology: an ordered account of the meaning of salvation.

Spiration: the procession of the Holy Breath from Father and Son within the Christian Godhead.

Spirit: in classical philosophy, an entity free from the limitations of matter.

Spiritus: a Latin word for breath or spirit, used as a translation for the Hebrew word "**ruah**" and for the Greek word "**pneuma.**"

Stereotype: the superficial characterization of the members of an out-group by the members of an in-group.

Subordinationism: the doctrine that the Son and Breath are inferior in being to the Father and that the Breath is inferior in being to the Son.

Substance: that which exists in itself and not in another as in a subject of adhesion.

Supreme: that than which none greater can be conceived.

Symbol: that which mediates the evaluative grasp of significant relationship.

Theological Specialty: one of eight interrelated fields of theological inquiry, which are distinguished from one another by their data, operational procedures, and results and ordered with respect to one another in such a way as to produce cumulative and progressive theological results.

Theology: an organized account of God.

Transcendental Categories: categories which are predicable of any reality whatever.

Transvaluation: an evaluative process which replaces one frame of reference with another and then uses a term from the abandoned frame of reference in the novel frame of reference in such a way that some of the term's former meaning is retained even though it acquires novel connotations and/or implications through its use in the novel frame of reference.

Tritheism: the doctrine of Joachim of Flora, especially his teaching that Father, Son, and Breath only resemble one another and constitute a social collectivity akin to human societies.